I0167586

Anxiety Is NOT the Enemy
Managing and Controlling Anxiety
in Your Everyday Life

Michael Raulin, PhD

Copyright

No part of this book may be reproduced or transmitted in any form
or by any means whatsoever, electronic or mechanical,
including photocopying, scanning, recording, or by any
information storage or retrieval system, without
written, dated, and signed permission from the author.
.

© Michael L. Raulin
2022
ALL RIGHTS RESERVED

ISBN: 979-8-9859925-1-9

Copyeditor: Stacey Lenn, (aka Grammargal)
Cover Design: Tanveer Ahmad

Table of Contents

Preface

For many people, anxiety is an unpleasant state that interferes with their functioning and makes their lives miserable. They are constantly anxious about their performance, what people think of them, or whether they can succeed in a world that keeps demanding more of them. They worry about their future, from career success to their relationships to whether they will be able to retire comfortably. However, anxiety is also a valuable resource that contributes significantly to our functioning. It pushes us to plan for challenges, such as building skills that make us more competitive in the marketplace, strengthening relationships that provide support when we need it, or making decisions that enhance our financial security. We do these things because they make us worry less. In this book, I demystify anxiety by explaining what it is, what factors influence it, and what value it provides. I will also cover methods to help people to manage their anxiety. What I do not do is encourage people to think about eliminating their anxiety. Without anxiety, we are defenseless. Anxiety signals the need for alertness, adaptation, and preparation.

Anxiety is normal. Granted, anxiety can become excessive, and when it does, it might qualify as an anxiety disorder. I cover the most common anxiety disorders in this book and the treatment options for those disorders, but I also focus on normal anxiety and how to manage that anxiety. With proper management and understanding, it is possible to keep one's anxiety generally below uncomfortable levels. More importantly, adequate management can keep anxiety below the level that interferes with performance and above the level needed to optimize performance. You read that correctly; too little anxiety reduces our performance and, in the process, makes our life more difficult.

You will learn about anxiety and the processes that create anxiety. You will also learn how to manage anxiety and how severe anxiety disorders can be treated. You will not learn enough to treat anxiety disorders, but the skills you will learn will give you a sense of control you may not currently feel. They will also give you the ability to plan your life with the belief that you can deal with whatever life throws at you.

The focus of this book is on understanding and effectively using the anxiety that is a part of everyone's life. People who feel overwhelmed by anxiety tend to view their anxiety as the enemy. It is not; it is critical to our survival and success. It is my sincere hope that I convince you of that fact. Moreover, I hope that understanding how to manage anxiety gives you the confidence to take on the challenges in your life.

I am deeply indebted to several people who helped move this project along and contributed immensely to the project's success. I wish to thank Lexi Rager for a very thorough and helpful review. I am also indebted to my copyeditor for this book (Stacey Lenn) and cover designer (Tanveer Ahmad). These people helped to make this book a better product.

Mike Raulin
MikeRaulin@gmail.com

Chapter 1

The Nature of Anxiety

Anxiety is a fact of life. It may not be the most pleasant fact, but it is a reality. If you are breathing and thinking, you will occasionally get anxious. Sometimes you get very anxious, and you do not like it. You may even hate it. You beat yourself up over being anxious. You think of your anxiety as a weakness that holds you back. You look at people differently and are convinced that they are looking at you differently. You can sense how pathetic they think your anxiety is, and that knowledge alone feeds your anxiety. But there is a surprise awaiting you. They are just like you. They are breathing and thinking and occasionally feeling anxious. Their anxiety may even occur more frequently than yours and may be more intense. And they are convinced that you view them as pathetic. It is a crazy house of mirrors.

There are so many emotions in life. There is excitement, love, disgust, depression, joy, and surprise, and they each have their place in people's lives. Anxiety, however, tends to be in a class of its own. It does not seem to have a place, at least not a place that feels comfortable. It can overwhelm other emotions, become the focus of our attention, and disrupt every aspect of life. It truly feels evil, yet, like breathing, it is essential to our well-being.

This book reviews the nature of anxiety, the factors that trigger anxiety, and the mechanisms that control anxiety. I do not try to tell you that anxiety is not an issue, but I do try to convince you that it is not your enemy. By the time you finish this book, you will realize that anxiety is a valuable resource. You will also learn that it is possible to manage anxiety and sometimes even control it. But most importantly, you will learn how it can make your life better, improve your performance, and add to your self-esteem.

Are you skeptical? Good! I want you to make me prove that you can learn to control your anxiety and use it to your benefit. To make it happen, you must take some risks, so I am asking you to give me a chance to show you what is possible. Take those risks, try some new strategies, and see whether they work. The potential rewards make the risks worth taking.

Anxiety and Fear

Fear and anxiety often feel like different levels of the same experience. That feeling is wrong. Anxiety and fear are two different processes generated by two different brain regions. They are also triggered at different times, and they serve different purposes.

Fear is a primitive response triggered by a mechanism in the brainstem. The *brainstem* is just above the spinal column, and it is the oldest part of the brain in terms of evolution. This fear response is often referred to as *fight-or-flight syndrome*, although a better name might be *flight-or-fight syndrome* because the first instinct is to flee danger. It is triggered when the organism "believes" that it is in danger. I put the word "believes" in quotation marks because it means different things to different organisms. Human beings, with our advanced brains, may have a strong sense of danger that we can articulate. More primitive organisms are unable to experience and think about danger but rather may be responding to primitive information, such as a quick movement toward the organism. The fight-or-flight response prepares the body to run for its life if possible or to fight to the death if escape is impossible. I discuss this fear response extensively in the chapter on panic disorder.

Anxiety should be thought of as apprehension. It is a sensation that there might be danger in the future and that we need to be prepared for it. Fear is a response to an immediate threat; anxiety is a response to a potential future threat. We experience anxiety because we can think hypothetically about the future. Frankly, imagining the future is one of our most remarkable skills. By thinking hypothetically about future risks, we can plan for them and be ready to handle them if they occur. The unpleasant sensation of anxiety motivates us to prepare to handle potential risks. If we take steps to prepare, our concern about those risks decreases, and consequently, our anxiety decreases.

The evidence is overwhelming that a fear response is universal in every animal with a modest brain. This response activates the body to have a better chance of surviving a life-or-death situation. The fact that the fear response has been maintained by evolution is a testament to the value of this response. We know what the sense of fear feels like to us. We can sense most of our body's responses to the situation, but we also have a powerful emotion that we might call *dread*. We feel like we could die if we do not handle the situation appropriately. It is not clear that lower animals, such as lab rats, have the same feelings. Those feelings are part of our conscious brain and may not be a part of the experience of animals with less sophisticated brains (Gazzaniga, 2018). But the fear response that prepares that animal for flight or fight is present, even if their experience does not include the feelings we experience.

Consciousness is one of those mysteries that people have debated for millennia. Consciousness is our awareness of our thoughts, feelings, and processes. Our brain does not just assess situations and select and implement actions; we are aware of the processes and, to a degree, control those processes. We think about our situation and what we plan to do. There is general agreement that the experience of conscious awareness is somehow a process involving brain activity. Still, the exact nature of that activity is unclear, and the purpose of consciousness is also unclear. It is presumed that consciousness evolved in much the same way that other genetically influenced capabilities evolved. If so, other creatures may possess consciousness, although they do not have the language skills that would allow them to communicate their internal sense of the world. If you have a pet, your interactions with it might convince you that it has a sense of itself and its relationship to you. You get that sense from watching its behavior and expressions. It may very well be that your dog has a sense of consciousness, just like you do. For now, that is one of those mysteries we are still trying to solve.

We know that human beings can and do think hypothetically about future events. There is laboratory evidence that many animals can also do the same. If those future events are potentially risky, we will likely experience anxiety, which may also be true for other animals. I have had several dogs, and they have been an essential part of my life. During four particularly rough months, three of those dogs died. They were all older and had wonderful lives, but their loss was painful. The fourth dog, who was several years younger than the other three, showed increasing distress with each of the deaths of the other dogs. Moreover, after losing all his siblings, he showed enormous distress whenever left alone. I do not know what he was thinking; I do not even know if he could think. But my interpretation was that he recognized that the other dogs had left, and he was insecure that he would be left behind. His facial expressions and behavior when left alone gave that impression. In other words, it may very well be that the experience of anxiety is not unique to human beings.

Anxiety signals that danger is possible and that we should take action to reduce its likelihood or its impact if it were to happen. Unfortunately, anxiety produces exactly the opposite response in some people; they try to avoid the anxiety by ignoring it and thus procrastinating when they should be acting. Think about the situations that make you anxious. If you have a job interview, you are likely to be worried about how you will perform in the interview. You can reduce that anxiety by increasing the likelihood that you will perform well during the interview. How can you do that? You do your homework. You make sure that your resume is impressive and free of all typos. You research the job and the company to demonstrate that you understand what the job involves. You think about how your skills and experiences uniquely prepare you for that possible job. By thinking about those things in advance, you are ready to give solid and persuasive responses to questions that might be asked. You might also think about how you might respond to some off-the-wall questions, such as how you might handle a truly unlikely crisis at the company.

4

You cannot predict everything that will happen in the interview, but the more things you can predict and prepare for, the more confident you will be that your interview performance will be impressive.

Will that preparation eliminate the anxiety? Of course not. You cannot predict everything, and therefore there will still be some doubt about whether you can handle the situation. But your anxiety will be reduced by the preparation, and if the preparation is thorough enough, the anxiety will be reduced dramatically. We take such steps every day to reduce our anxiety. We purchase insurance in case we are in an accident; we install smoke detectors in case there is a fire; we study for upcoming exams so that we are prepared to do well. All of these represent investing time and energy to reduce potential risks in the future. The important words here are "in the future." Anxiety is always future oriented, although the future may be weeks or minutes from now. If you must give a talk and you are anxious about public speaking, you are likely to be anxious long before the presentation and will still be anxious as you walk to the front of the room to give your talk.

In conclusion, fear is triggered by present danger, whereas anxiety is triggered by potential future danger. Fear and anxiety are triggered by different brain mechanisms (the locus coeruleus versus the amygdala), which serve different purposes. Fear is an intense feeling but is also a physiological response that prepares the body to run for its life or, if that is not possible, to fight in a last-ditch effort to survive. Anxiety does not include this massive innervation of our physiology for immediate action. Instead, it produces an aversive feeling that can be reduced by taking specific action. That action is usually some preparation to reduce future risk.

If fear and anxiety are so different, how is it that most people experience them as just different levels of the same phenomenon? The reason is that they share an aversive feeling that psychologists call **negative affect**. Negative affect is a part of many negative emotions. You not only experience negative affect when you are anxious or fearful but also when you are in physical pain, depressed, or extremely hungry. You can think of negative affect

5

as an amplifier of an aversive state, which increases one's desire to take steps to reduce that aversive state.

Evolutionary Contributions

Evolution has shaped species since the beginning of life. Broad systems, such as the circulatory system, gradually developed to serve critical needs. There is little doubt that evolution shaped hundreds of characteristics in virtually every species. Many of these characteristics have proved to be so successful that new species maintained the basic designs as they diverged from existing species. For example, the heart and circulatory system are remarkably similar in a wide range of animals. Digestive systems work in much the same way in many species, although there is more diversity in digestive systems because species have evolved to feed on different plants or animals.

Although our high school biology training has led us to think of evolution as something from the past, the process of evolution is ongoing and will continue to be ongoing. Most evolution occurs over centuries or millennia. But evolutionary changes can occur over hours. For example, doctors that specialize in the treatment of infectious diseases understand that if disease-causing bacteria are not wiped out completely through treatment, what may be left is a small number of treatment-resistant bacteria, which quickly multiply and overwhelm the body.

Dramatic evolutionary activity is occurring in the human brain. This is not something that occurs over hours or days but rather tens of thousands of years, but there is more change going on in the evolution of the human brain than in virtually any other system in the human body. The reason is that humans are changing the environment so rapidly that our brain is being challenged in ways it has never been challenged before. Such challenges spur evolutionary pressures that lead to adaptation. However, that adaptation takes tens of thousands of years while we struggle with demands that our predecessors could not even have imagined. Other systems evolved in more primitive creatures a long time ago and were passed on because they worked. The brain is what differentiates human beings most dramatically from other living creatures. Our brain is magnificent. I have always argued that you do not need to be religious to look at the functioning of the human brain and see it as miraculous. As you will see in this book, the brain is one of our greatest assets, but at times it is also a significant burden on our functioning.

Because of the way evolution is typically taught, we tend to focus on genes and how they evolve over time. Indeed, evolution would not be possible if it were not for our genes and for the fact that our genes occasionally are copied incorrectly. We call such incorrect copies **mutations**; most mutations are seriously detrimental, and the result is that the organism does not survive. Mutations are random, and random processes rarely produce positive results. But on rare occasions, the mutation may prove to be beneficial. If the mutation is beneficial, the organism with that mutation will have a selective advantage, which means that the organism may be more likely to survive and consequently more likely to reproduce and pass on those mutated genes. This simple process, which is repeated millions or billions of times, can lead to gradual changes in organisms. When members of a species are separated physically from other members of the species, each subgroup may experience different selective pressures. The result is that mutations that might have been unfavorable in the previous environment could be favorable in the current environment. Consequently, a single species gradually diverges into separate species if the members remain physically separated and therefore cannot interbreed.

A four-paragraph description of the process of evolution is hardly sufficient to understand the subtleties of this amazing process. But it should give us enough information to understand the topic of this book, which is the role of anxiety and how that role has been shaped by the changes in the environment in which we find ourselves. For now, I simply want to introduce an idea that I repeatedly cover in later chapters. *Evolution always involves an interaction of genes and the environment.* Genes that work in one environment may not work in another environment. Consequently, if the environment changes, the direction of evolutionary development also changes. Perhaps a massive environmental event may make certain foods unavailable. It might be a change in the climate that favors the growth of certain plants over other plants. Any organism that is capable of surviving with the plants that are still plentiful will have an advantage over organisms that can only survive on plants that are now rare or nonexistent. If there were no environmental changes, there would be little evolutionary pressure. In fact, many evolutionary theorists believe that the process is best described by something called **punctuated evolution** (Gould, 2007). This model suggests minimal evolutionary change most of the time, but rather dramatic and rapid evolutionary change when the environment changes dramatically.

There have certainly been periods in which such dramatic evolutionary change has occurred. For example, approximately sixty-five million years ago, a massive asteroid hit the earth near the current Gulf of Mexico (Black, 2022). The result was a mass extinction of much of the life on this planet, including the dinosaurs. Smaller creatures, such as the mammals of that period, were able to survive because they either required less food than the much larger dinosaurs or were able to consume food that the dinosaurs could not process. That event was certainly traumatic for dinosaurs, but without it, it is unlikely that human beings would ever have evolved. Frankly, dinosaurs ruled until a catastrophic event wiped out their food sources and changed the course of evolution.

Fortunately, we do not get hit by asteroids often, but the planet has gone through ice ages and periods of significant warming, and there have also been shorter periods of significant climate change due to massive volcanoes. We are going through an evolutionary change of our own making today. The world has changed more in the last hundred years than in the previous ten thousand years, and it is human beings that have been behind that change. I am not talking about climate change. We are operating in a world that is vastly different from the world of a hundred years ago, and we are doing it with bodies and minds that likely take tens of thousands of years to adapt. Think about it. Just a few thousand years ago, humans lived in very small groups of hunters and gatherers. Just one hundred years ago, travel was a long and arduous task. Just five hundred years ago, even the largest cities would be considered small by today's standards. Today, we can literally travel halfway across the planet in twelve hours; it was not that long ago that such travel would be unthinkable. We can be in routine contact with people in every corner of this planet, and we must deal with the challenges of working with thousands of different people instead of the small group that was the norm a few thousand years ago. Our bodies and our brain may be evolving, but they are not evolving nearly as fast as we are changing our world.

If you have been around for a while, you have lived through many of these dramatic changes. I have been around for a while. When I was a kid, my phone number was 44. That is not a typo. That was my actual phone number in a small town in central Wisconsin. When I moved to a larger town at the age of ten, my new phone number was 773. It was a few years later that phone numbers were standardized at seven numbers, although trying to remember seven numbers was considered so difficult that people typically resorted to using verbal mnemonics for the first two numbers. For example, when that process changed in the town I was living, my new number was Harrison 3 followed by four numbers. The first two letters of Harrison (HA) correspond to the numbers 42. If you grew up in the era of cell phones, you might never have noticed that below each of the numbers 2 through 9 are three to five letters from that era. Area codes did not exist because the process of making a long-distance phone call involved one operator talking to another and then talking to another, with each operator physically plugging in a connection from your phone to the phone you intended to call. There was no email; there was no Internet; the idea of something like Google was unthinkable. Everything in the library was either a book, magazine, or newspaper. The phone I carry in my pocket today has more computing power than the computer that served a campus of sixty thousand students when I was in graduate school. Moreover, that phone is my portal to virtually all the information in the entire world.

Those are just some of the changes in a single lifetime. They may not even be the most important changes. In less than two hundred

9

years, we have gone from most people working on farms to produce the food we eat to having less than 2 percent of our population able to produce all the food needed by our country and enough to export massive amounts of food to other countries. Travel across the country was possible when I was a kid, but few people engaged in such travel. Now, it is routine to get on a plane and travel hundreds or even thousands of miles in just a matter of hours. There was virtually no fast food when I was a kid; now, most restaurants in the United States are fast-food restaurants. The nature of our diet has changed dramatically, and not always for the best. However, the dramatic improvements in agriculture and transportation have meant that starvation, which was a serious concern to past generations, is rarely a problem unless war disrupts the system.

The implication of such massive change in such a short time to the environment is that we are almost certainly not well adapted to our current environment. There has not been enough time for our bodies and our brains to catch up with all these changes, and the worst part is that the changes are accelerating rather than decelerating. This creates a lot of problems for people, and one of the most significant problems is that we are subjected to situations that are difficult to handle and therefore a source of anxiety.

Value of Fear

Fear is our most primitive behavioral response. It is certainly one of the first behavioral responses to have evolved, and it is triggered in the oldest evolutionary part of the brain (the brainstem). This behavioral response prepares the organism to either escape or fight when faced with a potentially life-threatening situation.

When we think of fear, we think of the feeling that is associated with it. However, this behavioral response probably had no feeling associated with it when it first evolved because it evolved in creatures that did not have the brain capacity to have feelings or even conscious awareness. Many modern creatures still possess this fear response without the feelings associated with it. The

10

feelings are unnecessary; they probably are the result of cognitive abilities that evolved to make us aware of some of the activity in our brains. In most cases, this behavioral response achieves the same thing in us that it does in most other species. It gives us a better chance of surviving a life-or-death situation. In that respect, it remains a wonderful evolutionary tool for survival.

As you will learn later, the system that evaluates potential life-or-death situations is far from perfect, and sometimes it signals danger when in fact no danger exists. In that case, we experience what is called a *panic attack*. I discuss those in detail later and have an entire chapter devoted to the consequence of such panic attacks.

Value of Anxiety

Whereas fear mobilizes the body to respond to immediate threats, anxiety mobilizes the mind to anticipate future threats and prepare for them. This is an incredible resource. Again, it is perhaps the single most important asset of human beings. We can think hypothetically into the future and imagine both good and bad outcomes. This planning about the future is primarily done by our prefrontal cortex, and it is perhaps our greatest cognitive gift. We can use that information to prepare ourselves to handle whatever we encounter in the future. We no longer must wait for the danger to trigger fear, which in turn helps us survive that danger. We can take action that prevents the danger, warns us ahead of time if danger is likely, and allows us the time to react before the danger becomes imminent.

Our ability to use anxiety to improve our ability to function in difficult situations is the reason why anxiety is not the enemy. Anxiety is a resource, and it is a resource that is underappreciated because of the uncomfortable feelings associated with it. The idea that anxiety represents a weakness is simply ridiculous. Those who are not anxious are usually those who are not thinking clearly. The world is a dangerous place, and it is predictable that we will face danger as part of our everyday lives. The more we anticipate that

11

danger and feel anxious about that danger, the more likely it is that we are motivated to prepare before it arrives and either prevent it or handle it safely.

Risks in Those Who Rarely Get Anxious

One way to appreciate the value of anxiety is to imagine what it would be like not to have anxiety. Like pain, anxiety is a valuable signal that something may be wrong. There is a group of individuals who have significantly less anxiety than the rest of us. We call them psychopaths or sociopaths. The official diagnostic label is **antisocial personality disorder** (American Psychiatric Association, 2022). There are well-documented physiological differences between people with and without this diagnosis. One characteristic is that psychopaths tend to be underaroused, which is to say that the psychopath is motivated to create situations that are stimulating. This often translates into thrill-seeking behavior.

Psychopaths also show another physiological characteristic that is even more important in shaping their behavior. All of us are influenced by a pair of motivational systems called the behavioral activation system and the behavioral inhibition system. The **behavioral activation system** is influenced by potential rewards. It is what drives us to seek success and rewards. The **behavioral inhibition system** is influenced by potential losses. It is what drives us to behave in a way that minimizes the risk of such losses. In psychopaths, the behavioral inhibition system is not working well. These individuals are very good at seeking rewards but very bad at avoiding behavior that can lead to losses. Consequently, they engage in illegal activity because they do not fear the consequences of being arrested and sent to jail. Avoiding jail is a powerful incentive for most of us to avoid illegal activity. A good part of the behavioral inhibition system is anxiety.

The behavioral inhibition system does far more than just keep us out of jail. It is one of the most important elements in shaping a society in which people respect the rights of other people. For example, one of the reasons why we treat people fairly is that we

12

would likely be ostracized if we tended not to treat people fairly. The discomfort about potentially being ostracized has us constantly asking what people expect of us. Psychopaths do not ask that question, and that is one of the reasons why they lie, cheat, and steal if it is in their best interest.

For a good part of my career, I specialized in the treatment of anxiety and anxiety disorders. Almost without exception, my clients would describe their anxiety as if they viewed it as a weakness. When I would ask them their goal for treatment, it invariably was to remove the anxiety. They were delighted to find out that there was a group that experienced little anxiety, but their delight quickly faded when I explained that that group was called psychopaths. I rarely had to explain why psychopaths experience little anxiety or the fact that the lack of anxiety was probably contributing to the antisocial behavior that defines this disorder. This is the second reason why anxiety is not the enemy. Not only does anxiety protect us by having us prepare for potential danger, but also anxiety helps to socialize us to be the kind of caring and fair individuals others can love and respect.

Chapter Summary

Anxiety is part of our evolutionary history. Unlike fear, which is the most basic emotion, anxiety is far more subtle, more complicated, and more useful. Fear prepares the body to respond in a life-or-death situation. The preparation involves physiological changes that allow us to run faster to escape or fight harder if escape is impossible. It is an immediate response to an immediate threat. In contrast, anxiety is not an immediate physiological response, but rather a subtle change in our comfort level triggered by the idea that we may at some point in the future face a serious threat.

It is our ability to think hypothetically about the future and to imagine potential dangers that produces anxiety, and it is anxiety about potential dangers that drives behavior that reduces our risks. That is why anxiety is not the enemy; it is the energy behind human achievement because it motivates preparation that reduces potential danger and increases the likelihood of success. It also shapes our development in a way that encourages pro-social behavior that respects the rights of others and thus permits us to work together through mutual trust.

Section I

Managing Everyday Anxiety

Managing anxiety is possible, although not easy; eliminating anxiety is virtually impossible. The reasonable conclusion is that your goal should be the management of anxiety. Some people prefer to think of it as the management of stress because there is an unfortunate stigma associated with being anxious. However, these two concepts represent the same thing. You manage anxiety by keeping it to a level that allows you to function effectively and with reasonable comfort. It is a balance. If you are like the typical person, the balance you want is to eliminate anxiety. Who in their right mind would want to experience the discomfort of something like anxiety? However, we perform better under moderate anxiety. If you have something due tomorrow, you are likely to be more focused so that you can meet that deadline. Work on the same task with a deadline a month from now, and you are unlikely to be as focused and productive. We may not like the discomfort of anxiety, but it does focus one's energy, at least until it crosses a threshold. Everyone has experienced anxiety or stress that paralyzes their functioning. Such extreme anxiety or stress can be controlled, and it should be controlled.

I start this section by talking about the various triggers for anxiety and what makes those situations a trigger. Triggers are personal, so things that trigger anxiety in me may not trigger anxiety in you and vice versa. Triggers are also complex. They involve more than just a situation; they also involve our reaction to the situation. For example, if you are anxious in a performance situation, like giving a talk to a group of people, the way you interpret the situation can affect whether you experience moderate and normal anxiety, which can keep you on your toes, or an anxiety level that turns your mind to mush. This is the focus of chapter 2.

15

Chapter 3 moves beyond the experience of anxiety to the behaviors that are influenced by anxiety. Some of those behaviors are good; other behaviors are terrible. For example, if you must give a talk, the anxiety you feel in the days before the talk encourages you to prepare a great talk and rehearse it to the point that you can deliver it effectively. If you beg off giving the talk because of anxiety, you are putting yourself at a competitive disadvantage. That may reduce the anxiety but at a steep price.

Chapters 4 and 5 cover the topics that you are most likely interested in:. How do you control or manage anxiety, and how can you use those techniques in everyday situations? There is a principle that is critical in understanding this task. *We are programmed to learn anxiety quickly and to unlearn it slowly.* Learning anxiety quickly keeps us vigilant, more focused, and more careful in our decisions. When there is the potential of risk, such anxiety serves us well. However, sometimes our sense of risk is overblown, or the risk that once existed no longer exists. In that case, we need to reduce our anxiety. We can reduce our anxiety, and we do reduce our anxiety all the time. Think of the things that once made you very anxious but you now handle with little or no anxiety. With exposure and successful responses to those situations, we gradually learn to trust ourselves and therefore are less anxious. The key word here is *gradually*. Nature equipped us to unlearn anxiety but unlearning such a valuable safeguard too quickly is not a good idea. It may be that the risk we anticipate in a situation only occurs intermittently. If so, we might well enter that situation two or three times without experiencing negative consequences. If two or three experiences were enough to quell our anxiety, we might well enter the situation without the alertness inspired by anxiety and would fall victim to the risks of that situation.

The final chapter in this section (chapter 6) deals with manipulating the environment and your response to the environment to manage your anxiety responses in new situations. There are always new situations in life. We move to new locations, take on new jobs, meet new people, and face new challenges. Note that I used the term *manage* here rather than *control*. Our bias in new situations should always be to expect potential problems, and that means that we should be a bit anxious. If we manage our anxiety to the level that keeps us alert until we are reasonably sure that the new situation is safe, we are better off. We can keep anxiety in check if we take steps so that we feel confident in our ability to handle challenges. There is a lot to be said for the attitude of, "Been there, done that."

This entire section focuses on normal anxiety. The next section introduces anxiety disorders, which represent anxiety levels or anxiety responses that clearly interfere with our functioning. By the time we get to that section, you will appreciate that anxiety truly is normal and that most anxiety does not warrant a diagnosis.

Chapter 2

Anxiety Triggers

Everyone experiences anxiety. It is a natural part of life, but it is found more commonly in some situations than in others. If you are comfortable with your driving skills, you may experience little anxiety driving on a quiet street or even on an expressway. Add some snow or ice, and your anxiety increases dramatically. Anxiety in that situation is not only normal but also helpful. The wise decision might be to listen to your anxiety and not go out when driving is dangerous. If you have no other choice, the next best wise decision is to drive slowly and carefully.

In this chapter, we talk about the typical things that trigger anxiety. Some of the triggers we talk about will resonate with you, but not all of them. By understanding your personal triggers, you can plan for and therefore manage the anxiety that results. It is possible to manage the anxiety that seems to come out of the blue. However, it is much easier to manage anxiety if you know when to expect it and are prepared to respond accordingly.

What Makes You Anxious?

The best way to understand anxiety is to start by making a list of all the things that make you anxious. The list probably has hundreds of items from your actual experiences, but curiously enough, you can probably list thousands of other items that you have never experienced but feel confident would make you anxious. In other words, you have a built-in list of anxiety-producing events and situations. Once you create the list or a reasonable subset of the list, you can look for commonalities and, in the process, develop a strong understanding of how anxiety works for you.

When you create such a list, the first thing you will notice is that there is a large group of situations that create anxiety for everyone. There is also a large group of situations that create anxiety for most people but not everyone, as well as a large group of situations that create anxiety for a few people but not for most. In psychology, we refer to that as **individual differences**. Every person is unique, even identical twins, and that uniqueness is also expressed in what makes us anxious. We start this section by focusing on those situations that trigger anxiety in all or most individuals.

Situations that Make Almost Everyone Anxious

One situation that triggers anxiety for virtually everyone, at least initially, is public speaking. I emphasized in the previous sentence "at least initially" because with practice one gets very good at public speaking and experiences little or no anxiety while doing it. This principle is going to be a key theme throughout this book, but for now, this is just a tease for the rest of the book.

Another situation that generates anxiety for most people is taking tests, and the more important the test is, the greater the anxiety. If the test is only worth 1 percent of the grade for the course, the anxiety may be present, but it is not likely to be overwhelming. If the test represents 80 percent of the grade for the course, the anxiety is likely to be intense. Unpredictable tests tend to produce more anxiety than predictable tests. Think back to when you were in school. What did you feel when your instructor walked into class and announced, "Put your books on the floor. We are going to have a pop quiz"?

Many people get anxious about meeting new people, interviewing for jobs, or going out on first dates. Many golfers express anxiety about hitting the first drive on the first hole because, often, there are dozens of other golfers watching that first shot. It can be so embarrassing to hit a truly bad shot while everyone is watching. It is common to feel anxiety when you are asked to do something that you have never done before and are not sure you have the skills to be successful. That anxiety is likely to be more intense if people are observing or if you know that success or failure will be clearly visible. Most people feel anxiety when trying to sell something for the first time, especially if what they are trying to sell is themselves.

There are also situations that create anxiety for most people that are very different from the situations described so far. For example, driving in the middle of a snowstorm or a serious storm of any sort increases anxiety dramatically over driving in good weather. Standing on the edge of a cliff makes most people nervous; if the edge of the cliff has loose rocks, virtually everyone is going to be nervous. If in addition to the loose rocks there is a high wind, anyone who is not anxious is insane. A situation like that is clearly dangerous. Being threatened by someone with a gun, coming across a grizzly bear in the woods, or driving across Kansas when you see a tornado bearing down on you leads to instant anxiety. In fact, it is more likely that what you feel in those situations is fear, which is the body's response to an immediate threat.

Finally, danger need not be present for you to be anxious. In fact, much of our anxiety is not a response to a situation but to the possibility that a situation may occur in the future. We call such anxiety *anticipatory*. A classic example of anticipatory anxiety is the nervousness that you might feel waiting to go into a job interview or waiting for your turn to give a presentation.

You are probably aware that there are situations that make you anxious but do not appear to make other people anxious. You may be less aware of the fact that there are situations that make some other people anxious but do not make you anxious. We tend not to focus on anxiety unless we are experiencing it. We will talk about situations in which anxiety affects some people more than others, but before I do that, I want to point out an important fact. When we are anxious, we know we are anxious because we can feel it; when someone near us is anxious, we cannot feel what they are feeling. We judge their anxiety by what we can observe. A person might feel anxious but give no external indication of that anxiety or

20

indications that are so subtle that no one notices them. Without external indications of anxiety, we would incorrectly judge them to not be anxious. This principle is very important in later chapters because you will discover that it is much easier to hide your anxiety than to control it.

Situations that Make Some People Anxious

There are many situations in which we see dramatic individual differences in how anxious someone feels. Cataloging all these situations would be of little value. Instead, I want to focus on the variables that typically account for such individual differences. These variables can be divided into four general categories: *time dimension*, *behavioral demand*, *experience*, and *motivation level*.

One dimension that might influence the level of anxiety is the time between the thought about a potential risk and when that risk is likely to occur. For some people, thoughts about potential risk are almost as intense as facing the risk directly and immediately. The anxiety that they are likely to experience just moments before the situation may be close to the anxiety that they experience when first imagining the situation. For others, a risk far in the future, even if it is a serious risk, likely generates little or no anxiety until the risk is more immediate. Although this dimension may interact with some of the other dimensions, it tends to be relatively stable. There is no correct answer about the optimal anxiety response along the time dimension. Experiencing high levels of anxiety at any point in time may be disruptive simply because the anxiety prevents the person from functioning at an optimal level. But significantly delaying an anxiety response might leave the person with insufficient time to prepare to deal with the difficult situation. Moreover, life is complicated, which means that we deal with many difficult situations, and it is rare that we can ignore all the other situations to focus on only one.

We often get anxious about situations in which we have little or no control. Most people, especially younger people, get anxious at the thought of dying, even though death is inevitable. But even with an existential issue such as death, a careful analysis of the nature of our anxiety often reveals that our focus is on behavior. It is true that we all die, but most of us want to do it with dignity. Dying with dignity is a behavior; it involves focusing on others even as our own body gives out. It involves behaving in such a way that others are inspired and increase their admiration for us. If we imagine dying of a painful disease, we might well be anxious about both the pain and our ability to die with dignity given such intense pain.

Most of the things that make us anxious are not such existential issues as dying. Most involve situations in which we are required to handle some difficult situation, and the way we handle that situation has a significant impact on our future. The level of our skills in handling such situations and our experience in such situations has an enormous impact on our level of anxiety. People with excellent social skills, who have extensive experience meeting new people in a variety of situations, are unlikely to experience much anxiety about meeting someone new at work, at a party, or at a family get-together. Their experience tells them that they are likely to be successful. People with limited experience meeting new people may have much less confidence in their ability to handle the situation and therefore are more likely to be anxious about it. But even someone highly skilled socially, with considerable social experience, may be anxious about meeting the parents of someone they hope to marry. Despite their skills and experience, their desire to make a good impression on these extremely important people in their lives may heighten their anxiety.

There is a cliché in psychology that the best predictor of future behavior is past behavior in a similar situation. Clichés are often dismissed, but that is a mistake. Clichés exist in part because they are so clearly true that there is little to debate. People successful in certain situations routinely tend to be successful in those situations in the future. Of course, there is no guarantee of that, but if you were a betting person, bet on the person who has been successful in the past. Our experience with success or failure has an enormous impact on how confident we feel when facing new but similar situations. If we have generally been successful, our anxiety will only be modest because we have a reasonable expectation that we will be successful again. If we have generally been unsuccessful, the best prediction is that we will be unsuccessful again, and as a result, we will be anxious.

Sometimes, unsuccessful experiences can decrease our anxiety. If we have never failed at something, we may have an unrealistic expectation that failure will overwhelm us. However, if we take on challenges and sometimes fail, we now have experience in how we handle failure. The truth is that everyone fails. Some people fail more often than others, but the only way to be certain that you never fail is to never take risks. Failing to take a risk means that you will never accomplish anything, which might well be labeled a failure in and of itself. The people that we call winners are not people that win all the time; they are the people who come back from losses. I am a big believer in competitive sports for young people. I believe that such sports teach important life skills, such as dedication, tenacity, teamwork, and sportsmanship. But one of the most valuable lessons in sports is that you can be badly beaten one week and come back and win the next week. A loss is not the end of the world, but if the loss leads to giving up, it can have a huge negative impact on your life.

The final dimension that can have an impact on our level of anxiety is our level of motivation. If you plan on playing chess with a friend, the possibility of losing will not make you terribly anxious unless you believe that you absolutely must win. For most people, a chess match is not that important. But there are always things that are important. It might be the possibility of losing a friendship, a job, or a chance to change your life. If the emotional stakes are high enough, the anxiety will be intense. This is a delicate balance. We increase our success rate by being more highly motivated and doing what is necessary to be successful. However, if that level of motivation is so high that the anxiety overwhelms us, we are not likely to be able to perform at our best. This is a game that we play with ourselves as we try to manage anxiety. We learn to tell ourselves that it is important enough to work hard, but not so important that we are going to be devastated if we are unsuccessful.

Situations that Rarely Make People Anxious

It is often enlightening to look at those situations that rarely make people anxious. Those situations often have important things in common. They are usually situations in which there is little at stake. When we are getting together with friends to have a drink or a meal and just chat, we are not likely to experience anxiety. These people are already our friends, so we feel we are not likely to lose them during a casual encounter. But get together with the same people to talk about an issue that could be highly contentious, such as their excessive drinking, and the situation is different. There is a risk, and so we feel anxious. One reason that we enjoy getting together with friends is that we are relaxed in such situations because we expect them to go well, but a second reason is that such positive interactions with friends are invigorating. If we have had a tough week, with lots of things going wrong, we might look forward to getting together with friends on Friday night. When we are around people who make us feel good about ourselves and are not likely to judge us, we are rarely anxious. One reason we work so hard to find good friends is that spending time with them is good for our mental health.

Let me take a moment to point out the obvious. Not everyone you know makes you comfortable. Some people just seem to be judgmental all the time, and it is perfectly normal for you to feel uncomfortable or anxious when you are around them. Some people are unpredictable, one moment being quiet or friendly and the next moment angry and hostile. Those people make us anxious because we never know what to expect. One reason most people prefer not to hang out with their boss is that they do not feel they can be themselves with someone who is judging their performance at work. People that make us anxious for any or all these reasons can be thought of as *high-maintenance friendships*. We all have such friends, and they can be very good friends. They may be people who love doing things our other friends do not love. But some friends naturally make us more anxious. If we restrict ourselves only to those individuals that never make us anxious, we will only need a single hand to count our friends. Even in the most intimate relationships, such as between lovers, there are always potential situations that make us anxious. But if we have a history of resolving problems when they arise with that individual, our experience allows us to manage any anxiety we experience.

What do all these situations have in common? On the surface, they seem to fit into more than one category. Many situations that make us anxious are situations in which we must perform and, more importantly, are judged on our performance. Other situations involve potentially dangerous elements, which represent a risk to our well-being. The risk might be injury or death, but it could also be the risk of losing our job or being humiliated in front of friends or colleagues. Finally, recognizing that much of our anxiety is not a response to a situation but rather a response to our own thoughts is an important insight that is critical when we talk about managing anxiety.

The word *apprehension* is often used to refer to all these situations. We are apprehensive about a situation in which the outcome is uncertain. Moreover, it is often a situation in which we are not sure that we can handle at least some of the possible aspects of the situation. Note that we are talking about two unknown issues: what might happen and how well we can handle it. People hate the unknown. We really hate the unknown when there is risk associated with it or at least potential risk, and our response to situations with those two unknowns often includes anxiety.

When Do You Get Anxious?

Now that we talked about situations that make most people anxious, let's look more closely at the situations that make you personally anxious. I am guessing that most of the items in the previous section are on your list. Some of those items are considered minor because they generate only minor anxiety. I am betting there are others on the list that make you wince; those items produce intense anxiety for you. In fact, those items may disrupt a significant portion of your life because of the anxiety they produce.

Using the situations described earlier, you probably have a list of things that make you anxious. However, there are probably other situations that make you anxious. For example, perhaps you are one of the people who are anxious when you are alone. You may be more comfortable meeting new people for the first time than being in a situation in which you are by yourself. Perhaps there are certain people in your life that always make you anxious. It might be your boss, a particular friend or acquaintance, or someone you know from work. Try to construct as complete a list as you can and, in the process, give the items a rough ranking. By *rough ranking* I mean which of the items consistently produce strong anxiety, which items produce moderate anxiety or variable anxiety that is only occasionally strong, and which of the items produce modest anxiety that is easily managed.

You now have a reasonably representative list of things that make you anxious. What can you do with that list? The task of creating that list is the first step in learning to manage your own anxiety. The most common mistake people face in managing their anxiety is looking for a solution that works in every case. There are few such solutions, and frankly, the ones that exist are not particularly good. One solution that unfortunately many people with anxiety use is drugs or alcohol. Frankly, if you drink enough, you can pretty much numb any level of anxiety. In fact, if you drink enough, you can kill yourself, literally! A blood-alcohol level of 0.50 percent is lethal for almost everyone (roughly six times the legal limit for driving while intoxicated). There are anti-anxiety drugs that can be taken safely in high doses, but with a high enough dose, just staying awake can be difficult. Pretty much any anxiety that is present is stifled with such high doses. However, as you come off those drugs a few hours later, you will experience massive rebound anxiety. The longer you take the drugs, the more intense the rebound anxiety.

I am not going to tell you that drugs and alcohol are evil. That is not my role. Later in this book, when we talk about anxiety disorders, you will find there are drugs that can significantly reduce some of the anxiety and make it easier for you to manage the rest. However, we are not talking about anxiety disorders here.

We are talking about normal anxiety. It may not seem normal because of its intensity. It may even seem to be a disorder because of its intensity. But anxiety is nevertheless a normal response to a variety of situations.

What I present in this section, and even in the section on anxiety disorders, is an alternative management system. The alternative works, but it requires work on your part. The major disadvantage of the alternative approach to managing anxiety is that you must manage each of the situations that produce the anxiety. There are techniques, for example, that are amazingly effective at reducing public speaking anxiety. Those techniques might be somewhat helpful for managing anxiety about job interviews or driving in a snowstorm, but for the most part, reducing anxiety in those situations requires a specific approach geared to those situations.

How Do You React to Your Anxiety?

Now that you have a list of things that make you anxious, you need to think about something else. What do you do when you are anxious in each of those situations? Again, each situation is different. In some situations, you do your best to escape the situation when it occurs. Other situations you might avoid completely. Sometimes escape or avoidance is impossible. That is a terribly uncomfortable situation to find yourself in. How do you respond when that happens? Do you find yourself saying nothing and trying to blend into the woodwork? Do you find yourself talking too much, as if the talking somehow can ward off the uncomfortable feelings? Do you find yourself trying to deal with the situation but in a manner that is ineffective or even embarrassing?

I know it is hard to go through that long list of things that make you anxious and think about those anxiety-producing situations. Just thinking about them increases your anxiety, which gives you a clue about the nature of anxiety itself. But go through the list or at least a subset of the list. Think about each situation and list the ways you deal with it. You do not have to show the list to anyone.

27

There is no need to be embarrassed, although many people working on such a list are embarrassed. Pat yourself on the back for taking the first steps toward taking control of your anxiety.

Since each person is unique, I cannot predict what your list will look like precisely. What I can predict is that you will likely discover that there is a limited number of responses you use when you are in an anxiety-producing situation. You may never, for example, talk too much when anxious, or you might be like me when I was younger and cannot stop talking. You will probably find that your typical response to many anxiety-producing situations is to either avoid them if possible or escape from them if you can. That kind of procrastination is perfectly normal. That is the kind of behavior that is driven by anxiety. In the world in which human beings evolved, that type of behavior was adaptive. It is less adaptive in today's world. Moreover, if you routinely avoid or escape situations that make you anxious, you will never face your anxiety and learn how to manage it. The entire theme of this book is to recognize anxiety and learn how to manage it effectively and encourage you to face that anxiety. It is the only way for you to learn that you can manage it.

What Things Do Not Make You Anxious?

This has been a tough chapter. I have asked you to confront your anxiety by listing all the things that make you anxious and then to confront it even more by listing the things you do in response to that anxiety. I want to end the chapter on a high note. Yes, indeed, there are things in your life that make you anxious. Some of the things that make you anxious are inhibiting your ability to function as effectively as you would like. They may even be embarrassing you or severely affecting your self-esteem. We can deal with that, and I will show you how to do it in this book.

Right now, I want you to look at the other side of the anxiety issue. Some things make you anxious, but there are many things that do not make you anxious. Moreover, there are things in your life that once made you anxious but no longer make you anxious. I want to start with that second category. I want you to make a list of at least ten things that no longer make you anxious. They might be things from work or school. They might be things in your social life. They might be activities that you truly enjoy. What they have in common is that there was a time when they were anxiety producing, but that time is in the past. You overcame your anxiety in those situations.

So, take a few minutes and make your list. You are likely to find that your list falls into predictable categories. I am guessing that you can list several people that once made you anxious who no longer make you anxious. They might have changed, but it is more likely that you changed your response to them. I am also guessing that there are tasks that once made you anxious and no longer make you anxious. It is entirely possible that those tasks still make you anxious in some situations but no longer make you anxious in other situations. Put together your list to give us something to work with.

Now that you have your list, do your best to organize it. Find categories in that list. Ask yourself if any of those categories overlap the categories of things that still make you anxious. Do your best to remember what it was like before you conquered your anxiety with these items. Then, see if you can remember what you did to conquer your anxiety. You did conquer it; you were once anxious in those situations, and you are not as anxious or perhaps not anxious at all now. Remember the principle I introduced in chapter 1. We are programmed to learn anxiety quickly and to unlearn it slowly. We know how to unlearn it, but we do not often use optimal strategies for unlearning. Perhaps you used optimal strategies for some of your anxieties, but I am betting that most were suboptimal, and yet those strategies still worked. Imagine what you can do if you optimize those anxiety management techniques.

Chapter Summary

Anxiety is uncomfortable, and in some cases, anxiety can be so intense that it disrupts functioning and therefore qualifies as a psychological disorder. For these reasons, many people think of anxiety as problematic. It certainly can be problematic, but in most cases, anxiety is a natural response to the situations that we face. In this chapter, we looked at the situations that trigger anxiety as well as situations that do not trigger anxiety. This is the first step in analyzing your anxiety responses and whether they present a problem. In future chapters, we will look at ways to manage your anxieties. In general, the most effective anxiety control techniques are focused on individual situations and the mastery of those situations.

Chapter 3

Behaviors Driven by Anxiety

One of the more interesting and useful ways of looking at anxiety is to imagine the reasons why it evolved. Remember, anxiety and fear are not the same. The fear response, which is shared by almost every organism with even a primitive brain, drives the fight-or-flight syndrome. Basically, it prepares us to run like hell or fight like hell if our life depends on it. Anxiety feels like a milder form of fear, but it is not. Different brain mechanisms are involved in fear and anxiety, although some situations may trigger both.

In this chapter, I focus on the anxiety that we have called *apprehension*. This is anticipatory in nature. The situation that is generating the anxiety is not yet there, and yet we are responding as if it were. On the face of it, that seems like the worst of all possible worlds. Not only are we anxious about a particular situation, but we are also anxious about it even before it occurs. In fact, we are anxious about it even if there is only a possibility that it will occur. But, in fact, as you will see in this chapter, it is the best of all possible worlds. Our amazing ability to think hypothetically about the future and to visualize risks long before we face them is one of our greatest strengths. In my opinion, the only strength greater than that ability is our ability to work together with others as a team. We are the best possible social animals, and a good part of our success is because we are stronger as a group. The fact that we can anticipate problems and prepare for them contributes mightily to the success of our species and to our individual success. Unfortunately, it contributes to most of our anxiety in the process.

How Anxiety Works

When I talk about emotions in my classes, I often present the following hypothetical situation. Imagine that you spent years developing the perfect computer program to drive a vehicle. I used this example twenty years ago when the idea of a computer driving a vehicle was science fiction. As I write this paragraph now, we are very close to having self-driving cars and trucks. In fact, as you read this, self-driving cars may be routine. The fact that science fiction has, in a relatively short time, turned into science fact gives us some great material to work with.

Now, imagine that you want to add one more feature before you turn your computer program over to the task of driving cars and trucks. What you want to add are human emotions. Why might you want to add emotions? Well, the entities that have been most successful in driving cars and trucks in the past are human beings, and they have emotions. Therefore, it stands to reason that emotions are an important part of human functioning and should be included in our computer program. My guess is that you are not persuaded by this argument. In fact, my guess is that you find this argument silly. Why would you want your self-driving car to be emotional? You certainly do not want your self-driving car to suffer from road rage and step on the gas to run someone off the road because the program got angry. You probably think that one of the advantages of having a computer program is that it does not "suffer" from emotional influences.

Note that I put the word *suffer* in quotation marks. From the standpoint of performing a complex task like driving a car or truck, emotion adds little and often influences behavior that is not only suboptimal but also potentially dangerous. This obvious fact leads us to the central question of why we have emotions.

We know quite a bit about emotions. We know that most of the brain mechanisms for emotions are in what we call *midbrain structures*. In human beings, those midbrain structures are almost completely covered by the massive cerebral cortex that differentiates human beings from other animals. Other animals have a cerebral cortex, but no other animal has anywhere near the size of the cerebral cortex that human beings have. Moreover, the cerebral cortex has a much larger role in what human beings can do compared to the cerebral cortex of other animals. Most of our perceptual processes are controlled by the cerebral cortex. Virtually all our thinking, memory, and reasoning are controlled by our cerebral cortex. Much of our personality and the behaviors that are part of our personality are heavily influenced by the cerebral cortex. But we are still emotional beings, and those emotions can have powerful impacts on our lives. Anxiety is just one of those emotions.

Many of the emotions that we experience as human beings are also experienced by other animals. They are a part of the evolutionary history of animals. If you have a pet dog or cat, you understand they experience emotions. You can often see the emotions on their faces, just as you can read emotions on the faces of human beings. Our faces were part of our communication system long before our species developed language. Even today, we trust the information transmitted through facial expressions at least as much as what people tell us. If you ask friends how they are doing, and they tell you, "Fine," you will accept that answer if their facial expressions confirm their response but will doubt the answer if their faces tell you that something is bothering them.

We have a massive brain (primarily our cerebral cortex), which is capable of amazing feats of thought, perception, and reasoning. But we also have an older part of the brain that generates drives and emotions that are more primitive but still have an enormous impact on our behavior. We know from research that the parts of our brain that generate emotions are an earlier evolutionary achievement compared to the parts of our brain that we use for solving problems. The nature of evolution is that it builds on existing features. Any change in an organism that increases the likelihood of survival and reproduction is favored in the next generation if that change is due to a change in the genetic template for the organism. To use the language of geneticists, those organisms with traits that give them a survival advantage are more likely to pass on their genes, and therefore the next generation will have more individuals who carry those favored genes.

Some of the midbrain structures produce what we call *drives*, which is a strong impulse to engage in certain behaviors. Hunger and thirst are examples of drives, and clearly, hunger and thirst are important to our survival. That is as true today as it was a hundred million years ago. Anxiety is in a different category. Anxiety creates an uncomfortable situation that influences behavior. Hunger and thirst represent uncomfortable situations that drive very specific behaviors. When we are hungry, we want to eat; when we are thirsty, we want to drink. But when we are anxious, it is less clear what we want to do because anxiety can be triggered by so many different potential sources of risk. The best way to reduce the risk, and therefore the anxiety, depends on the nature of the risk.

Narrowing our discussion of emotions to the very specific emotion of anxiety, we can take the information we learned in the last chapter and begin to build a model of why nature included anxiety in our evolutionary development. Let me be clear that much of what I am saying here is speculative, and it is entirely possible that some of these speculations are incorrect. However, the speculation provides insights that are helpful in the management of our own anxiety.

It is difficult to separate the interaction of two aspects of our brain functioning that evolved at different times. Today, for human beings, anxiety is typically a response to a thought about what might happen in the future. It is also a signal when the current situation might have some risk. Think of it as an alert status a few steps below the highest alert status, which is the fear response. Soldiers consider *red alert* to mean a fight that is happening now or will happen very quickly, but they have lower alert statuses when the risk is high but not imminent. We do know that our fight-or-flight response is more likely to be triggered when we are anxious, which is one of the reasons there is such a strong relationship between anxiety and fear. So, we might speculate that anxiety serves the purpose in lower animals, less capable of thinking hypothetically into the future than humans, of being more alert when faced with a potentially dangerous situation. Their analysis of potential danger is likely primitive compared to what we can do. For example, they may be anxious because they are in a place that was dangerous in the past. It may not have been the place that was dangerous; perhaps it was a predator that was in that place in the past. We can make that distinction because we can think, but more primitive creatures that are unable to think at that level are more likely to survive if they remember only that there was something about this place that was dangerous.

Our ability to think about the future supercharges this potential danger signal, and that is what anxiety is: *a signal of potential risk.* When we can anticipate the risk before it occurs because of our ability to think about the future, we can prepare for the risk. What an amazing ability that is. It means that if we think about potential risks from predators, we can plan actions to avoid those predators or use our intellect to devise ways of fighting off those predators. We almost never face predators in today's modern world, but we do face risks that can be life-and-death and much more frequent risks that threaten our comfort.

If we have a job interview scheduled for tomorrow or next week, it is only natural to be anxious about our performance in that interview. Anxiety is uncomfortable, so our natural reaction is to try to reduce that anxiety. One way to reduce it is to cancel the interview and never go on another interview. However, that is not a very good choice because, in today's world, the way we hunt or gather our food is by getting a job and earning money to buy food from a grocery store or restaurant. However, there is a second and more effective way of reducing anxiety about the interview. We can prepare for the interview so that we are more confident that we can perform well. This strategy is central to all the management procedures discussed in this book. It will be coupled with one other strategy. That second strategy is a set of procedures that reduces our experience of anxiety. The second strategy is discussed in more detail in the next chapter.

35

Anxiety that Drives Withdrawal

Anxiety, like all emotions and drives, influences behavior. One type of behavior driven by anxiety is withdrawal. There are times when that is a perfectly reasonable response, and anxiety is an appropriate signal that that response should occur. Unless you need to drive in a blizzard, it would be wise to not do it. If you have never driven in a blizzard, trust me, you will be anxious. I lived in Buffalo for twenty-five years, so I have had lots of experience with snowstorms. The anxiety you feel driving in a blizzard, or even imagining driving in a blizzard, is a sufficiently strong signal to postpone any trip you have planned or to cut it short if necessary.

Driving in a blizzard is one of many situations that would be handled best by avoiding them. A blizzard is just one example of the power of Mother Nature. A hurricane certainly qualifies as something to avoid, either by staying off the road in a safe place or fleeing the hurricane before it arrives. Pilots understand you should not challenge certain weather conditions in a plane. Thunderstorms can be powerful enough to push a plane into the ground or even rip the wings off. But there are other situations that also would be better off avoided. For example, taking illegal drugs represents a risk. The risk includes the possibility that you might be arrested, and the long-term effect of the arrest could be enormous. But there is also the possibility that you could become addicted to a drug. Moreover, illegal drugs are not processed as carefully as prescription drugs. Therefore, it is entirely possible that the drugs you purchase on the street may be potentially dangerous or even lethal. That is especially true now that the drug fentanyl is often used to spike other illegal drugs. Many people likely avoid using illegal drugs because of the anxiety from these potential risks. Clearly, the anxiety is not high enough to prevent everyone from using illegal drugs. If it were, we would not have such a huge market for illegal drugs.

What other classes of behavior might be avoided because even the thought of engaging in them generates anxiety? Getting into a fight that you almost certainly would lose would classify. Getting into any fight should classify because it is entirely possible that the fight will get out of control and lead to serious consequences. You might be bigger and stronger and able to win a fistfight with a particular individual, but what if that person is carrying a weapon? Risking the loss of something significant (e.g., money, your job, or an important relationship) might be something that you want to avoid. You can imagine hundreds of activities that might involve such a risk, the vast majority of which you should avoid.

The avoidance covered in this section is not problematic; in fact, it is desirable because it reduces our risk. We need to make the distinction between effective behavior driven by anxiety and ineffective or detrimental behavior driven by anxiety. We want to encourage the former and discourage or deal with the latter. The next couple of chapters deal with this issue.

Anxiety that Drives Engagement

The more primitive response to anxiety is to avoid the situation or escape from the situation. But there is another response, and it is one that should be cultivated. Anxiety represents the feeling one has when there is doubt about whether a difficult situation can be properly handled. Effective preparation can reduce that doubt. Routinely preparing for such situations can reduce most doubt in many situations.

For example, if one is anxious about giving a public talk, devoting one's effort to preparing for that talk and for building one's skills so that the talk is high quality reduces future anxiety when a talk is scheduled. Remember that anxiety is learned quickly but unlearned slowly. In general, anxiety is unlearned if there is evidence that the anxiety is unnecessary. If you are anxious about talking but you prepare and, as a result, give an excellent talk, that reduces your anxiety the next time you have to give a talk. However, you do not want all the anxiety to be removed. Why do you not want that to happen? Because if the anxiety is eliminated, you do not experience the discomfort that motivates you to put in the time needed to be prepared for the next talk. Outstanding speakers routinely experience mild anxiety about upcoming talks that can only be relieved by preparing a solid and effective talk. If forced to say a few words with no preparation, they may well do a fine job, but they recognize that preparation would have made their remarks stronger and more persuasive.

Remember that anxiety is a signal that there might be risk and that preparation might help you to reduce or eliminate that risk. To decide on the best course of action, you need to interpret the reason behind the anxiety. It is perfectly reasonable to be anxious about a job interview or a public talk. There could very well be a lot at stake in both cases. If you fail to impress in a job interview, you may lose the chance for a great job. Moreover, you may make the kind of impression on the person interviewing you that will haunt your career for years. Give a great talk, and people will remember you; give a terrible talk, and they are even more likely to remember you, and not in a positive way. However, both situations allow you to prepare. There is no guarantee that things will go smoothly with the right preparation, but the probability that they will go smoothly increases. There is no guarantee that with the right preparation you will always succeed, but the probability of success does increase. The anxiety that you experience in the job interview or while giving the talk can be managed, but you do not want to manage the anxiety that is anticipatory. Anticipatory anxiety is the motivation for the hard work that it takes to be prepared. That principle will be very clear in the next chapter.

When Anxiety Is Critical

Life always contains challenges, and sometimes life contains risks. Anxiety is an important motivator in both situations. I spent a good part of my career working with people who experienced serious and sometimes debilitating anxiety. Technology for managing anxiety has improved dramatically over the last few decades. But I always found that my priority with clients was to convince them that anxiety was not the enemy. If one has been suffering from anxiety for any length of time and has experienced the restrictions that such anxiety imposes on one's life, it only makes sense to see anxiety as the enemy.

How do you convince someone who has been suffering from anxiety to think about anxiety differently? I already shared the strategy that I used successfully. I simply point out that there is a group of people who experience very little anxiety. Clients with anxiety problems immediately want to know how to join that group. When I point out that that group has a different diagnosis, my anxious clients are surprised. From their perspective, if you just get rid of anxiety, there are no other problems in life. When I tell them that the diagnostic term for that group is *psychopath*, they are usually shocked but rarely surprised. One of the reasons why psychopaths behave the way they do is that they do not experience the kind of normal anxiety that shapes people's behavior. Therefore, they engage in risky behaviors of all types, from driving too fast and experimenting with drugs to getting into trouble with the law. They do not experience the anxiety, guilt, or shame that you and I would experience if we lied to a friend or people rejected us as evil.

One of the greatest advantages of normal anxiety is that we tend to experience it in situations in which we are behaving in an antisocial manner. We are naturally social creatures, and the threat of losing the trust and goodwill of friends and family is more than enough to influence us to behave in an appropriate manner. However, the appropriate level of anxiety to shape prosocial behavior but not interfere with our other responsibilities in life is a delicate balance. At any given time, that balance can be disrupted. Like many things in life, there is a natural balance that we call *homeostasis*. Often, if we deviate from that homeostasis, natural mechanisms tend to bring us back to the appropriate balance. That is not always true with anxiety, but there are ways of taking control of our anxiety.

Anxiety is far too important to our survival and our normal development for us to try to eliminate it. If that was your goal when you picked up this book, you picked up the wrong book. You can handle anxiety; you may not like anxiety, but you can handle it. Anxiety will make you better if you manage it so that you can function at near-optimal performance. That is the focus of this book.

Chapter Summary

Anxiety almost certainly evolved over a long time, and it is found in most advanced animals. It may be more pronounced in human beings because of our ability to think hypothetically about the future and to imagine things that represent risk or danger. Other animals may be able to imagine the future, but it is unlikely that they can do it as well as we can. This ability is a two-edged sword. On one side, the ability to anticipate potential risks gives us an enormous advantage in that we can prepare to deal with those risks. On the other side, we experience the uncomfortable feeling of anxiety. That uncomfortable feeling perhaps makes us miserable, but it also motivates us to prepare.

Anxiety tends to motivate behavior. One type of behavior is escape or avoidance. That behavior is adaptive if there is high risk and no good reason to take on that risk. That behavior is not adaptive, however, if we are avoiding situations that are important to confront if we wish to be successful in life. The second behavior influenced by anxiety is any behavior that reduces anxiety. That is a very productive use of anxiety. It is what gets us to study earlier for an exam or prepare for a job interview. The anxiety in this second situation is still uncomfortable, but the discomfort is well worth it given the benefits we experience from being motivated to plan.

Chapter 4

Anxiety Control Techniques

In this chapter, I cover the topics that are probably the reason you purchased this book. Most people concerned about anxiety want to know how to eliminate it. I hope by now I have convinced you that eliminating anxiety is not a good idea. Anxiety has a lot of benefits. What we focus on is not the elimination of anxiety but rather the management of anxiety.

There are two aspects of anxiety that are particularly disruptive for people. The first is that high levels of anxiety can interfere with our performance. Almost everyone has experienced a situation in which their anxiety was so high that they panicked. By panic, I mean that they could not think straight. Perhaps this has happened to you. It might have been an exam on which you could not remember things that you knew you should be able to remember from your studying. It might have been a social situation in which you were meeting someone and something about the situation made you so anxious that your conversation was embarrassing. Such situations can be incredibly humiliating. The techniques that we cover in this chapter and throughout the book can help dramatically with that level of anxiety.

The second negative aspect of anxiety is that the anxiety itself is an embarrassment. When we meet someone for the first time, we do not want them to see us as so anxious that they wonder what is wrong with us. When we are giving a talk, we do not want the audience to hear our voice crack or see our hands physically shake. When we are on a first date, we want to be relaxed, calm, and charming. If we are obviously nervous, we are less likely to make a good impression. You will learn that it is easier to hide your anxiety so that others do not see it than to control your anxiety. If you hide your anxiety often enough in a specific situation, your anxiety will gradually go down. Remember, anxiety can be unlearned, but it is unlearned slowly.

There is a second reason why you want to control the observable aspects of anxiety. If you are nervous about giving a talk in public and you focus on that anxiety, the anxiety will build. Anxiety is one of those emotions that feeds itself. If we sense that our hands are shaking, that observation alone accelerates the shaking and the other physiological manifestations of anxiety. If we then try to think about what we want to say in our talk, the anxiety makes it hard for us to remember what we want to say, and that fact causes us to be even more anxious. Realizing that we cannot think straight may very well lead to panic. [Just a reminder: the panic we are talking about here is not the same thing as panic attacks, which are uncued fear responses. I talk about this in more detail later in the book.]

Our experience of anxiety is deceptive. Moreover, our strong sense of what anxiety is and how it works is inaccurate. We experience anxiety as a feeling, and we experience the physiological manifestations of anxiety as a response to that feeling. We are anxious for a reason, and our hands are shaking because of our feeling of anxiety. There is also a third component to anxiety, which is the behavior influenced by the anxiety. So, there are three elements to anxiety: the feeling, the physiological arousal, and the behavior influenced by anxiety. However, research shows that our feeling and physiological manifestations of anxiety are not as closely connected as they seem, and the behavior can operate independently of both aspects of anxiety (Lang, 1985).

We experience the feeling of anxiety and the physiological manifestations as if they were the same thing. But research shows that it is possible to change the physiological manifestations of anxiety and still have the feeling present or vice versa (Barlow, 2002; Lang, 1985). There is also evidence that suggests our impression that feelings come first and physiological responses are secondary may not be accurate. For example, one model of emotion suggests that the feelings we experience are the result of reading our physiological state and labeling an emotion based on the physiological state present (Friedman, 2010). Yet another model of emotion suggests that we read our physiological state to determine whether we are emotionally aroused and then judge which emotion we are experiencing based on our interpretation of the situation (Dror, 2017; Schachter & Singer, 1962). Of course, sometimes our interpretation of the situation is wrong and, therefore, our emotional response seems unreasonable. Both models of emotion are counterintuitive, but there is sufficient research consistent with these models that we should not dismiss them.

We do not need to go into depth on the decades of research on emotion. But we do need to recognize from that research that emotion is a far more complicated topic than it feels to us. When talking about managing the specific emotion of anxiety, we will use separate techniques for managing the physiological elements, the psychological feelings, and the behaviors that are influenced by anxiety.

Managing the Physiological Aspects of Anxiety

One aspect of anxiety is the physiological responses that occur when we are anxious. Those are automatic responses, but with a little practice, we can moderate them, thus increasing our sense of control. In this section, we talk about how we moderate these responses.

The Physiology of Anxiety

Take a moment to think about what your body feels like when you are anxious. Your body clearly is responding when you feel anxious. You are physically tense; it is not an accident that we use the word *tense* to refer to both the tension in one's muscles and the feeling of being anxious. Your heart is also beating faster. Some people are very sensitive to that increase in heart rate, whereas others are much less sensitive. However, today everyone can become sensitive to such changes in their heart rate by purchasing a smartphone with heart rate detection capability. It will be interesting to see what effect routine access to such information will have on our emotional responsivity.

Whether you can feel the heart rate or not, your heart rate does increase when you are anxious, and the more anxious you are, the more it increases. It is easy to measure heart rate. You can feel your heart rate by lightly placing a finger over the artery near your wrist and counting the pulses. That process is called *taking one's pulse*. You can easily measure the heart rate electrically with two electrodes properly placed. When the left ventricle of your heart squeezes to push that blood out into the body, its action is innervated by a strong electrical signal to the muscles of that part of the heart. That electrical signal is so strong that it is easy to pick up with electrodes on the skin. Finally, there are inexpensive instruments that fit over a finger and will read your heart rate (and other variables, such as blood oxygen level). These instruments are now routinely used in doctor's offices and can be purchased online for about $20.

Why would we want to measure heart rate? It can be a valuable indicator of the level of anxiety and has allowed us to study anxiety responses in the laboratory. With cheaper and more portable heart rate measures, scientists are now able to study anxiety in the real world, giving us insights that have informed many of the suggestions in this book.

When you are anxious, your palms tend to sweat. Your face may also sweat, but typically your palms sweat first. Without going into the physiological details, different mechanisms control palmar sweating and the sweating associated with temperature regulation. Normally, our body uses sweat to cool itself. The evaporation of sweat from our skin moves heat away from our bodies. That sweating tends to occur on the face and the body, including the chest, back, and underarms. The sweating that occurs on one's palms is controlled more by the anxiety level of the individual. It is a different mechanism. It does not take sophisticated instruments to detect that your palms are sweating; you can feel the sweat on your palms. Moreover, you understand that the sweat on your palms is related to anxiety. Therefore, you might be embarrassed to shake hands with someone if you are feeling anxious because they will have no difficulty detecting your sweaty palms.

The amount of sweat on the palms is a sensitive indicator of the amount of physiological reactivity that one is experiencing from anxiety. It can be measured with two large electrodes on a person's hands. What you do is pass a current between the two electrodes. If there is no sweat, little current passes because the skin shows high resistance to the flow of electricity. However, sweat is highly conductive, which means that much more electricity flows between the electrodes. With this measure, called the *galvanic skin response* (GSR), we can detect very low levels of anxiety that would not be apparent from just feeling the palms for sweat. We typically use large electrodes for this measure because the large electrodes spread out the flow of electricity. This prevents discomfort, which besides being annoying would interfere with the measurement of anxiety.

Measuring palmar sweating provides an even more sensitive index of an anxiety response than measuring heart rate. The first responsibility of the heart is to move oxygen to the body using the bloodstream. Clearly, the heart responds to anxiety, but that response may be overwhelmed by the primary duties of the heart. In contrast, palmar sweating is more specific to anxiety. Much of our understanding of anxiety is based on being able to measure the physiology of this response as people deal with challenging situations in the laboratory. The advantage of having such physiological measures is that we do not have to rely on our insights about our anxious responses to situations. Unfortunately, we are not always consciously aware of the things that make us anxious

Finally, your breathing is also affected by your anxiety level. When you are anxious you tend to take shallow breaths. Therefore, you are getting less oxygen into your body, and so you feel the need to breathe more frequently. Therefore, your breathing becomes shallow and rapid, and, in extreme cases, so shallow and rapid that you are hyperventilating.

Managing Your Breathing

When you are anxious, your breathing tends to become shallow and rapid. This is one symptom of anxiety that you can control. We may not be able to stop our breathing, but we can deliberately take deep breaths. Deep breaths have an immediate calming effect. Deep breaths help whether you are very anxious or only modestly anxious. They even work when you are not particularly anxious. Many smartwatches now routinely encourage the wearer to take deep breaths for one minute to slow their heart rate and to make them feel more relaxed. It works; it is one of the easiest anxiety management techniques to master, and it has an immediate effect.

The optimal way of controlling your breathing is to take deep breaths using your diaphragm. When you take deep breaths from your diaphragm, you see a slight bulging of your stomach just below the rib cage. When practicing these deep breaths, it is helpful to stand in front of a mirror with your hand resting just below your rib cage. This allows you to see the movement of the diaphragm and learn to control it more effectively. The optimal breath is nice and deep and held for several seconds. If you have never done deep breathing, try it right now. You will be surprised by the immediacy and power of such breaths. You may have been taught that it is best to breathe in through your nose. That is more for comfort than anything else. Air that passes through our nose is moisturized better, which is easier on our lungs and on our throat.

Deep breathing immediately relaxes your muscles and slows your heart rate. You may even feel a little lightheaded, and some people who experience significant anxiety find that lightheadedness disconcerting. There is nothing dangerous about that feeling, so instead focus on how relaxed your body feels. The nice thing about deep breathing is that it only takes a minute or two, and you can even do it if you are hyperventilating. However, deep breathing works better if you do not let the anxiety build to the level of hyperventilation. Unlike medications, you never have to worry about overdosing on deep breathing. You can easily control the timing of breathing. If you are anxious about giving a talk, take

46

regular deep breaths while you are waiting to speak. Just before you get up to talk, take one more nice deep breath.

When you first practice deep breathing, you will find that the most effective practice is to exaggerate your breathing. By exaggerating, I mean really emphasizing the movement of the diaphragm and lifting your shoulders to expand the lungs even more. This gives you greater lung capacity and helps to increase the flow of oxygen from the lungs into the bloodstream. Although effective, everyone around you will see what you are doing. However, you do not need to exaggerate your deep breaths for them to be effective in managing anxiety. You can take nice deep breaths without anyone noticing. Once you have learned to take deep breaths, practice taking those breaths in a manner that is stealthy. In that way, you can use this technique in virtually any situation.

Managing Muscle Tension

How many times have you told yourself to relax when you feel that your anxiety is high? How many times have others told you to relax because they thought your anxiety was high? My guess is that you will not be surprised to hear that such advice is close to worthless. We are terrible at getting ourselves to relax, but there is a trick that works well. It is not as easy as the deep breathing just described, but it does work. With training and practice, you can develop a remarkable level of control over your anxiety using this technique.

The trick is to relax your muscles. When we are anxious, our muscles are also tense. We are not good at commanding our anxiety to go away, but we can learn to control our muscles. We learn to control our muscles all the time. If you learn to play golf, type, ride a bike, or drive a car, you have learned to control your muscles in a very precise way to achieve a particular goal. You move every muscle in your body through a process of tension and relaxation, and some of those muscle movements are amazingly complex.

I will be covering in detail the process of **progressive muscle relaxation** in the chapter on behavioral techniques for treating anxiety disorders (chapter 12), which is what we call this muscle control technique. I will introduce the logic and the general strategies here.

Almost everything we do uses our muscles, and therefore, we are rather skilled at learning to control our muscles. Progressive muscle relaxation takes advantage of this skill to create a feeling of calm by reducing the tension in our skeletal muscles. To learn this skill, we simplify the process by dividing the body into separate muscle groups that can be individually controlled.

The technique that I have always used divides the body into sixteen muscle groups. It is not the only muscle relaxation procedure, but it is one of the oldest and probably the most systematically studied of the available techniques. By focusing on a single muscle group at a time, one can learn to feel the tension and reduce it on command. This is more challenging than learning to take deep breaths when you are anxious. Commanding your muscles to relax on cue takes practice and for some individuals is a difficult task. Some people simply try too hard. They try so hard that they increase rather than decrease the tension level. I have found that for those individuals, asking them not to try to relax the muscles but rather allow those muscles to relax is more effective.

The strategy is to learn to visualize the tension in each muscle group and then find a technique that allows that tension to dissipate. To make that easier, the person is instructed to gently tense the muscle. This gentle tension highlights the specific muscle, which allows the person to see the muscle clearly. Most people initially want to do the relaxation procedures with their eyes closed so that they can focus more completely on the feeling of tension and not be distracted by other things in the environment. Most people prefer to do the exercises in a recliner because it supports the body as the muscles gradually relax. A quiet location that is at a comfortable temperature also helps one to relax.

Initially, it might take twenty minutes or more to relax all sixteen muscle groups, but the time needed decreases with practice. Even still, this is not something that one can do in most situations to relax before facing a stressful situation. However, many clients discover that it is very effective in helping them to fall asleep more quickly and get a better night's sleep. But to make this technique more effective at managing anxiety, we combine the muscle groups to speed up the process. With enough practice, people can learn to quickly scan their bodies for pockets of tension and to relax their bodies on command. That means that you can do more than take a deep breath before going into that job interview; you can fully relax your body with just a few seconds of focus.

Although it takes practice to get good at progressive muscle relaxation, it is well worth the time and energy. The level of relaxation you can experience with this technique is greater than you can achieve with deep breathing alone. Moreover, sometimes it is just nice to kick back and really relax. After a busy day, a few minutes of significant relaxation feels wonderful, without the potential risks associated with other relaxation techniques, such as having a couple of stiff drinks. Finally, relaxation can help you in situations that have little to do with anxiety management. Muscle tension interferes with a smooth golf swing and being able to relax your muscles often improves the consistency of your swing. Although it is counterintuitive, being relaxed allows you to swing faster without swinging harder and, as a result, increases your distance.

Managing Heart Rate and Palmar Sweating

Controlling your breathing is easy to learn. Controlling your muscles is more difficult, but with sufficient practice, you can get very good at it. Heart rate and sweating of your palms are more difficult to control. Fortunately, the combination of breathing and muscle relaxation often achieves the goal of reducing these signs of anxiety. So, we will not be talking about additional anxiety control techniques for these variables.

I do want to point out one thing. People can hear your voice crack or see your hands shake if you are anxious. What people cannot detect is whether your heart rate is increased or your palms are sweating. However, if your palms are sweating and you shake their hand, they can detect your sweaty palms. But that problem is easy to solve. If you know you get anxious at job interviews and that your hands sweat when you are anxious, there is a simple fix. You only need to control the sweat on your palms for the few seconds that it takes to shake the hand of your interviewer. You can do that by wearing an absorbent pair of pants or an absorbent skirt. As you get up when you are called for the interview, casually slide your hand across that absorbent material. If the material is truly absorbent, you will be amazed at how quickly your hand dries and your handshake feels fine. Five minutes later, your palms may be sweaty again, but it makes no difference because your interviewer cannot see it. When the interview is over, repeat the process as you get up, and you can leave with a warm handshake. Most people put their hands on their legs or on the arms of the chair when they stand up. With just a little bit of practice, you can make it look so natural that no one will be the wiser.

The heart rate may be easy to measure, but it is not observable unless someone has special equipment or decides to take your pulse. Even if you are sensitive to your own heart rate, no one else will know. The risk with your heart rate is that you might focus on your heart, and that focus feeds your anxiety. That can be controlled with cognitive techniques that I cover extensively.

Managing the Behavioral Consequences of Anxiety

The topic of this section is huge, and many of the subtopics will be discussed in the next two chapters. But I want to introduce this concept because, in many ways, managing the behavioral consequences of anxiety is more important than managing the anxiety itself.

When we talk about behavioral consequences, I want to make a distinction between *voluntary behaviors*, such as avoiding the situation, and *involuntary behaviors*, such as your hand shaking

50

due to excessive muscle tension. These are very different phenomena, and they are handled in very different ways.

Anxiety is a signal that there might be a risk. When it comes to managing your behavior, your first task is to judge the legitimacy of the signal and the potential costs or risks that you face. Driving during bad weather and doing work on your roof during a windstorm are both risky; in fact, they might be extremely risky, and it would be smart to listen to your anxiety about doing those things. In such situations, the wise move is to not engage in behavior that has such a high risk.

Job interviews are anxiety-producing for most people, especially early in their careers. But job interviews are required if you want to get great jobs. Therefore, avoiding job interviews could destroy your career or, at the very least, slow your career. You may get your first job with only a brief interview or maybe just an application. If you do exceptionally well in the job, you might be promoted repeatedly. If you dread the thought of job interviews, advancing through promotions may sound inviting, but it locks you into a single company and into the goodwill of the people who run that company. If you want control of your life, you need to overcome your anxiety about job interviews so that you can, if you want to or feel the need to, find another job with another company. Avoiding job interviews at all costs is an example of potentially problematic behavior influenced by anxiety. Here, you do not want to listen to an anxiety signal. Even if it were possible to avoid all job interviews, the cost of doing that is almost certainly too high.

Sometimes you want to listen to the anxiety and adjust your behavior to avoid it. For example, you may decide to wait until the snowstorm stops before you go to the grocery store. There may be times when you cannot take that good advice. If a family member is seriously hurt or about to give birth, you might have to deal with the adverse weather to get them to a hospital. Again, if you know that you can manage anxiety, you feel that you have the freedom to make good decisions.

At other times, the anxiety drives you to do things that are clearly not in your best interest. These are usually either escape or

51

avoidance behaviors. In such situations, you either need an enormous incentive or the confidence that you can manage your anxiety to allow you to proceed. Let's suppose that you are anxious about dating, which is a rather common anxiety. Both the sexual and the emotional drive to find a partner is so strong that many people who are anxious about dating somehow get themselves to do it. If they meet the right person, the rewards of connecting with that person often decrease their anxiety dramatically. The good thing about dating is that if you are successful, you do not have to continue to do it. You make a commitment with someone who agrees to make a similar commitment, and you formalize that relationship in terms of an engagement and/or a marriage.

What about the behaviors that are simply observable manifestations of your anxiety? When you are anxious, you may start to shake. You must be extremely anxious, virtually terrified, for your entire body to shake. But high levels of anxiety cause your hands and knees to shake. Why is that? Because those are the two parts of your body that are least anchored when you are standing. Your hands are at the end of your arms, and if they are not resting on something, they tend to shake when your muscles are tense. Don't believe me? Stretch your arm out and squeeze your hand very tightly. As the tension builds in your hand and arm, the trembling is clearly visible. There is an easy fix. If you have a podium, just rest your hands on the podium. That provides enough of an anchor that the hands do not shake. Do not grab onto the podium. That is clearly visible and makes you look desperate. Never put your notes on a sheet of paper that you must hold. Put your hand out and let it tremble, and you will see that the trembling is mild. Now hold a standard sheet of paper and let your hand tremble, and you can see the trembling from a block away. One reason we encourage people to use 3 x 5 cards for their notes when speaking is that the 3 x 5 cards tend to be cupped in the hand and therefore never visually amplify the motion of a trembling hand.

Voices crack when you are anxious because of excessive tension in the body, including the vocal cords. Deep breaths are usually enough to calm the body sufficiently to prevent your voice from cracking, and if you become skilled at muscle relaxation, you should have no difficulty in preventing this obvious sign of anxiety. If you own a guitar or can borrow one from a friend, you can see this effect easily. Tighten the string, and it vibrates at a higher frequency. What you are doing is creating greater tension, and the natural physiological responses to anxiety increase tension and thus increase the frequency of the vocal cords. Pausing for a moment and taking a deep breath certainly helps, but one of the things that you can also do is simply move your chin down a bit. Pulling your chin down reduces the stretch of your vocal cords, which lowers the frequency and reduces the likelihood of your voice cracking. In most cases, you only need to do this for a few seconds because just seeing that you have control of your voice makes it more likely that you truly can control your voice.

This last point is critical in understanding anxiety. I talked about this point before, but I am going to take the time to reiterate it here because it is so important. When we perceive ourselves to be anxious and believe that others can see our anxiety, our anxiety increases. Said another way, anxiety feeds itself. So, the first goal in managing anxiety is learning how to hide it. You will still be anxious, but the people who are observing you will not be able to tell. Anxiety that you can hide is much less likely to spiral out of control. The information in the last two previous paragraphs gave you ways of hiding anxiety in a public speaking situation. We also talked about how you can hide sweaty palms by removing the sweat for a few seconds before shaking hands. Once you incorporate such techniques, the dreaded spiral of anxiety is much less likely.

It is common for people to misjudge their level of anxiety because they are comparing apples and oranges. This may have happened to you. Perhaps in a class in which you were required to give a presentation, other students told you later that you did a great job and that they were amazed at how comfortable you were speaking. You were amazed that they thought you were comfortable because that was not how you felt. Where did their false impression come from? Their impression was not false at all. They could see the visible signs of anxiety, and you were able to perform without showing those signs. They could not see how you were feeling.

53

From their perspective, you had no anxiety because there were no signs of anxiety. But when we look at our own performance, we not only see the behavioral signs of anxiety but also experience internal feelings. We often feel that we are more anxious than everyone else in a public speaking situation because we see more of our anxiety than they see. We see both the external signs and the internal feelings; they only see the external signs. It is so important to realize that if you do not look anxious, people will assume that you are not anxious. That is why I tell clients with anxiety that my first goal is to teach them to hide their anxiety, and only then do I show them how to manage it.

Reducing Anxiety by Improving Performance

Anxiety may be an accurate signal that we are being asked to do something that we are not confident that we can do. In fact, we may be confident that we cannot do what is expected of us. Almost everyone experiences public speaking anxiety initially, but as one gets better at public speaking, the anxiety gradually decreases. Most social anxieties involve situations in which we are required to perform and are being judged by other people. Certainly, public speaking anxiety fits into this category, but almost every public behavior qualifies. If you go to a party, you are expected to behave in certain ways, and if you do not feel comfortable that you can behave appropriately, the idea of attending the party will make you anxious.

Some of the best things in life, such as dating, can create a lot of anxiety because people dating almost certainly are evaluating the other person. We may be comfortable evaluating people, but we are often uncomfortable when we know that they are evaluating us. We are more confident dating someone who is like us and has similar interests because we believe those similar interests will result in them judging us positively. Worrying about being rejected or disappointing others can be a major source of anxiety.

Whenever we are dealing with anxiety in social situations, we must consider that the person's performance is indeed being judged.

54

Therefore, anything that can be done to improve that performance in advance reduces anxiety. Focusing only on anxiety in such situations will backfire. People may be less anxious, but if they are unskilled, they will be judged negatively. Such judgments can leave serious scars, which can result in intense anxiety in the future when faced with similar situations.

The problem with this situation is that the limited skills that lead to poor performance will almost certainly increase anxiety. That increased anxiety likely leads to avoidant behavior. If you avoid engaging in situations in which you are unskilled, your skills never improve. Moreover, if you are a younger person, you are competing with other younger people who are engaging in that behavior and in the process improving their skills. It becomes a vicious cycle. The anxiety leads to avoidance, and the avoidance leads to increasingly pronounced skill deficits relative to your peers, which leads to poor performance and thus anxiety and avoidance, and so on. I will be talking about this in more detail when I talk about the treatment of social phobias.

Thinking Differently About Anxiety

So far, I have talked about how you can manage the physiological sensations associated with anxiety and the behaviors that are driven by anxiety. There is another element that is critical in understanding anxiety. I have hinted at that element without specifically naming it. That element is how we think about anxiety. When anxiety spirals out of control because we can see manifestations of anxiety and know that others can see it, that spiral is being controlled by our thoughts. Humans experience anxiety because we can think about potential risks, which sometimes can be scary.

If you are going on a job interview in a few days, chances are you will experience anxiety repeatedly between now and the job interview because you are thinking about how the interview might go and all the ways it might go badly. That process is advantageous, even if it is uncomfortable. If we spend time thinking about how an interview can go wrong, we can use our minds to identify ways in which we can turn the situation around to our advantage. For example, let's assume that there is a gap in our resume that the interviewer might ask about. If we recognize that such a gap is there and might be raised in the interview, we can think of ways to answer the question that will not hurt our chances and may even improve them. Perhaps the gap was because the company that you worked for went bankrupt and the job market was tight, with few jobs available. Perhaps you used that time to build skills so that you would be more competitive for jobs. If your response to the question acknowledged those items, you have diffused the situation and given the interviewer reason to be impressed. You basically took lemons and made lemonade by using the time you were not working to be a better employee. More importantly, your worrying about how you would handle that question encouraged you to develop an excellent response to the question.

The anticipatory anxiety that most of us feel as we imagine potentially difficult situations is not a problem. Such anxiety drives us to be better prepared for difficult situations. It encourages us to think about alternative strategies. The best planners and leaders always anticipate problems, and when problems occur, as they inevitably do, these leaders are usually better prepared to handle them. Many people have described Bill Gates as a constant worrier (Becraft, 2014). He was always concerned about potential failures, and as a result, when problems arose, he and his staff had already anticipated those problems and were ready to handle them. I cannot say if that is true for every successful business leader, but I would give you 10 to 1 odds that it is true for most of them.

Anticipatory anxiety rarely spirals out of control, and it certainly has the benefit of motivating behavior that can reduce risks in the future. Anxiety that is more likely to spiral out of control is the anxiety that we experience when we are in the middle of a situation. I am going to continue to use the example of public speaking because it is a situation that creates anxiety for just about everyone and almost everyone has had enough experience with it that most readers can connect with my descriptions and explanation.

I have already talked about how anxiety can feed itself, and earlier in this book, I talked about how difficult it is for people to not think about a topic by trying to not think about it. The way to not think about a topic is to focus your attention on something else. Our attention is a limited resource. For us to process information, we need to focus most of our attention on what we want to process. There is a classic illustration of this phenomenon conducted by Daniel Simons and one of his students. College students in a psychology experiment were asked to observe a video of people, three dressed in white and three dressed in black. Their task was to count the number of times the people in white passed a ball. The people were moving, so it took considerable attention to focus on the three people in white and whether they passed the ball. What made this study so classic is that a guy in a gorilla suit walked right through the middle of the scene, stopping for a moment and thumping his chest, before walking off the screen. Many of the subjects who were counting the passes did not even notice the gorilla, even when asked in a way that might trigger a memory of the gorilla (e.g., "Did you notice anything unusual or did anything move across the screen?"). When shown the film a second time without having to count the passes, those subjects were shocked that they had not noticed the gorilla. Those who saw the gorilla could not believe that everyone did not see it because, in their mind, it was so obvious. [YouTube clip: https://www.youtube.com/watch?v=UtKt8YF7dgQ.]

If focusing your attention on other things can cause you to literally miss the presence of a gorilla in the room, it can certainly distract you from paying attention to your own anxiety. You perhaps have heard that it is a good idea to imagine that your audience is naked because that thought is bizarre enough that you will focus on it rather than on how you are feeling. You can achieve the same thing by focusing on the audience and reading their eyes. You can see when one of your points is really connecting with audience members because their eyes light up, which means that their expression changes. We are good at reading such changes, and because we are interested in what other people are feeling and how their facial expressions express those feelings, it is easy for us to focus on that and ignore our own anxiety. What we are doing with these techniques is preventing our own anxiety from feeding itself.

Anxiety is not the only thing that feeds itself. If you have a headache, the more you pay attention to the pain, the worse the pain gets. What is happening is that by focusing on the pain, you feel the pain more intensely and your muscles tense up due to the pain. For most types of pain, tension increases the pain. You may have had headaches that simply went away when you got distracted by some other activity. This is the opposite process. When you are distracted, your pain does not build and eventually goes away.

Our thoughts influence all emotions, including anxiety. If we tell ourselves that we must control the anxiety, and we find that we cannot completely control the anxiety, we get anxious about not having control. If instead, we label the anxiety as normal and focus on the goal of performing well despite the anxiety, we have no reason to get more anxious. Most people who tend to experience consistent problems with anxiety believe that they should be able to eliminate the anxiety, which is an unrealistic expectation.

Putting It All Together

The material in this chapter can be used to deal with everyday anxiety. You may have spontaneously discovered some of the concepts discussed here, such as deep breaths as a way of calming yourself. Anxiety management skills give you ways of dealing with situations that make you anxious. In some cases, you want to listen to the anxiety and avoid potentially dangerous situations. But in the complex world in which we live, avoidance is often a poor choice and leads to long-term negative consequences. Therefore, facing your anxiety and managing it sufficiently to function should be your goal. If you face a situation that makes you anxious and you succeed, your anxiety will decrease the next time you have to face the same situation. But remember the rule: we are programmed to learn anxiety quickly but to unlearn it slowly. Therefore, the decrease in anxiety that you experience after success is gradual and requires multiple successes before the anxiety decreases significantly.

My goal in this book is not to eliminate your anxiety. My goal is to teach you how to manage your anxiety. Eliminating anxiety, even if it were possible, would almost certainly be to your detriment, although you may be more comfortable without anxiety. If you can manage anxiety, the anxiety you experience will be a benefit rather than a disability. It will motivate you to improve and prepare for challenges. It will drive you to create situations that are safer and therefore more comfortable. Often, you will achieve this goal by improving your skills in managing difficult situations.

Chapter Summary

Anxiety is a normal emotion that is triggered in many situations. It is uncomfortable, and the discomfort that it produces is sufficient to drive behavior. In this chapter, we talked about how one can manage anxiety through a variety of techniques. Some of those techniques involve physiological manipulation, such as taking deep breaths. Some of those techniques involve behavioral change, such as learning how to handle difficult situations more effectively. Finally, some of those situations involve rethinking your interpretation. For example, if your goal is to have no anxiety, the presence of any anxiety is distressing and tends to make you even more anxious. If instead your goal is to manage your anxiety so you can perform optimally, you are far more likely to reach that goal and therefore less likely to experience spiraling anxiety.

I talk about these anxiety management strategies in more detail in the next chapter, putting them to work in real-life situations.

Chapter 5

Managing Existing Anxiety

Chapter 4 covered several techniques to manage your anxiety. In this chapter, we go one step further, showing you how to use those techniques in everyday situations that tend to create anxiety. I want to remind you that the goal is not to eliminate anxiety. There is nothing about anxiety that is abnormal. Anxiety only becomes a problem when it becomes too extreme or prevents us from being able to perform the tasks we expect of ourselves.

Good versus Bad Anxiety

There is a popular belief that anxiety is bad because it is uncomfortable. I can certainly understand why people believe discomfort is not a good thing, but that position fails to understand the value of discomfort. Let's take an experience that is clearly uncomfortable and has nothing to do with anxiety: pain. Pain, like anxiety, is a signal. If we break a leg and try to walk on it, we will experience intense pain. The pain will be so intense that it will be virtually impossible to walk. The pain tells us that something is wrong, and it shapes behavior to avoid making the problem worse. In our modern world, we would seek medical treatment. In our evolutionary past, we would try to stay off the leg as much as possible to give it a chance to heal. If the leg did not heal quickly, that broken leg would probably be life-threatening to our evolutionary ancestors. They would not be able to escape from predators, nor would they be able to hunt or gather food.

There are medical conditions in which pain is effectively blocked, and the complications from not having pain can be enormous. If you are reading this while sitting down, you may be putting sufficient pressure on your bottom to cut off some of the blood supply. If you do that for any length of time, your bottom will hurt, and you will move around to allow the blood to flow again. But if you have a spinal cord injury, in addition to paralysis, there may be a loss of feeling below the spinal injury. Therefore, you could be sitting reading this book and cutting off your blood supply and have no sense that anything is amiss. There is no pain to tell you that you need to move around. Consequently, you can do severe damage to the tissue of your bottom by cutting off the blood supply for too long. The result could be a massive ulcer. As an intern, I worked in a spinal cord injury unit. I have seen some of those ulcers. Some were the size of my fist, going all the way down to the bone, and they required several surgeries to repair. They were truly life-threatening because trying to prevent infection in wounds that large is extremely difficult. Unless we have a spinal cord injury that prevents us from feeling the pain of sitting in one spot too long, we would never sit in one place long enough to kill tissue by cutting off the blood supply. The pain would be overwhelming, and as a result, we would adjust our position to avoid the pain. In this case, pain is a good thing because it prevents serious physiological damage to our bodies.

There is another pain that is experienced by many people who have spinal cord injuries. The pain probably originates at or near the place where the spinal cord was severed, although the pain often feels as if it is coming from another part of the body. For example, the individual may experience their feet being on fire, and the severity of the pain indeed reflects the description I just gave. Of course, their feet are not on fire, and moreover, they are getting no signals at all from their feet because of the spinal cord injury. The signals are almost certainly coming from the severed nerve ends that may be stimulated by nearby tissue or bone. It feels like it is coming from their feet because at one time those nerves ran all the way to their feet. This is an example of pain that serves no function.

Earlier, we talked about anxiety as a signal. Anxiety tells us that there may be a risk and motivates us to take action to reduce the risk. When it operates that way, it is valuable to our survival and to

61

our success. It is uncomfortable, but discomfort is not the criteria by which we should judge anxiety. Some people find anxiety so uncomfortable that they use escape or avoidance. Depending on the severity of the risk, such action might be warranted. It certainly would be reinforced because it would reduce the significant discomfort associated with being anxious. But the problem with avoidance is that we never get a chance to see whether we could learn to manage the anxiety or to see what advantage there might be in our life if we could control our anxiety. In other words, it prevents us from seeing possibilities, some of which may be valuable resources for us.

All anxiety should be thought of as a signal, and the signal should indicate that we need to act. The problem is that without more information, it is hard to decide which actions make the most sense. In the next section, we talk about how one might go about gathering the relevant information. Our gut response to anxiety is avoidance or escape. However, we can overrule our gut and choose another path. For example, the anxiety about going on a job interview may make us feel like we should cancel the interview. That is an action, and that action will be reinforced because canceling the interview will reduce our anxiety. However, canceling the interview will also guarantee that we do not get the job, and to the extent that the job would be a good one for us, we have suffered a significant loss. Because we have a strong and immediate sense of what we have gained (reduced anxiety) but have little idea what we might have lost (a great job), our tendency is to think that avoidance is the best strategy. We go for instant gratification, but the cost of such gratification can be very high.

Canceling an interview that makes us anxious reduces the anxiety, but it is not the only way of reducing the anxiety. We have talked about this before. Anxiety that we experience before a potentially risky event, called *anticipatory anxiety*, can motivate behavior that reduces the risk. It is highly unlikely that you will face a life-or-death risk in a job interview. The most likely risk is that you will not do a good job and therefore will not be hired. There is a small possibility that your performance in the interview will be so bad that the interviewer will always think less of you. If you live in a

62

small town, such an event might have serious consequences, but in larger cities, it is entirely possible that you will never see that interviewer again. If we focus on the most likely risk (poor performance in the interview that leads to rejecting you for the position), we now have a sense of what we should focus on improving (i.e., our interview performance).

What can you do to be better prepared for a job interview? Well, you could show up on time and appropriately dressed. Depending on the interview and the job, the appropriate dress might include either a business suit or just clean work clothes. If there is an application process, you could fill out the application in detail, emphasizing the features that make you a strong candidate. If you are expected to produce a resume for the interview, you can make sure that your resume is up-to-date and well-written and has no spelling, grammatical, or typing errors. Each of these things can be done well in advance of the interview so that you are prepared to make a good impression in the first few seconds. Evidence shows that people really do make split-second decisions, and if those decisions are negative, it takes a lot of information to change the person's mind (Demarais & White, 2005). Therefore, you want to go into the interview dressed for success and having completed everything that is expected of you.

What about the interview itself? Your anxiety likely gives you strong clues about the possible negative things that could occur during an interview. What questions could the interviewer ask that may be difficult to answer? It might be about your lack of experience in certain areas that would be important for that job. How can you answer a question that would not put you in a bad light? That is a perfect example of anxiety that can motivate you to think creatively about how to address a situation. For example, you do not want to lie, because the consequences of lying are serious. Most lies you tell will eventually be discovered. Some companies automatically fire someone who lied during an interview, even months after the interview. But you likely have arguments that strengthen your case, although they may not be sufficient to get you the job. For example, you could acknowledge that you do not have experience in that area, but you have a history of learning

63

new skills quickly and excelling in those skills. Be sure to have specific examples to support your argument. Now you have a way to handle the question you feared the most. It may not be handled perfectly; perfectly handling that question would be to get those skills or experience before you go in for the job interview. But that option may not be available to you. It is entirely possible that you will be the best candidate even though you do not currently have all the skills that the company was hoping to find in their new hire.

Analyzing Triggers

In the previous section, we talked about ways of using anxiety as a signal to prepare yourself to be more successful. However, the presence of anxiety is not enough to tell us what we need to do to be better prepared. Our typical response to anxiety is to reduce it as quickly as possible, and that usually involves avoidance. But if we can tolerate anxiety long enough to analyze the situation, anxiety can often be our single best asset. You heard that right! Anxiety not only is not the enemy, but also it can be your best asset because it can dramatically improve your performance and therefore the trajectory of your life. That is quite a promise, and I certainly would understand why you would be skeptical. Let me see if I can convince you of the value with some examples.

The best way to understand the meaning of anxiety signals is to compare the situations in which we feel anxious with situations in which we feel little or no anxiety. For example, we might feel anxious in situations in which we are meeting new people, but once we get to know those people, the anxiety all but disappears. Alternatively, some of the people that we meet continue to make us anxious. In fact, for some people, the more we know them and the more we are around them, the more anxious we are. Those are not accidents. Our anxiety is telling us something important.

We have talked about anxiety as a signal that the situation might be dangerous. Let's look more closely at that signal because there is a second aspect that we have not talked about. We can think of anxiety as a response to the idea that danger may exist coupled

64

with a question about whether we can handle the danger. There is danger all around us. Every time we get into a car and travel at high speed, there is the potential that a terrible accident might happen. Some people are aware of the danger to the point that they are terrified of driving. Most of us, however, understand that traveling at seventy miles an hour could be dangerous if we hit something or if something hits us. But we experience minimal anxiety because we feel confident that we can avoid such tragedies. How do we avoid such tragedies? We make sure that the car is in good shape so that we are not concerned that the brakes will give out or that a tire will blow out. We make sure that we are in good shape by not drinking and driving or driving when we are so tired that we cannot keep our eyes open. We make sure that the environment is safe. If we are driving on a well-maintained expressway, we feel confident going seventy miles an hour. If, however, we are driving on a dirt road with lots of potholes, we are not foolish enough to try to do that at seventy miles an hour. We slow down for bad weather, and when the weather is bad enough, we may decide not to go out on the road at all.

These are some of the ways of managing anxiety through a constant analysis of the situation and an adjustment to that situation. There is an additional way of reducing anxiety. The more experience you have with driving, especially if you have been able to avoid accidents, the more confident you are in your ability to handle whatever occurs. There are exceptions to this general principle. The first exception has to do with young drivers, who often have a level of confidence that is not warranted by their experience. Not all young drivers have this, but many do, which is why the insurance rates are so much higher for these drivers. This overconfidence is more common in young males than young females, and therefore young males often pay the highest insurance rates.

The other exception to this general rule is that not all driving is the same. If you live in mountainous areas, you may often drive on roads that have thousand-foot drops along the edge. Driving for months or years on such roads can gradually become routine. If you live in major cities, you may drive in bumper-to-bumper traffic that barely moves or drive on multilane expressways moving at high speed with people changing lanes rapidly. With experience, these conditions seem normal. If you live in San Diego, you almost never drive on snowy roads, and so snow may seem terrifying. Someone with the same driving experience along the eastern edge of Lake Michigan may drive on snowy roads a hundred days a year. They may respect the risk associated with snowy roads but are no longer intimidated by it.

These driving examples give us a clear indication of a principle associated with anxiety. Anxiety is a signal that there may be a risk that we may not be able to handle. If we repeatedly demonstrate to ourselves that we can handle that risk, the anxiety will diminish. Note the careful choice of words. The anxiety will not disappear, nor should it. It will decrease but not disappear, because there is still a risk. However, because we have ample evidence that we can handle most sources of risk, the anxiety will be much lower. Remember the principle that we are programmed to learn anxiety quickly and to unlearn it slowly. If you have lived in snowy areas your entire life and have been able to drive in the snow for years, you are likely to experience only modest anxiety on a snowy day. If you hit a slippery patch and spin out into the ditch, your confidence about driving in snow will be dramatically affected. It does not take much for us to become anxious again. If another car loses control and spins out and hits you, the consequence is likely to be more severe on your anxiety. The reason is that such an incident indicates that your safety depends on both your ability to drive in the snow and the ability of all the other people who share the road with you.

Let's look at several classes of situations that often produce anxiety. In that analysis, we look at the variables that predict the severity of the anxiety and how quickly the anxiety either increases or decreases depending upon our experiences.

Meeting People

Unless you are a hermit who lives off the grid, you are likely to meet people as a regular part of your life. Meeting new people can be anxiety-producing in some situations, while other situations may produce little or no anxiety. For example, let's assume that you are a toll collector. You might meet people every twenty seconds as they pull up to your booth and hand you the money for using the highway or bridge. Most people would consider such a situation to be low-stress and not something that would produce much anxiety. In fact, many people would consider the situation to be such low stress that they would be bored in a matter of days. In contrast, politicians often meet people almost as frequently as toll collectors do. Many people could not imagine being a politician, shaking hands, and talking to one person after another for hours on end. They would envision lots of problems and might experience intense anxiety about how well they could handle such problems. In these scenarios, we have two individuals, involved in very different careers, both meeting lots of people but apparently experiencing situations differently enough to warrant different levels of anxiety. Why is that?

The biggest difference between the politician and toll collector examples is the expectations of the people they meet. Toll collectors simply collect money. Individuals pull up to a toll booth expecting to give them money, and their only expectation in return is to get the correct change. If the toll collector says, "Have a good day," that may be a bonus, but it is not an expectation. In contrast, politicians might get anything from an overly friendly conversation with someone they had never met to someone swearing at them because of their political positions. They may be asked about their background, their beliefs, their values, and what they will be doing about a certain issue. No toll collector has ever had to address that many questions. Finally, it is rare for someone meeting a politician not to judge that person. Have you ever judged a toll collector? Unless you pull up and the toll collector is obviously making a personal call and ignoring you, you likely have completely forgotten the experience and that person within seconds after pulling away from the booth.

These simple examples illustrate two of the most important variables that contribute to anxiety when we meet new people. The first is the complexity of the behavior expected of us. The second is whether we are likely to be judged.

Imagine being a politician. Imagine running for office for the very first time. You have little experience shaking hands and introducing yourself to strangers, so going door-to-door will be difficult. Walking up to strangers in a mall and introducing yourself will also be difficult. You have never done that before, so you anticipate that you may not be able to do it well. You also anticipate that some people will not respond well, and in fact, you are right about that. With experience, you find that most people respond positively if you smile and quickly explain why you are doing this strange thing of walking up to a stranger and offering to shake their hand. You also discover that you can quickly read the people who do not want to talk with you and that you can diffuse the situation by simply thanking them for their time and quickly moving on. Over time, you experience some people who respond badly, and you discover that a sincere apology and an immediate withdrawal will diffuse even that situation. Perhaps, a seasoned politician explained all these things and maybe even role-played the situations with you to give you more confidence. It does not matter where the experience came from. If your experience shows that you can handle a variety of situations and handle those situations well, your anxiety will go down.

My first encounter with a politician in a public setting occurred when I was fourteen years old and working in a store. I was frankly a little shocked when my US senator walked up to me and introduced himself. He was very friendly and obviously confident, but frankly did not waste a lot of time with a fourteen-year-old who could not vote. He moved on quickly to other people, most of whom were as shocked as I was to see their US senator. In most cases, the senator spent less than ten seconds with someone, simply greeting them with a friendly smile and a handshake and leaving a very brief message. The two messages I remember hearing were, "If I can be of help, do not hesitate to call my office," and, "I hope you will support me in next year's election." On two occasions, he spent more time with people who recognized him and raised some issues. He seemed to listen carefully to the issues being raised and always thanked the person for their feedback.

I have often wondered what might have happened if I had followed this politician for an hour. I suspect I would have gotten bored because the few examples I just mentioned from my less than five minutes of observation probably represented 90 percent of his repertoire of responses. He was certainly capable of more; in full disclosure, he was a well-known and generally well-respected senator. But his task that evening was to spend a couple of hours in one town in his state shaking hands with potential voters and giving them a story to tell other potential voters when they got home. He wanted to be seen, and on that evening, he had set himself up to do just that. Was he anxious? I have no idea, but my guess is he was not. He had done this so often in so many towns and handled himself well that he almost certainly expected that he would be able to handle whatever happened.

I could not imagine doing what that senator was doing that evening. It would take great effort for me to even try to do what he was doing. I later learned that this senator would spend between four and ten hours with this kind of handshaking every time he was in the state, and he had been doing it for years. I am told that the modern equivalent of what he was doing is to get on the phone and ask potential donors for money. Politicians often must spend several hours every week and sometimes several hours every day making these calls to potential donors to have sufficient money to be successful the next time they run for office. The fact that politicians learn how to do these challenging tasks and do them with little or no distress is an indication that either (1) they do not experience the situation to be potentially dangerous or (2) they have overcome that anxiety through their experience. The second option is the most likely one.

I suspect that there are very few politicians who describe themselves as shy. That does not mean that they are naturally outgoing; what it means is that their level of anxiety in meeting new people is low. I also suspect that most successful politicians are successful in part because they have developed excellent social skills in meeting new people. Moreover, they have refined their

69

skills in a variety of social situations. It is a very different skill to talk with someone for twenty seconds compared to talking with someone for twenty minutes. Some people are more comfortable with the former, whereas others are more comfortable with the latter situation. But the key point for this section is that both situations represent skills. The way you behave when making brief conversations with people is clearly different from the way you behave when you have a more extended, and therefore more personal, conversation with someone.

I want to draw on another situation from my high school days. It was the first time I had ever gone to a wake. The mother of a close friend had passed away. Prior to this wake, I had never even seen a dead body, and I had no idea what to say. I found myself overwhelmed even with my close friend because I had no idea what to say or do. I did not stay long, and I did my best to blend into the woodwork. But what I remember about the situation was how there were several people at the wake who amazed me. They seemed to be very comfortable; they easily moved from one person to the next, and whatever it was that they were doing, it always seemed to be the right thing.

Unfortunately, I have attended a lot of wakes and funerals since then, and as I get older, the pace at which I attend such events increases. I guess all my friends are getting older, and so their parents are much older and more likely to die. I have learned through experience that the people who amazed me at the first wake that I attended were people who had simply done it many times before. Some did it professionally, such as the minister at this first wake. They had worked with grieving individuals as part of their job. I also learned that there are no perfect words or perfect actions. You can say the same thing to one person after another, and if you say it with sincerity, it will be accepted and appreciated. Saying something like, "I'm so sorry for your loss," or, "Is there anything that I can do?" works well.

The examples of a politician meeting with constituents or a minister at a funeral or wake illustrate an important point in social interactions. There are expectations in most social interactions. If you know those expectations, you can behave properly. If you have experience in those situations, not only are you likely behave properly, but you are likely to be able to do it with finesse. Those are specific social skills, and if you have the social skills needed for a specific situation, you are likely to be confident and therefore unlikely to be anxious. The toll collector also had a set of social expectations, but they are minimal, so it takes little training and experience to be comfortable in such a job.

Every social situation demands things of us. In fact, social situations demand things from everyone involved. The demands may not be identical for everyone. If you are a student talking with the professor, there are clear expectations of behavior for both parties, but they are not the same expectations. If you are two people who meet on a bus and strike up a conversation, the situation is likely to be more balanced.

Finally, because each situation demands different things, there is no such thing as "being good with people" in general. There are many people who are exceptional at their work with people in their profession. They are warm, polished, helpful, and effective in meeting new people and dealing with whatever issues are part of their careers. They can do that because they are experienced and have learned the unique skills demanded of their situation. The same skills might be ineffective in other social situations, such as striking up a conversation with someone they barely know on a golf course. As polished as they look when they are working, they might completely lack polish and finesse if they were out on a first date. The take-home principle here is that all social situations have expectations. If we have both a clear understanding of those expectations and the skills to meet them, we perform well, we expect to perform well, and consequently, we are likely to experience little or no anxiety.

Handling Danger

Meeting new people may make us anxious, but it is not likely that we will be attacked by someone we just met. There are situations in which danger does exist, and that danger may even be life-threatening. Firefighters, police officers, pilots, and soldiers all

71

face life-and-death situations as part of their job. Are they anxious about that? Of course, they are! Years ago, when I was learning how to fly, I had several pilots share with me the same quotation: "There are old pilots, and there are bold pilots, but there are no old bold pilots." This cute quotation accurately reflects a principle associated with flying planes. That principle is that it is potentially dangerous, and if you do not keep that danger in mind and behave accordingly, you can end up dead.

There will always be dangerous jobs, and for those of us who do not have dangerous jobs, there will always be situations in our lives that pose danger. Let's start by focusing on dangerous jobs. We have already talked about how when faced with life-or-death situations, the fight-or-flight response is engaged. This is our body's reaction to a situation that might end our life. We engage our entire body, 100 percent, to prevent that outcome. If we can escape, we are prepared to run as fast as we can. If escape is impossible, we are prepared to do whatever is necessary to survive, which means that we will literally fight to the death.

But what if your job involves a high probability of facing such life-or-death situations? Your fight-or-flight response is not engaged just because you might face such a situation. It is only engaged when you face life-or-death situations. What is engaged is the awareness of the potential of such situations. Again, that is our strength. We can think hypothetically about the future; we can identify risks that are probable, and because we can do that, we can prepare for those risks. Of course, thinking about the idea of dying, even though there is no immediate risk, makes us anxious. This anticipatory anxiety is an incredibly valuable motivator. It is more than aversive enough to encourage us to take steps that reduce the danger and, thus, our anxiety.

When our back is against the wall because we are overwhelmed by fear, we are not good at thinking and problem-solving. In those situations, we tend to engage in instinctual behavior and/or overlearned behavior. The fight-or-flight response is an example of instinctual behavior. By and large, there is little that we can do to change instinctual behavior, but it is possible to overlearn behavior so that we can use it in the most extreme situations. For example, if

72

you are a soldier, you may face other soldiers who are trying to kill you. Your job is to not die and to kill the soldiers that are trying to kill you. In modern warfare, you do not do that with your bare hands but rather with complicated weapons. If you are an infantry soldier, for example, and your weapon jams, you need to fix the jam efficiently in the middle of a firefight. The only way to do that is to overlearn the task.

Overlearning means learning the task so thoroughly and practicing it so often under so many difficult conditions that the task is automatic and can be done whenever needed. Being able to repair a jammed rifle in the middle of a firefight is a valuable skill if you are a soldier and you want to survive. However, that is only one example of a situation in which training for a dangerous situation can prepare people to survive that situation. Racecar drivers find themselves in the middle of high-speed accidents more often in a single afternoon than most of us do in a lifetime. Moreover, their instinctual responses are often the wrong responses to avoid being caught in such accidents. If we are driving on the expressway and an accident occurs in front of us, our instinct is to steer away from it and brake. However, on a racetrack, the optimal response often is to hit the gas and try to go around the accident before one of the careening cars hits you. If you are a pilot flying a plane and your airspeed drops too low, your wings lose lift and you enter what is called a *stall*. A stall has nothing to do with the engines but rather with whether the wings are producing sufficient lift to keep the plane in the air. When your wings stall, the plane falls, and the instinctual response is to point the nose upward so that you can gain altitude before you hit the earth. If you do that, your wings will continue to stall, and you will hit the earth. The correct response is to point the nose down, which allows the plane to gain airspeed and thus allows the wings to start doing their job again. Pilots are trained to do this response by repeatedly stalling the plane at high altitudes and pushing the nose down in response until that behavior is second nature. You do it at high altitudes because that gives you more time to recover from a stall and therefore is less dangerous.

We have talked about occupations that have potential danger, but the people in those occupations do not usually expect to die. Good pilots expect to have safe flights even when things go wrong. They are confident in their skills and in the procedures that they follow routinely to minimize risks. They inspect their plane before a flight and go through detailed checklists to make sure everything is ready to go. They not only want to protect their own life and well-being but also the lives of everyone on their plane. Their risk is objectively low, which is easy to confirm by looking at the statistics on airplane accidents. But the risk is low because there is risk, and that risk drives behavior to minimize it. Moreover, high-risk occupations have a long history of analyzing the risk and building procedures and safeguards to minimize risk. On those rare occasions when a plane crashes, the investigation that follows looks at every aspect of the plane's operation and the crew's reactions. The result is improved equipment, better backup systems, and better training to avoid similar problems in the future.

The examples above only touched the surface of the specialized training that people in dangerous occupations undergo. The key element that pulls all of these examples together is that (1) there is a realization that danger is possible, (2) that realization creates anxiety, which motivates people to reduce the danger through preparation, (3) part of that preparation is to identify optimal strategies through analysis, and (4) knowing the optimal strategies will not by itself help unless the individuals have overlearned those strategies and can perform them under the most difficult of situations.

I want to make one more point before we leave this section. Life-or-death situations do not always include a risk to the person expected to act. Surgeons, for example, are highly unlikely to die while performing surgery, but their patients may very well face life-or-death situations if a complication were to develop. Moreover, surgeons can deal with unexpected complications because they stay focused and continue to think clearly. Except for the group that we call psychopaths, people normally experience the risk of death in others as a life-or-death situation because of the process that we call *empathy*. Surgeons train hard to be prepared for almost any complication, and surgeons who perform the same surgery repeatedly have the kind of experience that allows them to respond quickly and effectively to most complications. That is one reason why it is advisable to have complex surgeries in hospitals in which the doctors perform the surgery every day. But there is always the possibility of complications that the doctor has never seen. Most surgeons do their best not to get involved with the patient and instead perform as if the situation was not life-or-death. That is one of the reasons why most hospitals discourage doctors from doing surgery on friends and family. It is not just surgeons that fit into this category. Most air traffic controllers approach their job as moving blips around on the screen in an efficient and safe manner. They go out of their way not to think of each of those blips as a plane with hundreds of passengers on board. This effort to block the natural empathy response improves their functioning and, as a result, improves the odds of survival for those individuals under their care or guidance.

Performance Situations

There will always be anxiety in performance situations if (1) the judgment of others is important to you and (2) there is doubt that your performance will be good enough. Both elements exist on a continuum. There are times when people are extremely anxious about how they will be judged and other times when there is almost no anxiety about being judged; there are situations in which it is almost certain that one will be successful and other situations in which it is equally certain that one is likely to fail.

There are other factors that affect performance situations. For example, the size of the audience when one is giving a public talk often affects the level of anxiety. However, these factors tend to have less of an influence on anxiety level than whether one is being judged and whether one expects to be successful in the judgment.

Performance situations are like the dangerous situations we just discussed in that there is predictability and, in most cases, time to prepare. If you know you are going to be judged and if the judgment of the people who will be evaluating you is important, you can take steps to be better prepared and therefore decrease the likelihood of failure. This is one of the positive attributes of anxiety. We are anxious about the situation before it occurs, and that anxiety drives behavior that reduces the risk.

The second element in performance situations (likelihood of success) is interesting in several respects. The most interesting aspect is that the relationship is not linear. In a linear relationship, the amount of anxiety increases in direct proportion to the likelihood of failure. The relationship between the likelihood of success and one's level of anxiety appears to be curvilinear, which leads to some unusual behavior. If, for example, there is little chance of failure because the task demanded of you is one that you have mastered, there will be little anxiety. If there is a strong chance that you could fail, the anxiety will be much higher. But curiously, if there is little chance that you will succeed, it appears that people invest less in the task and, consequently, experience less anxiety. It is as if they are going through the motions before accepting the inevitable failure. The greatest anxiety is usually in the middle range. One of the curious consequences of this fact is that some individuals, when faced with a task at which they might succeed but nevertheless has a high probability of failure, structure the situation so that the probability of failing is much higher. Failing when it is inevitable appears to be less emotionally destructive than failing when there was a chance of success. This process is referred to as **self-handicapping**.

The most important principle in performance anxiety is that one can influence the probability of success through preparation. The anticipatory anxiety is a motivator for that preparation. Typically, the level of anticipatory anxiety is a good indicator of how much time and energy one should put into the preparation.

I will use an example from my own life. I have taught courses with classes that ranged from five to five hundred people. I talked to live audiences of a thousand or more people and was often interviewed on live television, where the audience was measured in hundreds of thousands. But the most anxiety-producing talk I ever gave was to a group of one hundred people. However, those one

76

hundred people were probably half of the most important people in my discipline in the world. If I did a good job, my reputation would be enhanced; if I blew it, my professional reputation might never recover. I rehearsed that presentation more than any presentation I had ever given. I spent months preparing that presentation at a time in my career when I often created such presentations in a matter of hours for other audiences. I swear I could have been in a coma and would have been able to give the presentation because it was so overlearned. As you might have guessed, the presentation went well. If I had blown it, I probably would not be here writing this book. At that time in my career, I experienced little or no anxiety talking to the public but clearly experienced intense anxiety talking to groups that were important to my professional reputation.

New Situations

New situations should always produce anxiety because if we have never experienced the situation before, we cannot possibly be confident of success. Just like performance situations, new situations can benefit from preparation. It is rare that a situation is new to everyone; however, it is common that you will face a situation that is new to you. If others have experienced the situation, you can learn what to expect in that situation through research. With the Internet, we can learn about almost anything that we are likely to face in a situation that is new to us.

There is another element of new situations. We talked about how confidence in a situation grows if you have been successful in that situation repeatedly. At some point, you experience little anxiety because you expect the probability of success to be high. But there is general confidence that can build over time if one has enough successful experiences in a variety of situations. The popular phrase, "Been there, done that!" illustrates the concept. It is not unusual for successful individuals who are older to experience less anxiety in new situations because they have the general expectation that they can handle those situations. Why do they have that expectation? Because, in the past, they have faced many new situations, and in the past, they have been successful far more often than unsuccessful. They may also have had experiences in which they were unsuccessful but handled the situation with grace. Being successful is better than being unsuccessful but being graceful when things do not go smoothly is a pretty good second option. You can enhance this growth by routinely taking time to analyze both your successes and failures. Identify the skills and strategies that led to a successful outcome. Do the same for unsuccessful outcomes. The result is you will have an inventory of reasons why you are generally successful and, therefore, an argument for expecting to be successful in the future.

Analyzing Your Responses to Anxiety

We have spent most of this chapter discussing the most common triggers for anxiety. That list is nowhere near complete because everyone has their own unique triggers for anxiety. That said, the range of triggers we discussed reflects the typical ways in which people experience their anxiety. In this section, we will take it to the next step. Once you know what makes you anxious, you need to understand how that anxiety affects you. If you add this second element to your analysis, you will have the tools to minimize your anxiety and maximize your likelihood of success, even if the anxiety cannot be dramatically reduced.

Nature of Your Anxiety

Everyone has experienced anxiety, but what we have not experienced is other people's anxiety. If our hands shake when we are anxious, we can see that; we can also see it if it happens to other people. That is an example of a visible anxiety symptom. However, the feeling of anxiety is not visible. We are aware of our own anxious feelings, but we are unaware of the anxious feelings of other people. If they are feeling anxious but their voice is strong, they appear to be decisive, and there is no visible shaking, sweating, or blushing, then we likely will interpret them as calm and in control. We might even go so far as to compliment them on how well they did and express our amazement that they were not more anxious, only to learn that they felt quite anxious.

The point of this discussion is that most of our focus is on our feeling of anxiety when we should be focusing on the visible manifestations of anxiety. If you want to be able to control your anxiety, the first thing you should work on are those things that other people can see. In most cases, there are ways of managing those elements. If you are anxious on the inside and no one can tell, from their perspective, you are not anxious. They will be impressed, and when you think about it, that's 90 percent of your goal in situations that produce anxiety. You want to be able to impress people even when you are anxious.

Some individuals do indeed have observable physiological responses that are part of their anxiety. Their face may flush as if they are extremely embarrassed; they may sweat tremendously, especially from their face; their voice may easily crack when they are anxious, or their body may physically shake. Some of these responses can be controlled with medication; if you are one of the people who experience them, you may want to talk with your doctor or with a psychiatrist who may be more familiar with those medications. Other symptoms can be controlled with techniques that we have already introduced here and will discuss in more detail in the last section of the book. Muscle relaxation techniques, for example, can have a strong effect on muscle tension, which is the cause of physically shaking when you are anxious. Your hands may sweat when you are anxious, but if no one sees your hands sweat, they will have no evidence of your anxiety. We have already talked about how absorbent clothing is an amazingly effective way of removing sweat from your hands with a casual motion before shaking hands.

Most people who experience anxiety show few observable signs of anxiety unless their anxiety is intense. They feel anxious, and the feeling may be so intense that they feel out of control. But the people around them, unless they are highly trained and observant, are unlikely to pick up on the subtle physical manifestations of that anxiety. These individuals only need to focus on performance and not on hiding their anxiety from observers. If they are giving a public talk, they need to have a good talk that is well-rehearsed. If they are in a job interview, they need to be prepared for most of the questions they are likely to be asked and to be knowledgeable about the company they hope to work for. If they are meeting new people, they need to be good at conversation. Most people incorrectly believe that means they should know everything and be able to talk about anything. A much more effective strategy is to ask the people you are meeting about themselves and then carefully listen to what they tell you.

All these things represent skills, and the more practice you have, the more skillful you are. Moreover, many of these skills can be learned with tutoring. Therapists who work with people who experience anxiety are usually very good at providing that kind of tutoring because it is a major component of their treatment program. But you can also get tutoring by purchasing books on the topic. There are thousands of self-help books on almost any topic imaginable. Some of them are outstanding, many of them are excellent, but a few of them are, at best, misleading and, at worst, counterproductive. If you use the same principle you use when you search on the Internet (look for consistency across sites), it will not be hard to nail down some strategies that are likely to work for you.

Your Behavioral Response to Anxiety

In addition to the physiological manifestations of anxiety, there are behavioral tendencies that often go along with anxiety. Anticipatory anxiety is valuable when it motivates behavior that reduces anxiety by having you better prepare for the situation. But when that anticipatory anxiety leads to avoidance or escape, it is counterproductive. An extreme form of avoidance is to not go into situations that are making you anxious. That is a serious problem because many of those situations are important to your personal and professional life. A more common kind of avoidance is to not think about the situation. You have a difficult situation coming up and you are anxious about it; if you focus your energy on something else, you will forget about the upcoming situation for a moment and, in the process, reduce your anxiety. Unfortunately, you have thrown the baby out with the bathwater in that your anxiety was your primary motivator to be better prepared. It provides motivation because being prepared makes you feel more confident and therefore less anxious. Avoiding the anxiety may make you feel better in the near term, but you still must face the situation that is making you anxious, and now you will be doing it with a less-than-ideal level of preparation. If you are unprepared, you are far more likely to be unsuccessful, which makes the next time you must face a similar situation even more anxiety producing.

There are other examples of anxiety responses that are not in your best interest. Many people feel a strong need to "confess" their anxiety. They might be inclined to say something like, "I am sorry if I am not making a good impression, but I am very anxious right now." Their hope is that such a confession will elicit empathy on the part of the person they are hoping to impress. It might accomplish that goal, but it is more likely to accomplish the goal of eliciting pity. Pity is not likely to translate into a positive evaluation. There are ways in which you can confess your anxiety in a manner that is effective, but I am reluctant to encourage people to do that. It requires considerable finesse and skill because it generally involves making an effective joke about the situation. Unless you have the skills of a comedian, you are not likely to pull that off. So, the best advice that I can give you is that there is no reason to tell people that you are anxious. In fact, if you simply focus on performing, there is a very good chance that they will not even notice your anxiety.

Let me soften that advice and repeat a point that I made earlier. Although I discourage people from sharing their anxiety in a situation in which they are likely to be judged, I often encourage them to discuss their anxiety with friends and supportive individuals in advance of such situations. This process achieves two goals. The first is that it helps to plan strategies to perform more effectively as well as manage any anxiety that is expected. The second is that one invariably learns that the anxiety one expects to feel is entirely normal and likely shared by almost anyone in that situation.

There are other behavioral responses to anxiety that affect some people but not others. For example, some people become virtually speechless when they are anxious; other people simply cannot stop talking when they are anxious. Both behavioral tendencies can be managed with practice. Curiously, the same strategy can work for both. For example, try to get the other person to talk by asking them good questions and listening to what they say. With just a bit of preparation, you can have a wonderful repertoire of questions that serves almost every situation.

Other people get defensive and even angry when they are anxious. This response is more difficult to deal with, but there are strategies that are effective. For example, if someone says something that seems critical, you might respond initially by thanking them for their feedback. If indeed they are being critical, thanking them will put them off-guard and encourage them to be more supportive given your response. These skills are subtle and take practice to develop, but they are invaluable in many settings. One way to learn the skills is to watch people whose job it is to handle those kinds of situations. Press secretaries for politicians or corporations are often the people on the frontline dealing with critical feedback. Some of them are amazing at how well they do their job and the finesse that they bring to their job. Watch them perform, imagine using their techniques or even their words to deal with situations you are likely to face, and then practice. You do not always have to practice in the situation. Sports teams routinely practice away from the game, and many athletes practice at home. When you practice your responses to finesse difficult situations, practice out loud. You will quickly discover that it is not just the words you say, but the way you say them. Your tone of voice, body position, and facial expressions are all part of what you need to communicate.

To illustrate the importance of practicing out loud, imagine dealing with someone who made a very critical comment about you. Perhaps they said that your suggestions for dealing with an issue were useless. Moreover, assume that their tone of voice and facial expressions amplified the message that you were useless. It is hard not to feel defensive, and we are rarely at our best when we are defensive. In fact, some people learn to make people uncomfortable and defensive as a deliberate strategy to disrupt their ability to deal with the situation. Decades ago, it was a strategy heavily promoted for job interviewers because it was supposed to be better at detecting who was best able to handle stressful situations. It was called a *stress interview*. People who maintained their cool or had the skills to turn such attacks around did well. But psychopaths also did well because they do not respond with a lot of anxiety. Hiring psychopaths is not a good business model; hence, the technique is much less likely to be used today.

So, imagine a person telling you, "The advice you gave me was useless." How can you respond? Social psychologists have studied this situation extensively. If you respond defensively with something like, "The advice was fine, you just did not follow it," you are engaging in a tit-for-tat strategy that will escalate. If, however, you respond with, "I am sorry to hear it did not work. Tell me what happened, and let's see if we can find something that will work for you." How did that response feel to you? Now, read that sentence out loud. How did it sound? How did it feel? Did you notice that the tone of your voice can make a huge difference? Try different tones. Did you notice that you are automatically responding to the different tones of voice with different facial expressions? Now, try a specific tone, imagining that you are looking at the person who criticized you and expressing your concern about their frustration.

This exercise helps you to appreciate how some people always seem to say the right thing in a difficult situation. It is not just that they say the right words, but they get their tone of voice and facial expressions to drive their message home. When we discuss social anxiety and its treatment, I will emphasize the importance of rehearsal and that the rehearsal should always be out loud. It is even better to do the rehearsal in front of a mirror so you can see how you look to other people. Words are much less important than nonverbal cues, and this is especially true in difficult or emotionally charged situations.

83

Your Interpretation of Anxiety

It is almost impossible to ignore anxiety. It would be of little value to us if we could easily ignore it. When we are anxious, we are aware of that anxiety, and we respond to it. However, one of our responses is the way that we interpret it, and some interpretations can easily feed anxiety.

Anxiety is not a weakness, and yet many people feel that it is. When you interpret your anxiety, you give it new dimensions. If your anxiety convinces you that you are weak, you will feel unable to handle the anxiety or the situations that trigger it. If your anxiety convinces you that you are incompetent, you will feel the situation is hopeless. Hopelessness can lead to more problems, especially depression. Anxiety can feed anxiety, but it can also fuel depression.

The interpretations of anxiety discussed above are common and natural but not in your best interest. The way to overcome those interpretations is to offer new interpretations that are less destructive to your ego. For example, label the anxiety you are experiencing as normal and potentially valuable. That label will have you searching for the value of anxiety. Anxiety's value is its signal potential. Something is amiss or may be amiss in the future, and you need to be prepared to handle it. That is a truly valuable message and not a sign of weakness.

An alternative interpretation of anxiety is that it is the normative state of life. Many people have the misconception that life is supposed to run smoothly. It does not. Many things happen randomly, and except for rare events, such as winning the lottery, most random events are, at best, a nuisance. More often, random events are much more than a nuisance. They represent a threat to us. Given the nature of life and the randomness around us, one should expect anxiety to be routine. Something that is routine and experienced by just about everyone should not be thought of as pathological. If it is routine, it is normal.

To reframe anxiety in the ways described in this section, you must take deliberate charge of how you think about it. You need to

84

practice alternative interpretations. You need to repeat to yourself statements until they become habits. The statements might be something like, "Anxiety is not a weakness," or, "Anxiety is normal." These are powerful reinterpretations that take the damaging elements of anxiety and transform them into more positive propositions. If you have shared your feelings over casual conversations with friends and colleagues, you have already learned that feeling anxious is normal. Even more powerful statements focus you on the value of anxiety. Statements like, "This anxiety is telling me something important," or, "I will be better prepared because of the anxiety I feel now," accomplish this goal.

Accepting that Anxiety Is Normal

By now I hope that you have come to accept anxiety as a normal state. Everyone experiences it, although some people experience it more than others. The ones who experience more anxiety are not necessarily weak; in many cases, those are the individuals who are more successful in life because their anxiety drives them to be the most prepared for life.

There can be times when anxiety gets out of control, and in those cases, one might qualify for a diagnosis of an anxiety disorder. I will be talking about anxiety disorders in the next section of this book. Anxiety disorders are problems because they interfere with functioning. Anxiety by itself is rarely a problem because, in most cases, it improves functioning. It may be uncomfortable, but some things in life are uncomfortable.

Chapter Summary

In this chapter, we talked about ways of understanding anxiety by analyzing what triggers it and our responses to it. That information will help us to manage our own anxiety. It is important to realize that managing your anxiety is not the same as eliminating your anxiety. Eliminating your anxiety would be a foolish thing to do even if you had the power to do it. Without anxiety, we very likely would be less prepared for the hassles that we face every day. That said, most people would prefer to be able to manage their anxiety, minimize it to the extent possible, and do that in a way that does not interfere with other aspects of their life.

In the next chapter, we turn our attention to the management of anxiety. Our focus is on using the principles from this chapter to actively address the feelings and behaviors associated with feeling anxious.

Chapter 6

Strategies to Avoid or Minimize

Anxiety

Few people enjoy anxiety, but many people learn to manage anxiety effectively. The assumption that most people make is that anxiety is always uncomfortable. The truth is that there are situations in which anxiety does not feel uncomfortable. The first time you go on a roller coaster, you are likely to experience anxiety as the cars are pulled up the first hill. The anxiety is perfectly reasonable. Most people are afraid of heights because they cannot fly. Therefore, if something were to happen and they fell, the consequences would be severe. Most people are afraid of new and intense experiences because they are not sure if they can handle them. We have those feelings even though we know that it is highly unlikely that riding the roller coaster is life-threatening. In fact, if we thought it was life-threatening, electing to ride the roller coaster would be a truly dumb thing to do.

The interesting thing about experiences like riding roller coasters is that our feelings change over time. After a few rides on the roller coaster, many people really want to go again. How much do they want to ride that roller coaster again? Enough to stand in line for ninety minutes before they are given the opportunity. What is happening? Clearly, the anxiety that is very much a part of your first roller coaster ride has somehow been translated into another experience that we might call *thrilling*. This is a natural transition. It is not unique to roller coasters. People who skydive report the same phenomena. People who do intense performances in front of large crowds report the same phenomena. Anxiety is intense initially, but with repeated exposure, the person learns to manage the anxiety. But the evidence shows something very interesting.

The person's physiological responses normally associated with anxiety remain. However, the time course of these physiological responses shift. For example, naïve skydivers hit their peak anxiety just as they are leaving the plane. By peak anxiety, I am talking about the physiological reactivity that is part of the anxiety response. Seasoned skydivers achieve almost the same peak of physiological arousal, but they achieve that peak just before they exit the plane. When they exit, their physiological reactivity often decreases (Epstein & Fenz, 1965). I talk later about what might be behind this well-established phenomenon.

In this chapter, I focus most of our attention on how one manages anxiety. For most people, managing anxiety means minimizing anxiety, and we focus on how to achieve that goal. However, there are situations in which minimizing anxiety is not a suitable goal. We will talk about those situations, how to identify them, and what to do in those situations. For now, the take-home message is that anxiety can be managed, and, with practice, you can learn to manage your own anxiety.

Anxiety as a Behavioral Signal

We have talked about anxiety as a behavioral signal that there could be a risk in the future and that it would be wise to take that into account in your planning. Presumably, this behavioral signal is part of our evolutionary history, although it would be extremely difficult to prove that point. We have many behavioral signals that we share with other animals, and these signals drive critical behavior. The fact that we share them with other animals and that they are important to survival argues for an evolutionary origin, but from the standpoint of this book, the origin of anxiety is irrelevant.

What is relevant about anxiety is that it is a clear signal of distress and an indicator that attention and possibly action may be wise. In the previous chapter, we talked about analyzing the triggers of anxiety and the behavioral responses you have when you are anxious. That is the analysis that should be the initial response to any feeling of anxiety. What exactly are you anxious about? What situation or thought or piece of information triggered your anxiety? What are the actual risks that you face, in what situations will you face those risks, and when will those risks occur? What can you do to reduce those risks? And finally, are the risks that you potentially face too great given the potential rewards of facing them?

I wish I could tell you there were simple answers to each of those questions. In some cases, you can give reasonably good answers based on your own experience in the situation and on information that you can attain from other sources. However, there are situations in which you have limited information available and still need to decide on what to do. Finally, part of your decision rests on variables that are personal and a function of your own value system.

An example of a personal decision is how much risk you are willing to take. Implicit in this question is what return you expect for the risk you are taking. For example, applying for any job has risks, not the least of which is the blow to your ego if you apply and are turned down. However, there may be other risks as well. For example, it is entirely possible that you could be working for a company that would fire you if they discovered that you were looking for a job with another company. So, interviewing with another company risks your current job. Is that risk too great? The answer depends on how likely it is that you will be discovered, how likely it is that you will be hired by the new company, and how good the potential new job is compared to your current job. Unfortunately, in most cases, it is impossible to determine the likelihood of each of these risks, so the best you can do is make educated guesses.

There are other situations in which the risk is clear and the benefit less clear, and yet many people decide that the risk is worth it. For example, there are people who choose to go skydiving. Jumping out of a perfectly good plane may not seem like your idea of fun, but for some people, it is. They understand that there are risks, and they are certainly interested in reducing the risk as much as possible. They may choose to go skydiving because of the risks; those risks are how they have fun. They do not expect that their skydiving will increase the likelihood of their career success or help them to meet the right person to marry.

In full disclosure, I had a brief career in skydiving. It was brief because, on my second jump, the wind shifted dramatically and took me into a cornfield. I came down badly on my ankle, breaking my leg in four places and doing severe damage to both the ligament and tendon. Prior to that injury, I could dunk a basketball. After that injury, I could barely jump three inches off the ground. However, I do not regret my decision to go skydiving. It was a great experience, and it was an opportunity for me to demonstrate that I could control my own anxiety and handle a dangerous task. That said, I have talked to many people who went skydiving and told me that they were absolutely convinced that if anything went wrong, they would not have been capable of doing what was required to survive. I am sorry, but I think that is crazy. I did not tell them that, but it was what I was thinking. I would never have jumped out of the plane if I had not felt confident that I knew how to identify a problem and implement the required action to save my life. I do not have a death wish, and I have never had a death wish.

In part to illustrate the unusual nature of anxiety triggers, not only did I skydive when I was younger, but I also learned how to fly a plane when I was older. You would think that the combination of those activities would indicate that I have no fear of heights. But in fact, I do have a fear of heights. I am terrified of being on a ladder or on a roof that is more than fifteen feet in the air. When I was younger, I would force myself to do necessary homeowner's tasks because, frankly, I did not have the money to pay other people to do them. So I would clean the gutters, paint the house, and remove things that were on the roof. Once I could afford it, I stopped doing those things and paid other people to do them. The first house that I owned was two and a half stories. When the roof needed to be replaced, I got several bids, and one of the bids was turned in by an eighty-year-old gentleman who calmly walked around our roof to determine what was needed. When he came down, I expressed my amazement at how comfortable he was on the roof. He told me it was just a big hill, but I told him it was a big hill with a cliff halfway down. I would be happy to walk on the roof if someone could just lift it off the house and put it in the backyard.

Perhaps you have examples of similar situations in which you can and do handle situations that are anxiety-provoking while wanting to avoid similar situations because they trigger overwhelming anxiety. Sometimes, there are legitimate reasons that might explain the difference in your response to these similar situations. Sometimes, there are no obvious reasons that could explain the differential response. I could point out, for example, that more people die from falling off ladders or roofs than from skydiving. On the surface, that sounds like a reasonable argument. But if you are statistically sophisticated, you will realize that this argument is flawed. There are many more deaths from climbing on ladders than from skydiving because many more people engage in the former activity and would never consider doing the latter activity. The probability of risk is still higher for skydiving than for ladder climbing.

Avoiding the Anxiety Spiral

Anxiety feeds itself. If we are in a situation that makes us anxious, such as a job interview, and we notice ourselves getting anxious, we quickly start to get anxious about getting anxious. It becomes a vicious cycle that can quickly overwhelm our abilities to cope.

Most people have experienced this vicious cycle for themselves, so I do not need to tell you much about how it feels. The important point is what feeds this vicious cycle. It is a combination of two things. The first is a recognition of the anxiety building, which results in the person becoming anxious about being unable to control the anxiety. But there is a second element that is not obvious. That second element is the belief that anxiety must be controlled or something dramatically bad will happen. However, anxiety is normal. Many situations produce anxiety. By labeling such anxiety as pathological, we create the expectation that we should not be anxious. Consequently, the experience of anxiety is evidence that we cannot meet this unrealistic expectation. The

91

demand that we never be anxious is clearly unrealistic, and yet many people instinctively make that demand on themselves.

Adjusting Your Focus

The description above gives us two options to manage our anxiety in situations in which we feel our anxiety spiral out of control. The key word in the previous sentence is *manage*. It makes no sense to eliminate the anxiety. Anxiety is as normal as breathing; it is a natural response to routine situations. We can no more make anxiety go away than we can stop breathing. Therefore, our goal should be to control it to the extent that it no longer interferes with our ability to function.

One way to manage anxiety is to adjust our focus. What allows anxiety to spiral out of control is our focus on the anxiety. We are not very good at ignoring things, but we have serious limitations in our ability to pay attention to multiple things at the same time. This limitation of our attentional system can be an asset when it comes to managing anxiety. If we focus our attention on something other than the anxiety, it is impossible for us to focus our attention on our anxiety.

What are the things you might focus on instead of the anxiety? It depends entirely on the task and the situation you find yourself in. If you are in a job interview, you can focus on the interviewer and the questions the interviewer is asking. If you are about to give a talk and are waiting for your turn to speak, you can focus your attention on the people who are currently speaking. If you are driving over a long bridge and the thought of driving on that bridge makes you feel anxious, you can focus on the traffic and maintaining proper spacing between you and the car in front. If you are in a tight enclosure, such as an elevator, there really is no task for you to focus on, but there are certain topics you can focus your attention on. You might, for example, think about what you need to do later that day.

Again, the strategy is to break your focus on your anxiety by focusing on something else. Whenever possible, focus on things that will improve your performance. You will be highly motivated to improve your performance, so that focus will be relatively easy to maintain. If the situation does not allow that kind of focus, the best principle is to focus on things that are inherently interesting to you. That might be a list of the things you need to do, but it could be something like fantasizing about the ideal date with the person of your dreams.

Finally, sometimes you just need to relax and do nothing. We are not constructed to operate efficiently 24/7. Few people can even manage half that level of intensity. Our mental health demands a balance, and sometimes that balance includes putting your feet up and reading a trashy novel, binge-watching Netflix, golfing with friends, or simply doing nothing more than taking a nap. Relaxing is a fine art, and anxiety tends to disrupt the relaxation we all need. But relaxing is as important to your physical and mental health as eating well and getting sufficient sleep. If you find that anxiety is making it hard to relax, try relaxing by doing things you enjoy. You will find that such activities are effective at capturing your full attention, thus depriving the anxious thoughts of the energy to dominate your attention.

Challenging Your Expectations

It should be clear by now that the idea that we should be able to fully control our anxiety is unreasonable. So how could we possibly maintain this unreasonable expectation? The answer is simple. We usually have no idea that we are entertaining this expectation. Many of our cognitions are outside of our conscious awareness, and because they are outside of our awareness, we are unable to challenge them.

You might be asking yourself how we can have thoughts and have no awareness of those thoughts. Are they really thoughts if we do not know we are having them? Freud originally introduced the idea of the unconscious, and his treatment approach focused on bringing unconscious thoughts into consciousness so they could be evaluated and challenged. Whatever you think about Freudian theory and treatment, the evidence for unconscious thoughts is

93

overwhelming. Most of it came not from practitioners of psychoanalytic treatment but from cognitive psychologists studying the way people think, behave, and respond to situations. Let me describe two lines of evidence that illustrate this issue.

I am betting that you have experienced something that almost everyone experiences at one time or another. You try to remember the name of someone, and the harder you try, the more unlikely it is that you remember it. So you say to yourself, "To heck with it; the name will come to me later." Then you go on with whatever it is you were talking about. Sometimes the name never comes, and it is not the end of the world. But occasionally, while you are talking about something completely different, you suddenly remember the name and blurt it out. What happened? It is almost like there is some little guy running around in your head looking through all those places that that person's name could be, and then suddenly this little guy finds the name. You have no awareness of that process because you are focused on what you are talking about now. But your mind is still working on the frustrating problem from a few minutes earlier, and it is doing it completely outside of your conscious awareness. Just to be clear, there is no little guy who runs around your brain looking for lost memories, but it is a colorful metaphor.

The second example comes from some well-designed research. This research uses an instrument to present a visual image for a very short time. We do not need to go into the details of how this process works except to say that the researchers know exactly how to make sure that image is only available for processing for a few milliseconds. What do you see when images are flashed that quickly? At best you see a flash of light. If you ask people what they saw, they might report a flash of light, but they certainly will not report an image. If you show them pictures of five images and tell them one of those images was briefly flashed to them and ask them to select the image that was flashed, they will reiterate that they did not see anything. If you ask them to guess which image was flashed even though they did not see it, they, in fact, will select the correct image at chance level. In other words, they apparently have no idea what they saw.

Therefore, you might conclude that they did not see the picture because it was not on the screen long enough for them to see it. However, if we can show that flashing a picture changes a person's behavior in a reliable and predictable way, that is strong evidence that, even though the subjects believe there was no picture, they still saw a picture and processed it at a level below their consciousness. How do we do that? We can ask people to define a word. If we ask people to define the word *pen*, more than 95 percent of people will define it as a writing instrument. If we take another group of people and flash them a picture of a barnyard scene and then ask that group to define the word *pen*, almost 30 percent will define the word as an enclosure for animals. They tell us that they saw nothing but a flash of light, and they cannot even guess above chance what the image was. But at some level, they must have seen it because when asked to define the word pen, they give a lower-probability definition, "an enclosure for animals," far more frequently than individuals who did not see a brief flash of a barnyard scene.

You may not recognize some of your expectations because they are outside of your awareness, but you can infer them from the actions you take. If you find yourself catastrophizing about the anxiety you are feeling, you are probably telling yourself that being anxious is a catastrophe. That means you are telling yourself that it is unreasonable to feel anxious and that people will think less of you for being anxious. You may not hear yourself thinking those thoughts, but it is likely that such thoughts are behind your dramatic reaction to your own anxiety. As you will learn later in this book, challenging such ideas is effective in shutting down the spiraling effects of anxiety.

Chapter Summary

Many people believe their goal should be to eliminate their anxiety. Besides being an impossible goal, it would be a foolish idea. Anxiety motivates behavior, and that behavior is often desirable. If we are anxious about something we must deal with in the future, we are motivated to prepare to handle that something effectively. Such preparation is often the difference between success and failure.

One of the most feared aspects of anxiety is the fact that it can feed itself. Anxiety can spiral out of control because now we are anxious about being anxious. That becomes a vicious downward spiral, but it is a spiral we can cut off with the right actions. One way to prevent the spiral is to not focus on your anxiety, but human beings are terrible at not focusing on something. However, we have a natural limitation that we can turn to our advantage. That limitation is that we have limited attention, and so if we focus our attention on one thing, virtually all our attention will be withdrawn from everything else.

The second strategy for reducing this spiraling anxiety is to challenge the thoughts that are part of our anxiety. Those thoughts often involve statements like, "Anxiety is a weakness, and I cannot show weakness," or, "People will think less of me if I am anxious." These thoughts may be outside of our conscious awareness, but we can infer their existence from our actions and the thoughts that are part of our consciousness. Once these unconscious thoughts are recognized, we can challenge them and, by challenging them, reduce their power.

Section II

Anxiety Disorders

The first part of this book focused on the experience of anxiety, which is both a normal and desirable response. Note that I did not say it was pleasant. It is precisely the unpleasantness of anxiety that makes it so valuable because it encourages us to take steps that reduce the anxiety in most situations, thereby reducing our risk or increasing our chances of success. However, there are situations in which anxiety can get out of hand. When that happens, the anxiety can become maladaptive, and we say that the individual is suffering from an anxiety disorder.

The *DSM* (*Diagnostic and Statistical Manual*) is published by the American Psychiatric Association. It lists hundreds of psychological disorders, but only about half a dozen are considered anxiety disorders. That number is deceptive because almost every psychological disorder includes anxiety as a symptom. We consider a disorder an anxiety disorder if anxiety is the primary symptom. For example, most people who experience depression are also anxious, but depression is the primary symptom and has the largest effect on the person's behavior. The last chapter in this section deals with anxiety as a secondary symptom of other disorders.

In this section, we cover (1) panic disorder and agoraphobia, (2) generalized anxiety disorder, (3) phobias, and (4) obsessive-compulsive disorder. Note that the most recent edition of the *DSM* (*DSM-5-TR*, American Psychiatric Association, 2022) has obsessive-compulsive disorder in its own category with other related disorders, but in past editions, obsessive-compulsive disorder was considered an anxiety disorder, and it is certainly driven by very high anxiety levels.

The primary focus of this section is on describing what it is like to have these disorders from two perspectives. The first perspective is from the client's point of view. What do these symptoms feel like, and how do they affect the client's life? The second perspective is from the point of view of the loved ones of the client. These are not conditions that affect only the individual. Because these disorders can dramatically affect almost every aspect of a client's life, they also affect the lives of those who care about the client. I talk a bit about the research on what causes these disorders, but that is not my primary focus. This is not an abnormal psychology textbook, but rather a book intended for a general audience interested in understanding better both anxiety and anxiety disorders.

Chapter 7

Panic Disorder and Agoraphobia

Panic disorder is characterized by frequent panic attacks. A *panic attack* is a fear response that seems to come out of the blue. In other words, it is a fear response when there appears to be nothing to fear. If you are truly faced with a life-or-death situation, you certainly will experience fear, but you understand that your fear is both reasonable and appropriate. When that same intense fear occurs for no reason, it is common for people to imagine that they are dying or that they are going crazy.

Although panic disorder always includes panic attacks, panic attacks by themselves do not define a panic disorder. Many people have panic attacks who never develop panic disorder. To qualify for the diagnosis of panic disorder, an individual must develop intense anxiety about the panic attacks and an expectation that more panic attacks will occur. The anxiety about future panic attacks often drives agoraphobic avoidance. **Agoraphobia** occurs when one either avoids or immediately escapes from a situation that produces intense anxiety that one might have a panic attack. Panic attacks are disruptive to individuals with panic disorder, but agoraphobic avoidance is often the most disruptive part of this disorder. As you will learn, agoraphobic avoidance can be severe enough that the individual may be housebound, unable to work outside of the household and unable to carry on a normal social life.

Fight-or-Flight Syndrome

We have already discussed *fight-or-flight syndrome*, so you already know it is the body's response to a life-threatening

99

situation. This syndrome is the body preparing to run for its life and, if escape is impossible, to fight for its life. Although it is referred to as *fight-or-flight syndrome*, reversing the terms makes more sense (flight-or-fight). The reason for reversing this is that the instinct is to escape, and to fight only if you have no escape route available. Perhaps at some point in your life, you have been warned about the dangers of cornering an animal. If you corner an animal, the animal may very well believe that its life is in danger, and if it has no escape route, it will prepare to fight to the death. If it is a small animal, it may very well not have any chance of killing you as a potential predator, but it can certainly do damage in such a life-or-death struggle.

Fight-or-flight syndrome is one of our oldest evolutionary developments. It is triggered in the brainstem in a location known as the **locus coeruleus**. The syndrome is by no means unique to human beings. It is found in virtually every creature that has a brain, because creatures with even primitive brains will have a brainstem. The fact that evolution developed this response early and maintained it in virtually every creature that evolved since suggests how important it is to survival.

Panic attacks are fear responses, but they are false alarms. The brain is constantly processing information about the environment, and when that information suggests that there may be a danger, the fight-or-flight syndrome is triggered. But if there is no danger, we are puzzled by our fear response; the brain determined that danger is present, but it is a mistake because there is no danger. Every creature or object that is designed to respond to situations has the potential to respond incorrectly. You are all familiar with smoke detectors. They are designed to sample a small portion of the environment (that portion that might be smoke) and give off a very loud signal if they find enough smoke-like material to suspect that a fire could be present. Note all the qualifying words in the previous sentence. We all know that smoke detectors occasionally go off when no fire is present, which is another example of a false alarm. You might have burned something in the oven or even set it off when boiling water. If that happens, we reset the smoke detector or remove its battery for a while.

But our brain is far more complicated than a smoke detector. We cannot just reset our brain or cut its power when we experience the false alarm that is a panic attack. Instead, our brain tries to figure out what is happening and why. To us, the terrifying experiences that seem unwarranted are the most significant elements of what is happening. But it is unlikely that other creatures, such as rats, have the same experience of the fight-or-flight syndrome. They likely lack the brain capacity to interpret and feel such emotions. But they possess the brain capacity to activate the body to escape or fight for survival. Many of our emotions likely evolved in creatures much less complex than us, and the experience of those emotions in those creatures is probably different from what we experience. One of the things our brain development has allowed us to do is think about and interpret what is going on around us and in our own bodies.

False alarms are only one of two possible mistakes in a judgment situation. Let's focus on the simple example of a smoke detector to discuss these concepts. There are two states the smoke detector must recognize: fire or no fire. There are two responses the smoke detector can give: alarm and no alarm. Smoke detectors detect whether a fire is present by monitoring one or more substances that look like smoke; different detectors use different strategies to do this monitoring, and we need not be concerned about these differences for this discussion. If the level of the substance reaches a preset threshold, the alarm goes off. Below that threshold, the alarm does not go off. The first error, the false alarm (also called a *false positive*), is the smoke detector going off when no fire is present (i.e., the substance monitored is above the threshold but not because there is a fire). The second error, the *false negative*, is more than annoying. It could cost you your life. That error is the detector failing to go off when there is a fire, and as a result, you are not warned in time to escape. These two errors are inversely related. In English, as the probability of a false alarm increases, the probability of a false negative decreases. In a simple device like a smoke detector, the manufacturer determines the relative probability of these errors by where they set the threshold for the alarm to go off. All smoke detector companies set this threshold to minimize false negatives, which means that false positives will be more likely. Why do the set the detectors up this way? Because false positives are annoying, whereas false negatives are life-threatening. Clearly, one error is more serious and should be avoided.

The discussion of false positives and false negatives in a simple device like a smoke detector is complicated enough. Detecting danger of any sort with the multiple senses that feed information to our brain is unbelievably complicated by comparison. There are so many possible dangers and so many possible indicators of each danger. In our evolutionary history, predators were a major source of danger. Predators sneak up on their prey, so movement in the grass, a faint smell or sound, or a shifting shadow suggesting movement might indicate danger. But all these things occur all the time in nature. Grasses and tree limbs move because of the wind, which can also move sounds and smells and change shadows. Detection is uncertain, but those creatures that detected predators more often had a better chance of surviving. The cost was occasional fear responses that were unnecessary because no predator was present. Even today, we respond with alarm if we detect what feels like rapid movement coming toward us. It may only be a shadow moving, but it still feels dangerous because of our evolutionary history.

Take the simple discussion of false alarms in a smoke detector and the detection of potential predators in our evolutionary history and multiply it by a thousand, and you have an idea of the complexity of our brain's task of monitoring the environment for danger and triggering appropriate responses to allow us to avoid or survive that danger. It is no wonder that panic attacks occur. The mystery is why they do not occur more often.

The core element of the fight-or-flight response is that the body is immediately preparing to literally run for its life or fight to the death. To achieve those goals, the muscles of our body tense, which gives us a faster reaction time if we need to avoid an attacking predator. That tension also gives us more strength so that we can push and run harder and faster. Our heart starts to beat faster and stronger. This moves more blood to the muscles, which need an enormous amount of oxygen to be able to run for a long time. It can feel to many people like their heart is pounding in their chest, and in fact, it is. The muscle tension can give one a feeling that their chest is being compressed and that it is hard to breathe. It is often common for people experiencing this fight-or-flight response to believe that their neck is being tightened to the point that it is affecting their breathing and swallowing. All these physiological responses serve a single purpose: to be better prepared to fight or run, preferably the latter.

I cannot tell you what a fight-or-flight response feels like to a rat. Rats cannot tell me about their experience. I cannot even tell you what the fight-or-flight response feels like to my pet dogs, although I suspect that their experience is much closer to my human experience. I encourage you to be skeptical of this interpretation because I have not had any detailed discussions with either dogs or rats. However, I did extensive research with rats when I was in graduate school and have had dogs in my household for most of my adult life. I know from my studies that the cerebral cortex of rats is small, and the cerebral cortex of a dog is much larger, although well short of the size of the cerebral cortex of human beings.

We do our thinking in the cerebral cortex of our brain; we do most of our feeling in what are called *midbrain structures*, which are under the cerebral cortex in human beings. From an evolutionary perspective, the oldest part of the brain is the *brainstem*, which generally handles life-critical functions. If you suffer brainstem damage, you will likely die immediately because your heart will stop beating, your lungs will stop breathing, or both. Note that the fight-or-flight fear response is in the brainstem along with other life-critical functions.

Our experience of life is probably different than that of other species because we have the cognitive capacity associated with having a large cerebral cortex. One of the mysteries of our experience is called *consciousness*, which is the sense of ourselves as thinking creatures that evaluate and respond to the environment. We see something happen, we think about what it means and what we should do, we decide on an action, and then we act. That is exactly how it feels, and there is extensive research that shows that a good part of that feeling may be an illusion. For example, it generally takes about seven hundred milliseconds for us to become consciously aware of something, and yet there is evidence that we have started to act on an experience within four hundred milliseconds. In other words, even before we are consciously aware that something has happened, our brain has already decided on an action and begun to implement that action. Therefore, that action could not possibly be the result of a conscious decision to act.

Consciousness has been a mystery throughout recorded history. The ancient Greeks speculated on the nature of consciousness and the role it played. Later scholars speculated that consciousness had an existence independent of the body (the so-called *mind-body dualism*). We now believe that consciousness is a result of brain activity and not separate from brain activity, but still a mystery. People are trying to solve that mystery, but it has certainly proved to be a challenge (Gazzaniga, 2018).

Consciousness is critical to our understanding of anxiety and anxiety disorders because our awareness of anxiety affects both our behavioral responses and our emotions. We think about our anxiety and what it means. Sometimes those thoughts lead us to despair, and we give up on handling the anxiety we experience. However, as you will learn in the last section, we can take control of our thoughts, which can help us to manage anxiety and turn it to our benefit. We discuss that process in the chapter on cognitive therapy for anxiety disorders.

Developing Secondary Anxiety (Fear of Fear)

A panic attack can be terrifying. By definition, a panic attack seems to come on for no reason. Consequently, it can feel like you are going crazy or you are dying of something like a heart attack. You are literally feeling the fear that you would experience if you were in a life-or-death situation. The problem is that you are not in a life-or-death situation, so the fear must be interpreted as meaning something else. Clearly, you cannot trust your mind or your body, and that itself is a terrifying situation. So how do you respond? You begin to worry about when the next panic attack will come. Since, by definition, panic attacks come out of the blue, they are unpredictable. If they were predictable, they would not be so terrifying. Because you cannot predict them, you cannot prevent them. Moreover, you may not even be able to prepare yourself for them.

That is the situation that creates the secondary anxiety associated with panic disorder. It is bad enough that you must experience the terror of occasional panic attacks, but now you spend most of your time worrying about when the next one will come and how you will respond to it. As you will learn shortly, you expect that your response will be inappropriate and embarrassing. Sometimes that expectation is reasonable, but in most situations, you have more control than you imagine.

Avoiding Panic Situations (Agoraphobia)

The secondary anxiety associated with panic attacks, and not the panic attacks, is what drives agoraphobic avoidance. Agoraphobia is translated as either fear of open spaces or fear of the marketplace. Both fears can be found in individuals who have panic disorder. Although agoraphobia could occur with almost any anxiety disorder, it is far more likely to be found in panic disorder.

Agoraphobia is often the most disruptive part of panic disorder. It is what prevents people from leaving their houses and/or taking care of their everyday responsibilities. In some cases, the person may be willing to venture out, but only if they are with someone that serves as a "safe person." This person might be a spouse or close friend who gives the person with panic disorder enough confidence to be able to challenge the fear of having a panic attack. However, this dynamic can be very disruptive to relationships because it puts tremendous pressure on the safe person to always be available.

The situations that tend to be avoided when someone suffers from agoraphobia fall into two categories: situations that tend to trigger panic attacks and situations that would be difficult to escape from if one had a panic attack. It is common for these two categories to overlap, as we will see shortly. The reason why someone with panic disorder might avoid situations from which escape is difficult is the person fears that their attempt at escape will be so dramatic that it will draw everyone's attention and bring on ridicule.

Situations that Trigger Panic

Occasionally, there are specific situations that an individual has always feared, and those situations tend to be avoided when agoraphobia develops. For example, if people have always been afraid of heights, the natural fear they experience is likely to put their fight-or-flight response on a hair trigger. Consequently, they avoid those situations to avoid having panic attacks.

The more common situations that are avoided in panic disorder are ones in which the person has previously experienced panic attacks. There might be nothing special about those situations, and in many cases, there is no reason to view those situations as dangerous. However, because they have experienced panic attacks in those situations in the past, they expect to experience panic attacks again in the future, and therefore, they avoid those situations. This is not entirely unreasonable. The anxiety they experience in these situations increases the likelihood that panic attacks will be triggered. This makes sense if you understand how fight-or-flight syndrome works. It is normally triggered in situations that are life-threatening, unless it represents the false alarms associated with panic disorder. If we have reason to believe that situations could be life-threatening, our body is on alert, ready to respond at the first sign of potential danger. In other words, it does not take much to trigger panic attacks in such situations.

Situations From Which Escape Is Difficult

Many people with agoraphobia avoid such situations as bridges, elevators, planes, and crowded places. What each of these places has in common is that it would be difficult or potentially embarrassing if the person were to try to escape suddenly. For example, if you have a panic attack on an airplane, you desperately want to get off that airplane immediately. But the pilot will not be willing to land the plane immediately just so you can get off, so you are trapped. The fear of bridges rarely has anything to do with the idea that the bridge might collapse. Instead, the problem is that you might be trapped on the bridge and not be able to get off. That could easily happen if there is a minor accident in front of you and the traffic comes to a stop. You could not move forward to escape the situation. Within seconds, there would be traffic behind you that would also be unable to move, and therefore either going forward or turning around would be impossible. For the same reason, people with agoraphobia tend to fear tunnels, limited-access highways (expressways), elevators, and grocery stores.

You might be asking why grocery stores are on this list. When you first walk into a grocery store, leaving is easy. But as you fill your grocery cart, leaving becomes more problematic. If you are standing in line to check out with someone behind you, leaving your cart there and running out of the store will be very embarrassing. For the same reason, being in a classroom or in a small meeting can be problematic because leaving abruptly will draw attention to you.

Many people with agoraphobia fear that they will run out of the situation screaming in terror and that everyone will be watching them. They continue to feel that way even though such behavior is exceedingly rare. Moreover, they continue to feel that way even though they have had panic attacks and have been able to leave the situation without drawing undue attention. Again, the behavior in this anxiety disorder, just like every other anxiety disorder, is driven more by expectations than past experiences.

What Is It Like to Experience Panic Disorder?

As you might guess about a disorder that sometimes confines people to their homes for years, the experience of panic disorder is intense and often overwhelming. Panic attacks are incredibly intense and impossible to ignore when they occur. I have never met anyone who was not distressed by a panic attack, and that includes individuals whose panic attacks were triggered deliberately in the laboratory so that the physiology and psychology of panic attacks could be studied as they occurred.

It is relatively easy to trigger a panic attack. The most common way is to have individuals breathe a mixture that includes about 5 percent carbon dioxide. Carbon dioxide is the waste product of animal metabolism. We breathe in oxygen and use that oxygen and other nutrients to power our bodies. The oxygen is carried through the bloodstream to the various organs of the body. We think of blood as red because if we bleed, that blood is automatically oxygenated by the oxygen in the atmosphere. But blood is blue when it is no longer carrying oxygen. You can see examples of that in your own body. Arteries carry the oxygenated blood from the lungs through the body, and veins carry the depleted blood (i.e., no longer carrying oxygen) back to the lungs to be oxygenated. You can see those veins on the surface of your arm and the back of your hand, and you will note that they are blue instead of red.

The atmosphere contains about 20 percent oxygen and about one-half of 1 percent carbon dioxide. Most of the rest of the air is nitrogen. Plants use carbon dioxide for fuel and give off oxygen as a waste product, so the proper balance of plants and animals on the planet is important to the health of both. If you breathe a mixture of 5 percent carbon dioxide and 20 percent oxygen, you will feel like you are being oxygen deprived. Therefore, you will be gasping for air. This sounds crazy because you are getting plenty of oxygen and there is no need to gasp for air. The problem is that we did not evolve a mechanism for monitoring oxygen levels. Instead, we evolved a mechanism for monitoring carbon dioxide levels. That works fine if we are on the planet because as carbon dioxide increases, oxygen decreases. In other words, the level of carbon dioxide is inversely proportional to the level of oxygen. The system works fine if we stay in the environment in which we evolved. However, human beings have a habit of exploring new environments.

We did not evolve to fly, and by ourselves, we are not capable of flying, but we have the intellect to design machines that allow us to fly. As you increase your altitude, the density of the air decreases. The proportion of gases remains the same, but the total amount of each gas decreases as the density decreases. Therefore, at ten thousand feet we have considerably less oxygen than at ground level, and at thirty thousand feet, we do not have nearly enough oxygen to keep us alive. Planes handle that by pressurizing the cabin so that the density of the air in the cabin is comparable to that at an altitude of about seven thousand feet. This pressurized air is still a bit thinner than most of us breathe every day, but there is plenty of oxygen to keep us alive. If you are flying a small plane that is not pressurized, once you get above ten thousand feet, you probably will not have enough oxygen to keep you conscious. The problem is that your body thinks you have plenty of oxygen. That is because your body is monitoring the level of carbon dioxide. If the level of carbon dioxide is low, the body interprets that to mean that the level of oxygen is high because on the surface of the earth this inverse relationship is almost always true. Therefore, your body thinks you have plenty of oxygen, and you will happily fly the plane until you pass out from lack of oxygen. As you might have guessed, it is not good to pass out when you are flying a plane, which is why regulations require you to wear an oxygen mask if you fly above a certain altitude for a certain length of time.

You do not need to understand the relationship between carbon dioxide and oxygen or the fact that we monitor carbon dioxide as an indirect measure of whether we are getting sufficient oxygen. You can simply take my word for the fact that breathing 5 percent carbon dioxide will make you feel like you are oxygen-starved and, more importantly, will reliably trigger a panic attack in both patients with panic disorder and individuals who do not have panic disorder. Much of what we know about panic disorders is a result of laboratory studies conducted on individuals with the disorder who have volunteered to have panic attacks in the laboratory while being carefully monitored. I give those individuals great credit for enduring a terrifying experience to help scientists diagnose and treat other people with the disorder.

When I first started specializing in the treatment of anxiety disorders, I had the advantage of having a colleague who studied panic disorders in the laboratory. I wanted to understand at a gut level what panic attacks felt like, and I was able to experience them because her lab had the equipment needed to trigger panic attacks. Those experiences gave me real insights into the nature of panic attacks and why people with panic disorder respond so strongly to them. It also allowed me to talk in detail about my experiences of panic with my patients, which gave me a lot of credibility. I can tell you that knowing that the panic attacks were triggered by the level of carbon dioxide did little to reduce the uncomfortable and sometimes terrifying experience of a panic attack.

I want to make one final point. I experienced two panic attacks in my life outside the lab and several in the lab that were deliberately induced with carbon dioxide inhalation, yet I never developed panic disorder. Although panic disorders are defined by panic attacks, the attacks alone are not sufficient to trigger the disorder.

For the Individual

As uncomfortable as panic attacks are, most people who have a panic attack never develop panic disorder. They are distressed by the attack and often confused about what it was, but somehow, they reinterpreted the panic attack in a way that allowed them to discount it. How do they do that? They might, for example, say something like, "I should not have had that third cup of coffee." Sometimes, their interpretation is even simpler. They might see the experience as abnormal, but just an unpleasant sensation that will go away.

Why is it that some individuals respond to a panic attack far more dramatically than most individuals? The answer seems to be a personality characteristic that has a strong genetic component. This characteristic is called **anxiety sensitivity**, and it refers to the tendency to view symptoms of anxiety as dangerous and threatening. An individual who has an occasional panic attack but does not have anxiety sensitivity is likely to be less distressed by the experience because the anxiety symptoms do not feel as dangerous. However, people with anxiety sensitivity respond more strongly to panic attacks. Most people with panic disorder develop the disorder after their first panic attack, and most of those people show signs of anxiety sensitivity prior to developing the disorder. They clearly were more distressed by their anxiety than most other people well before their first panic attack. This last point is important because one might imagine that the development of a dramatic condition such as panic disorder might produce anxiety sensitivity. The fact that anxiety sensitivity appears to precede the disorder lends credence to the idea that it is a contributing factor.

People who develop panic disorder typically experience their first panic attack as terrifying. Their body is completely out of control, and there appears to be no reason for them to feel that way. Moreover, their psychological response is just as dramatic. They feel like they are about to go crazy or that they have already gone crazy. Even after the attack subsides, which most attacks do within twenty minutes, they are still terrified that something is drastically wrong. It is common for people with panic disorder to seek immediate medical treatment at the emergency room because they believe they are having a heart attack. It is relatively easy to establish that no heart attack has occurred, but ER doctors differ in their ability to handle these situations effectively. Doctors usually recognize that the individual had a panic attack, and some are empathetic in talking about panic attacks with the patient and encouraging them to see someone for treatment. Other doctors view panic attacks as not a real disorder because they do not view them as a medical disorder. Unfortunately, some of those doctors show little empathy and may even be annoyed by the continued concern of the patient. This kind of reaction from the doctor may increase the concern of the patient that he or she is going crazy.

111

One might imagine that an experience severe enough to convince people that they are dying or going crazy would have an enormous impact on their behavior. Individuals with panic disorder begin to obsess about future panic attacks. They do everything in their power to avoid such attacks, which includes avoiding situations in which the attacks have occurred in the past under the assumption that there is something in that situation that triggered the attack. Sometimes, people with panic disorder avoid very narrow situations, such as a particular building, but more often they avoid large categories of situations, such as all buildings more than three stories high. Because people with panic disorder are anxious about future panic attacks, the anxiety makes the trigger for those panic attacks more sensitive. That means that it takes less to trigger a panic attack, and therefore panic attacks are more frequent and occur in more situations. The result is that people gradually decrease the situations in which they are comfortable and begin to avoid more situations and/or places.

We talked about how panic attacks are false alarms, and any system that is designed to monitor a situation and make a differential response depending on the situation is subject to false alarms. The smoke detector in your home was a great example. Why is it so easy for us to ignore the annoyance of a smoke-detector false alarm and so difficult for clients with panic disorder to ignore their panic-attack false alarm? Part of the reason is that a panic attack is not just a loud sound designed to tell us that there might be a danger. It involves massive changes in our physiology and, as a result, massive psychological responses to those physiological changes. In other words, it is far more personal. Moreover, for those individuals prone to panic disorder, which usually means that they experience anxiety sensitivity, these responses are not only more personal but also more threatening.

To fully understand the impact of panic disorder on an individual, we need to separate the panic attacks and the anxiety about the possibility of future attacks. The panic attacks are incredibly aversive and therefore terrifying. They make the person feel completely out of control, in large part because they seem to come out of nowhere. Consequently, the person becomes extremely anxious that future panic attacks are likely, and that anxiety drives avoidance of situations that feel potentially dangerous. The person is constantly on edge and has severe concerns about their ability to control situations. The helplessness associated with this situation is a recipe for depression; therefore, it should not be surprising that secondary depression is often found in individuals with panic disorder. When we think about suicide, we often associate it with depression, but the risk for suicide is as high in individuals with panic disorder as in individuals with major depression.

Given the intensity of panic attacks and the intense anxiety about having more panic attacks, it is not hard to imagine how agoraphobic avoidance might develop. It is also easy to understand how disruptive such avoidance would be to one's normal life. If you cannot go to work or to the store to pick up groceries or to your child's PTA meeting, you cannot live up to the normal responsibilities of life. That fact alone is terribly traumatic and disruptive to one's life, but it has a secondary effect. People with panic disorder have the same level of responsibility as other people, and their inability to live up to that responsibility is devastating to their emotional well-being. They often feel like failures, people who are so weak that they cannot do even the simplest of activities. They become emotionally and socially withdrawn, which increases their sense of isolation.

For the Loved Ones

Having a loved one suffering from panic disorder is emotionally distressing. Your loved one is clearly suffering, although you may not be able to understand why they are suffering or have a sense of how you might help alleviate the suffering. For many people, the idea of panic attacks creating this level of disruption in a person's life is hard to imagine. Consequently, you may feel like your loved one is not trying hard enough to overcome their condition. Moreover, some of the things they report seem to be crazy, although they are clearly not crazy. So how is it that the person is unable to leave their own home because "they might lose control"? For years, the person was able to leave their house and carry on

113

their life, and from your perspective, it appears that nothing has changed. Frankly, it is common for loved ones of individuals with panic disorder to do their best to be understanding, but at some point, their empathy simply runs out.

I will discuss psychological treatments for various anxiety disorders in the last section of this book, including panic disorder. That information will give you an idea of how a disorder like panic disorder can be attacked and treated, but it will not give you enough information to serve as the therapist for a loved one with panic disorder. The complexity of the disorder is such that you really want someone who thoroughly understands the disorder to guide the treatment. However, it is often helpful to have one or more loved ones involved in the treatment of someone with panic disorder. The first reason is that the therapist familiar with this disorder can give excellent advice on the best way of supporting someone during treatment. The second reason is that it is not just the panic patient who is suffering. As a loved one of a panic patient, you are suffering as well. Your life is being disrupted, and the sense of helplessness experienced by panic patients may also be shared by you because it seems like there is nothing you can do. Therefore, you need support as well during this process. Moreover, the individual suffering from panic disorder may well be a good source of support for you, which may decrease your sense of hopelessness.

There is nothing you can do to make the panic disorder go away. Frankly, there is nothing a therapist can do to make the panic disorder go away. Psychological treatment of a panic disorder involves people with the disorder learning how to manage their anxiety and then using that information to challenge the anxiety until it no longer controls them. That is not easy; remember the principle that we are programmed to learn anxiety quickly and unlearn it slowly. The anxiety level in panic disorder is unbelievably high, so you can expect the process of reducing that anxiety level takes time and a lot of hard work. You cannot do that hard work for the affected individual, but you can be supportive during the process. Sometimes that support involves giving the person a gentle nudge; at other times, it involves heavily praising the efforts of the person even though progress is slow. It is hard work to provide this kind of support, and there are times that you may feel like you are nagging the individual. It is sometimes a fine line between encouragement and nagging, but you want to try to walk that line as best you can.

The good news is that panic disorder is treatable, even in individuals with severe cases. The even better news is that successful treatment often gives the person his or her life back. That is an intense motivator for individuals with panic disorder. As the individual becomes better able to manage his or her anxiety, you can take advantage of those gains by doing things that are meaningful to both you and the patient. Such activities are enormously reinforcing for both of you and make it easier for the affected individual to continue to challenge the anxiety.

Review of Treatment Options

There are two treatment approaches for panic disorder, which we discuss in more detail in the last section of this book. The first is a cognitive-behavioral approach that involves teaching people to manage their anxiety while gradually challenging the restrictions on behavior imposed by agoraphobia. The second approach uses medications to manage the panic. The medications used most often are selective serotonin reuptake inhibitors (SSRIs). This section outlines these approaches.

The cognitive-behavioral approach used in the treatment of panic disorder involves three components. The first component includes anxiety management techniques, such as deep breathing, muscle relaxation, and cognitive refocusing of attention. The value of these techniques is that they allow clients to manage their anxiety even during intense exposure to situations that normally trigger anxiety. The second component involves challenging unrealistic fears. Panic disorder often creates these unrealistic fears and leads many clients to seek medical help because they believe they are dying. The feelings are so intense that such fears seem reasonable despite overwhelming evidence that the fears are unjustified. This aspect of the treatment is important in motivating clients to do the third and most important element, which is exposure.

It is almost impossible to talk oneself out of anxiety. Self-talk is valuable in that it provides the motivation to challenge anxiety through exposure to the situations that trigger the anxiety. But it is the exposure to anxiety-generating situations that is the most valuable aspect of psychological treatment. Remember, we are programmed to learn anxiety quickly and to unlearn it slowly. Learning it quickly is advantageous because we can learn to be cautious in dangerous situations with limited exposure. However, sometimes we need to overcome that anxiety to function. We just do not want to abandon anxiety too quickly, so we are programmed to unlearn it slowly. We unlearn anxiety through exposure, and in almost every case, we can do the exposure in a gradual manner that keeps the level of anxiety manageable. During this exposure, the individual uses anxiety control techniques to minimize the anxiety and to give the individual a sense of control over the situation. The individual also uses cognitive restructuring techniques to challenge the gut feeling that the situation is truly dangerous.

Exposure to situations that trigger feelings of panic is critical in the behavioral treatment of panic disorders, but a second type of exposure is often included in the treatment. We call this second exposure type **interoceptive exposure**. In this aspect of the treatment, we have people with panic disorder expose themselves to the physical sensation associated with a panic attack. Those sensations often become triggers for panic attacks. *Interoceptive* means "internal physical feelings." For example, common interoceptive feelings associated with panic attacks include a racing heart, sweating, physical shaking, difficulty breathing, and hyperventilation.

The psychological techniques described above are very effective for most people with panic disorder (Craske, Wolitzsky-Taylor & Barlow, 2021). The treatment is different than what many people think of psychological treatment in that little time is spent talking about the anxiety and most of the time is spent challenging the anxiety. Therapists will often leave the office with their panic clients for exposure treatment. They might, for example, get in a

116

car and drive over bridges of various lengths to challenge the anxious feeling that bridges are dangerous because the person might be trapped on the bridge. Moreover, clients are encouraged to continue the exposure on their own in between therapy sessions. These exposure sessions without the therapist are usually less intense, but they are important in solidifying the gains made during therapy sessions.

Medications are also effective in the treatment of panic disorder. At one time, anti-anxiety drugs were used, but they are rarely used today. The reason for that is that the anti-anxiety drugs need to be at a very high level to be effective against the intense anxiety associated with panic disorder. At such high levels, it becomes difficult to reduce the dosage without triggering rebound effects. Even a slight reduction in the level of the anti-anxiety drugs produces a dramatic increase in anxiety and much more frequent panic attacks. Consequently, the drugs of choice for the treatment of panic disorder are SSRIs.

SSRIs are often incorrectly referred to as antidepressant drugs because that was the first disorder for which they were frequently used. However, research has shown that SSRIs are effective for many disorders, including panic disorder (Bandelow, Michaelis & Wedekind, 2017). SSRI medications do not produce an immediate reduction in anxiety but rather seem to calm the system so panic attacks are less frequent. By themselves, their effectiveness is limited, but to the extent that the individual is willing to challenge the anxiety through exposure because of the control they experience through the medications, the improvement can be dramatic.

Chapter Summary

Our understanding of panic disorders has improved dramatically over the past fifty years. We once thought panic attacks were simply intense anxiety attacks, but we now understand they are a different phenomenon. A panic attack is a fear response, which is a primitive response designed to help us survive life-or-death situations. We often refer to it as the fight-or-flight syndrome. It activates the body so that we can run faster or fight harder to survive.

As valuable as this reflex is, when it occurs absent a life-or-death situation, it is terrifying. The individual experiences these massive feelings, which often feel like the person is dying or about to go crazy. The intensity of this response is so strong that it produces almost instantaneous anxiety about being in any situation in which panic attacks have been experienced. Moreover, because this reflex action makes one want to flee, the person starts to avoid situations in which flight is either impossible or would be embarrassing. This is the agoraphobic avoidance that is often the most serious part of this disorder because it disrupts the person's life so dramatically.

Effective psychological treatment exists for panic disorder. It involves the management of anxiety through both physiological manipulation and cognitive challenge and the gradual exposure to those situations that have triggered the anxiety in the past. Medications can also be effective, primarily SSRIs, which seem to calm the system sufficiently so panic attacks are less frequent. One might think that anti-anxiety drugs would be the drug of choice, but they are often avoided because of the strong rebound effects when one tries to reduce the dosage.

Chapter 8

Generalized Anxiety Disorder

The diagnosis of *generalized anxiety disorder* refers to exactly what the label implies. Individuals with this disorder tend to worry a lot, tend to worry about just about everything (generalized worry), and tend to experience worry that does not go away. In many cases, these individuals function fine, but constant worrying wears them down emotionally. It is hard to be at your best when your energy is being sapped by this dark cloud that seems to constantly hang over you.

Generalized anxiety disorder, which is often referred to simply as **GAD**, is one of the more interesting anxiety disorders. As you will see, although the person experiences significant anxiety, it is not clear that it is the same anxiety found in other anxiety disorders or experienced by most people in normal situations. The term *worry* is typically used to describe the anxiety found in GAD. It is a cognitive process; the person is thinking about all the things that might go wrong, and those thoughts produce an uncomfortable anxiety state.

When Is Anxiety Not Anxiety?

We all know what anxiety feels like because all of us experience anxiety at least occasionally and sometimes quite intensely. But by now you probably realize your feelings may not accurately reflect what is going on. We feel, for example, that fear is intense anxiety. However, you now know that fear and anxiety are different concepts, they involve different brain mechanisms, and they serve different purposes. Worrying is certainly part of the anxiety that people sometimes feel. If you are anxious about a job interview, you will spend considerable time thinking about that job interview and all the things that might go wrong. That certainly is worrying, and anxiety is certainly part of the worrying in that situation.

Although almost constant worrying is the defining characteristic of GAD, it is common to have other symptoms present. These may include restlessness, irritability, difficulty in concentrating, and sleep disturbance. Some of these symptoms may be secondary to the worrying (i.e., a result of the constant worrying) instead of one of the core symptoms of this disorder. Less frequently, somatic symptoms such as nausea, diarrhea, and muscle cramps are reported.

What is surprising about generalized anxiety disorders is that the constant worrying that defines this disorder may, in fact, not be anxiety as we understand it. It feels to people with GAD like anxiety, and they describe it as anxiety. But anxiety is more than just a feeling. Anxiety involves specific physiological arousal that can be easily measured with electronic instrumentation. When we take such measures, it appears that anxiety in GAD lacks some key physiological components found in other anxiety disorders (Denefrio, Myruski, Mennin & Dennis-Tiwary, 2019).

One could speculate about why the apparent anxiety in generalized anxiety disorder seems to be an attenuated anxiety response, without the full range of physiological elements normally found in anxiety. It may be, for example, that individuals with generalized anxiety disorder have learned to manage their anxiety by shutting down part of the response, which makes the anxiety less threatening to them. We use the term **autonomic restrictors** to refer to individuals who show this attenuated anxiety response.

The term autonomic restrictor comes from our understanding of the **autonomic nervous system**, which is an automatic system that shifts our energy from a primary focus on maintaining our health to a primary focus on responding to immediate threats. The autonomic nervous system has two branches that tend to be mutually inhibitory. That is, when one branch is active, the other is inactive. The **sympathetic branch** of the autonomic nervous system is active when we are stressed; the **parasympathetic**

branch of the autonomic nervous system is activated when there is little or no stress. When the sympathetic nervous system is active, all our energy is directed to dealing with the challenges in front of us. When we say that we can give 110 percent, that statement may be true when we have sympathetic nervous system arousal. We can be more focused, exert energy for a longer time, and be able to respond more effectively. It all sounds perfect, except for one thing.

After reading the above description of the sympathetic branch of the autonomic nervous system, you are probably asking yourself why we cannot be in this supercharged state all the time. The reason is there is a cost. There is always a cost. When we are under parasympathetic nervous system arousal, our body is focused on taking care of itself. I like to refer to the tasks involved as the housekeeping chores of the body. We digest food, we remove wastes, we allow the body to heal from injuries, and we get the necessary rest to be able to be our best when that is necessary. It helps to think of this in terms of a real household. If there is something traumatic happening to you and your family, you are likely to focus your energy on dealing with their trauma. You are not going to worry about doing the dishes, washing your clothes, or vacuuming the rugs. By postponing those housekeeping chores, you have more time and energy to focus on dealing with immediate problems. Our body can do that, just like we can do it for a household. But our body can only do that up to a point. If we do not take care of our body through parasympathetic nervous system arousal, our health will deteriorate. No matter how much sympathetic nervous system arousal we have, if our body is no longer healthy, our ability to respond to difficult situations will be limited.

There is an important corollary to the idea described above. We are perfectly capable of handling periodic stress and anxiety. It does not normally take a toll on our bodies. However, it becomes a problem when the stress or anxiety is too chronic. When the stress is too chronic, we are under constant sympathetic nervous system arousal, and because that arousal inhibits parasympathetic nervous system arousal, our body is not taking care of itself. We do not have to vacuum the rugs every day or wash the dishes every day, but if we put it off too long, the house will be a mess to live in. The same is true with the housekeeping chores of the body.

Making Worrying Effective

Everyone worries, so what is the difference between worries that all of us experience and worries that are part of what we call generalized anxiety disorder? Like most anxiety disorders, the basis for the generalized anxiety disorder diagnosis is that the anxiety is either too intense or ineffective. In this case, the second definition seems to be the most important.

People with GAD worry a lot, but the worrying does not seem to do them much good. Consequently, they continue to worry. Moreover, they continue to worry even if they have taken steps that should reduce the need to worry. For example, they may be worried about how they will handle an upcoming task. Like most people who worry about such things, they act to be better prepared, but it does not seem to make much of a difference. They continue to worry despite the action. In fact, not only do they continue to worry, but also the intensity of the worry remains high despite the preparatory steps that they have already taken.

Worrying by itself accomplishes nothing. The only thing that accomplishes something is behavior. So, if you are worried about an upcoming event, you will have made yourself uncomfortable, but the worrying does not make the upcoming event less risky. What reduces the risk is behavior that prepares you for the situation. For example, if you are worried about a job interview, you can do your research and be well prepared to answer questions about how you fit into the company. You can make sure that your cover letter and resume are impressive and that there are no errors that could easily be corrected. You might imagine some of the toughest questions and how you would approach them. Those are behaviors; those behaviors decrease the risk of something bad happening because you are prepared for it.

In generalized anxiety disorder, the worrying seems to continue, perhaps in part because the behavioral element is often missing. In the normal course of things, our thoughts about potential risks increase our level of anxiety, which motivates behavior to reduce the risk and therefore reduce the anxiety. In generalized anxiety disorder, the anxiety goes on endlessly, in part because there is a reason to be anxious. Nothing has changed; the person spent time worrying but very little time doing something about it. Worrying produces the illusion of action because it feels like our worrying process is preparation. But if we want to reduce anxiety, we must translate the motivating power of anxiety into effective action. What constitutes effective action depends on the situation and on our resources. It is important not to let the idea of perfection get in the way of action. Perfectionism can lead to procrastination, which blocks any effective action. The goal should be to prepare as much as possible rather than to insist on being prepared for every possible eventuality.

Worrying has the potential to freeze behavior. We are so absorbed with our anxiety and overwhelmed by the idea that we are not prepared to face the challenges that we are unable to act. Consequently, there is no reason to reduce our worry because we are no more prepared than we were earlier. Moreover, we are now closer to the potential danger, or perhaps the potential danger is now more likely, and the result is that there is even more reason to worry. The intensity of our worry increases, and our ability to act to reduce the actual risk decreases. As you can see, this can quickly become a vicious cycle.

What Is It Like to Experience Generalized Anxiety Disorder?

Everyone worries, some people more than others, but worrying is not the same as having generalized anxiety disorder. In GAD, the worrying seems to be endless, and more importantly, the worrying rarely seems to be productive. Generally, when we worry about things, we typically take steps to reduce the cause of the worrying.

If we know that money will be short by the end of the month when our rent is due, we tend to be cautious about spending money so that we have cash on hand to pay our rent. Once we see that we have sufficient funds to pay rent, we typically stop worrying about the rent until the next month. That is an example of productive worrying because it leads to behavior that solves the problem we face.

For the Individual

People with generalized anxiety disorder do not just worry. Their worrying seems to be endless, and it often leaves them with a sense of hopelessness. No one likes to worry, but most people understand that worrying is part of their job. It does not matter whether they are worried about something at work or in the family; they consider themselves responsible for recognizing and solving problems in their everyday life. They would prefer not to worry but understand that worrying is a signal that they need to take some sort of action.

People with GAD feel the same way about worrying, except for the fact that they never seem to be able to follow through. They either are unable to take action that would reduce the worry, or they take the action, and it has no impact on their level of worrying. In that sense, they have insight into the nature of their disorder because they know that their worrying is not working. They also understand that when other people worry, they take action that reduces their risks and therefore reduces their level of worry. For the individuals with this insight, their inability to control their own worrying is a source of frustration and sometimes leaves them feeling helpless.

Some individuals with GAD have less insight into the fact that their worrying does not lead to the kind of action that would generally reduce the reasons to worry. For them, the worrying seems to be entirely legitimate, and because they are unable to reduce the causes of the worry, they also feel helpless. However, their sense of helplessness is because there is nothing they can do, or at least they feel that there is nothing they can do. To them, the world is constantly frightening and unpredictable and there is little they can do to make the world safer.

For the Loved Ones

If your loved ones suffer from GAD, you may experience some of the same helplessness they experience. Your helplessness is because there appears to be nothing you can do to talk them out of their anxiety. Even when you can see clearly that the individual could take actions that should reduce their anxiety, it is exceedingly difficult to get them to follow through. You may be frustrated because you sense that they are failing to take action that would help the situation. You may even be frustrated because you sense that they resist any effort on your part to help them to overcome their anxiety. It may seem to you that they do not want your help or that they would prefer to remain anxious. Moreover, even when you do get them to act, it often fails to have a significant effect on their anxiety.

In that sense, the worrying found in GAD is different from the worrying most people experience in their everyday lives. We all worry, and often we worry about things that are important enough to worry about. The worry drives behavior that increases our likelihood of being able to deal with a problem when it arises. Over time, we learn how to prepare for difficult situations, and consequently, we are less worried about how we will handle them. We expect that the same will be true for everyone, and when it is not true for a loved one with GAD, we are left puzzled. Below, we review behavioral strategies that tend to be effective for many people with GAD. Suggesting those strategies to someone with GAD may be helpful, but they seem counterintuitive, and as a result, the individual with GAD may be reluctant to do them. This may be a situation in which a therapist would have an advantage because the therapist presumably would be assumed to know more about this disorder. In addition, the therapist often finds it easier to remain objective when working with individuals with GAD.

Review of Treatment Options

Generalized anxiety disorder is certainly uncomfortable, but many people with this disorder function well enough that others are unaware of their difficulties. They suffer mostly in silence, although some individuals with GAD are anything but silent. Unfortunately, generalized anxiety disorder is more difficult to treat than some of the other anxiety disorders that appear to be more intense.

There are several strategies used in treating generalized anxiety disorder. One strategy focuses the individual on making the worrying more productive. This is typically done with behavioral therapy or cognitive behavioral therapy that challenges the individual to focus their worrying on what can be done to reduce the risk. By focusing on the behavior, the intensity of the worrying is often reduced, and the reason for worrying is typically reduced as well. If you prepare for what it is that you are worried about, there will be less need to worry.

Curiously, a strategy that seems counterintuitive is also effective. Instead of encouraging people to not worry so much, you encourage them to worry more and to systematically schedule a time to do the worrying. This is often combined with the idea that the worrying will not go away because the individual is not worrying effectively. Setting a time to worry hard and emphasizing the importance of taking the information from that worrying session and putting it to work stimulates the behavioral response that often overcomes the paralysis associated with constant worrying.

Medications have shown some benefits in the treatment of generalized anxiety disorders, but their effectiveness is limited. In addition, when medications are withdrawn, it is common to see rebound effects. There does not seem to be a magic pill that can turn off the worrying associated with generalized anxiety disorders.

Chapter Summary

Generalized anxiety disorder is characterized by a constant state of worrying, but curiously the anxiety associated with the worrying is not typical anxiety. It does not include the wide range of physiological sensations that are normally a part of the anxiety response. Everyone worries at times, but in GAD, the worrying is excessive and rarely productive. Worrying is productive if it leads to action that decreases the need to worry and, in the process, decreases the worrying.

GAD can be frustrating for those suffering from it because the worrying seems endless, and it often feels like nothing can be done. Unlike normal anxiety, which tends to be a powerful motivator for action to be better prepared to handle difficult situations, it is common for anxiety in GAD to not motivate such behavior. This can be frustrating for a loved one because it appears that the individual with GAD is not taking the kind of action that might reduce anxiety.

Psychological treatments focus on making the patient's worrying more effective and using their anxiety to motivate action to reduce the reasons for worrying. Medications are sometimes used, but their effects are limited, and rebound anxiety is common when the medications are withdrawn.

Chapter 9

Phobias

Phobias are intense fears of objects or situations. To qualify as a phobia, the fear must be significant enough that it prevents the person from carrying on with normal life expectations. For example, many people have a fear of snakes, and if you know little about snakes, that is a perfectly reasonable fear. Most snakes are harmless, but some snakes are potentially deadly. If you cannot tell the difference between a harmless and a deadly snake, it would be wise to steer clear of all snakes. But being afraid of snakes does not qualify as a phobia unless it is disrupting your life. If the only impact on your life is that you have vowed never to have a snake as a pet and that when you visit the zoo you avoid the building that houses snakes and reptiles, the fear of snakes is not really disrupting your life. Consequently, you would not qualify as having a snake phobia. If the idea of walking through the park or visiting the desert or playing golf is unimaginable because you might run into a snake, then your snake fear is disrupting your life and would qualify as a phobia.

We divide phobias into two general classes: specific and social phobias. The two most recent diagnostic manuals have renamed social phobias as **social anxiety disorders**. The distinction between social and specific phobias is important. Specific phobias refer to fears attached to objects or situations, such as being afraid of snakes, spiders, flying, or heights. In contrast, social phobias are performance-based fears. Someone with a social phobia might be afraid of speaking in public, meeting new people, or any situation in which they are likely to be judged. The fear is the same, but the fact that one is being judged with social phobias means that the treatment must focus on improving performance as well as managing anxiety levels.

Specific Phobias

Specific phobias are fears of specific objects and/or situations. There are literally hundreds of situations or objects that people might find fearful. Some of them make sense in terms of survival. Being afraid of heights is useful because, unlike birds, we cannot fly. If we were to fall off a ladder, there is a very good chance that we could be seriously hurt. Being afraid of snakes or wild animals that could be dangerous will reduce the likelihood that we will put ourselves in a potentially life-threatening situation. Other phobias seem to have been learned from specific experiences. Someone who is attacked by a dog or witnesses a dog attacking someone might well develop a fear of dogs. Even those of us who love dogs and have lived with them for years have no difficulty understanding how someone could be afraid of dogs after an experience like that. But the research shows that most people who are afraid of dogs have never had such an experience or witnessed such an event (Kheriaty, Kleinknecht & Hyman, 1999). Although one clearly could learn to fear dogs, it appears that most dog phobias are not learned.

Other specific phobias are variations of phobias associated with agoraphobia. Agoraphobia is the secondary fear often associated with panic disorder. The individual is afraid of having panic attacks and being in a situation that will either trigger those panic attacks or, if an attack happens, would make a graceful escape difficult. It is common for individuals with panic disorder and agoraphobia to be afraid of bridges, planes, elevators, tunnels, and expressways. In each case, the anxiety is not about the situation itself but rather the fact that these situations may leave a person trapped. If you are on a bridge and a traffic jam develops, within seconds you will be caught in the traffic jam and have no place to go. The same is true of tunnels and elevators and limited access highways such as expressways. These do not qualify as specific phobias because the person is not afraid of the object or situation.

That does not mean that everyone who is afraid of bridges or flying has agoraphobia rather than a specific phobia. Some people are truly afraid of bridges, and some people are truly afraid of flying.

The point I want to make is that it is not the fear itself that defines a specific phobia, but rather how it fits into the larger pattern of fears and whether there might be another explanation for that pattern. This analysis of the phobia determines the best way to treat the phobia. I talk more about that in the brief review of treatments later in this chapter and then again in the last section of this book on treatments.

In theory, anything could become a phobic object or situation. In practice, a relatively small number of objects or situations are likely to be phobias. Many phobias involve animals, from large animals like horses to the smallest of spiders. Other phobias involve potentially dangerous situations, such as heights or severe weather. Some phobias involve objects in which there is objectively little danger, but it can appear dangerous to someone who is unaware of how the object works. Think about a fear of flying. You have a massive metal object filled with people, luggage, and fuel, and somehow it magically flies. Of course, it is not magic. The operation of an airplane is well established, which is why we can build them and fly them safely year after year after year. Engineers build planes with structures that are rugged and able to handle a variety of situations, and pilots are trained to understand the operation of a plane and respond quickly when a problem arises. For this reason, tens of thousands of planes take off and land safely every single day. However, on those rare occasions when there is an accident, it usually captures the headlines, sometimes for several days. That difference in coverage in the news is one of the reasons most people dramatically overestimate the risks associated with flying.

In a similar way, long bridges and tunnels, elevators, tall buildings, and structures that appear to be impossible often generate a reasonable fear because people do not understand that the buildings are indeed safe.

Social Phobias

Social phobias are different from specific phobias in that they involve a fear of a situation in which the person will be judged. The most common social phobia is a fear of public speaking, but some people are afraid of meeting new people, doing job interviews, dating, and any social interaction in which the person is expected to perform at a level that feels like it is beyond their capacity.

The distinction between social and specific phobias is critical because treatment is different. If one is afraid of dogs or snakes, one can use gradual exposure, coupled with anxiety management techniques, to decrease the anxiety and thus the avoidance. If we do the same thing with a social phobia, we are likely to reduce a person's anxiety only to have it increase again when the person is in the situation and performs poorly. If people are afraid of public speaking and we do not help them to be more effective at public speaking, any effort to reduce the anxiety will, at best, be temporary and easily overwhelmed by the impact of poor performance.

Some people are more prone to develop social phobias than others, but many social phobias are natural and normal. They are the result of being unfamiliar with a social demand and not having confidence that one is prepared to meet that demand. Granted, some people naturally seem able to express themselves in words better than others, and those individuals will likely learn to be comfortable in a public speaking situation more quickly than individuals who are less able to express themselves in words. However, even those individuals with natural talent find initial public speaking situations to be anxiety producing. If despite their anxiety, they can give a reasonably good performance, their confidence will increase, and their anxiety will decrease with each public speaking occasion. However, few people are so naturally gifted that every public speech is solid and effective, so most people experience negative consequences associated with public speaking, which increases the likelihood that they will be anxious in the future.

Everyone knows examples of people who are afraid of public speaking, and most people understand those examples because they have their own concerns about public speaking. There are other situations in which anxiety is a common response in a social situation, but most people overcome that anxiety. For example, dating is a challenging social encounter in which most people experience significant anxiety over how they are being evaluated by their date. Yet many people continue to date until they overcome that anxiety. There are powerful motivational variables associated with dating. As a species, we tend to affiliate, and one of the most intense affiliations is with a potential sexual partner. With such a strong motivation, people tend to face their fears and eventually find relationships that are satisfying to both parties. It helps that both people on a date have the same insecurities, and therefore both people are motivated to try to make the situation go as smoothly as possible.

There are few natural motivations for public speaking. Sure, many people realize that public speaking is an asset that can enhance a career. But there is nothing close to the drive that one finds in a situation such as dating. Instead, one is faced with the challenge of doing something that is not natural and doing it with anxiety that is often strong enough to disrupt performance. However, public speaking, dating, and interviewing for jobs are all skills. A skill can be improved with practice and training, and if people are confident in their skills, they are likely to experience only modest levels of anxiety.

When we seek to treat social phobias, we split our focus between the management of anxiety and the improvement of the skills on which the person will be evaluated. For example, we teach people afraid of public speaking to be more effective at public speaking. We teach people afraid of dating to carry on conversations and engage in expected behaviors when one is dating. We teach people who are afraid of job interviews to be more effective in the job interview and to prepare more effectively for the job interview.

What Is It Like to Experience Phobias?

There is no single way to describe what it is like to have a phobia. It depends on the phobia, and it depends on how the phobia gets in the way of the person's goals and desires. Some phobias are little more than an embarrassment to most people. In this category are fears of animals, heights, or amusement park rides. Other phobias are more disruptive, such as a fear of driving over bridges, flying, or public speaking. These are often things that people are expected to do as a part of their everyday life, and they are expected to do them even if they are uncomfortable doing them. Finally, some phobias have extremely disruptive effects on a person's life. We have already talked about agoraphobia in the section on panic disorder. This phobia prevents the person from having any semblance of a normal life.

Because there is such variability in how phobias affect an individual, this section is longer than it has been in past chapters. Although I cannot cover every possible phobia, I will try to give several illustrations of how different phobias are likely to affect an individual and their loved ones.

For the Individual

For most specific phobias, the phobia is an annoyance and perhaps an embarrassment to the individual. People accept that it is possible to be afraid of dogs, snakes, or spiders. It may be a bit more embarrassing for males because they may be a part of a male society that has a rather macho image of fear. Some subgroups, for example, accept that a woman could be afraid of spiders but that a man should never be afraid of something they could easily kill. Even still, the emotional impact of the phobia is likely to be little more than embarrassment. Part of the reason for this is that many of these phobias are common enough that these fears are understandable to other people. Moreover, many of these fears are relatively easy to accommodate. If you are afraid of heights, it may be difficult to get a job as a roofer, but there are literally thousands of jobs that would never require you to face your fear of heights.

Although many people are comfortable around dogs and will happily pet them, it is common enough that people are uncomfortable around dogs that it is easy to avoid intimate contact. It is also possible to give a plausible excuse, such as you are allergic to dogs and if you were to pet them you likely would have difficulty breathing.

There are a few specific phobias that have a more significant impact on a person's life because they require the individual to avoid things that sometimes are difficult or impossible to avoid. There certainly are occupations that require air travel, but there are also thousands of occupations in which air travel is never required. Therefore, being afraid of flying is something that can usually be accommodated by your choice of occupation. Of course, it is not possible to drive to Europe or Japan, but one who is afraid of flying is typically not interested in such a trip anyway. Although flying is common today, there are a lot of people who do not fly and a lot of other people who avoid flying whenever possible. Again, the hassles associated with flying often can be used as an excuse to avoid it without raising an issue that might be embarrassing.

Social phobias tend to be more disruptive to a person's life and more embarrassing. Being afraid of public speaking is certainly a common experience. Most people experience at least some anxiety speaking in public, and therefore, acknowledging a fear of public speaking is only a minor embarrassment. For some occupations, it is a minor inconvenience; for other occupations, it could stall your career.

But for many people who have a fear of public speaking, their fear extends beyond the formal talk in front of a group of people. They are uncomfortable speaking up at a party or inviting people to a backyard barbecue. The extent of their public speaking phobia is severe enough that it interferes not just with their professional lives but also with their personal lives. Public speaking phobias are the most common social phobias, but there are also people who are extremely uncomfortable just meeting new people. For them, a job interview with a stranger might be overwhelming. Striking up a conversation with someone sitting next to them on a plane or bus would also be difficult. These are skills, and the more you do them, the better you get at them. If you avoid them for years, you will show a social clumsiness that is well outside the norm. The longer you avoid such situations, the more severe your social deficits are relative to your peers, and thus the greater likelihood that your behavior will indeed be embarrassing. Consequently, your anxiety about social situations will also be elevated.

What may be clear by now is that phobias of any kind restrict our lives. Some phobias restrict our lives more than others and, depending on our career directions, that restriction might be severe. But there is another element to factor into this analysis. There is always a sense of embarrassment, and sometimes that sense of embarrassment can be intense. Again, it will depend on the nature of the phobia and how it affects our lives. It will also depend on whether we can adequately hide the phobia within the context of our lives. But if you are forced to admit a fear that you are unable to overcome and that restricts your behavior, it is likely to be more than an embarrassing situation. It may be experienced as extreme humiliation and have a huge impact on your self-esteem.

For the Loved Ones

The impact of specific phobias on a person's loved ones depends on the nature of the phobia and how much it disrupts your loved one's life. If a person is afraid of snakes and its primary impact is that the person does not want to go for walks in the woods or visit the building at the zoo that houses snakes, the effect on their loved ones is probably negligible. If the phobia prevents someone from flying, that could have a significant impact on friends and family because it would mean that they either could not go on a trip that requires flying or they would have to go without the person who was afraid of flying.

The second factor that has an impact on loved ones involves the loved ones' responses to the individual's phobia. Some people can readily accept that fears may be intense enough that avoidance is a reasonable response. In such a case, they will at least have empathy toward the individual with a specific phobia. They may believe that the avoidance is unnecessary, but at least they accept that it is a reasonable response to the fear. Others, however, view the specific phobia as unreasonable and therefore respond negatively to the individual. Any disruption caused by that specific phobia is viewed as unnecessary. The result is that there can be considerable friction between the person with the specific phobia and his or her loved ones.

In contrast to specific phobias, social phobias often are more disruptive to the friends and family of the affected individuals. The most common social phobia, public speaking anxiety, is at least understood by most people. There are few people who have not experienced public speaking anxiety, and consequently, most people understand how people could be anxious about such situations. Moreover, it is possible to avoid almost all situations that involve public speaking, although the costs of such avoidance can be high depending on the level of education and the type of job that one has. It is almost impossible to become a manager if you are unable to speak in public, which means no matter how good you are at your job, you have created an occupational ceiling. This ceiling might severely affect your family because it limits your potential income. Many things limit our income that are outside of our control. If there is high inflation, your salary is unlikely to keep up with that inflation. If the job market is tight because the economy is hurting, there may be little opportunity for promotions and raises. But a social phobia like public speaking anxiety is in a different category because it involves self-handicapping. Even for a spouse or children who understand and empathize with public speaking anxiety, there might be some hard feelings if the income is less than what they would expect to meet the standard of living they desire.

Social phobias may also severely restrict an individual's social life, and consequently may influence the social life of their loved ones. Many social events involve couples, and if one member of the couple consistently wants to avoid those social events because of social anxiety, there likely is going to be resentment from the other member of the couple. It is not that every couple wants to be party animals; many couples prefer to have their social interactions involve smaller groups of people. If one member of the couple wants to be a party animal and the other prefers not to be involved in social interactions at all, there is likely to be tension. But even for those individuals who prefer to get together socially in smaller groups, having a spouse who does not want social interactions because of their fear is disruptive. Moreover, everyone needs social interactions, even those individuals who are fearful of social interactions. What this often means is that there is too much pressure on one's spouse or family member to provide for the social needs of an individual who is socially fearful. Meeting those needs makes it harder for the individual to meet his or her own needs.

Review of Treatment Options

Phobias are treatable, but to be effective in the treatment, one must understand the nature of the phobia and how it affects the individual. We cover the treatment of specific phobias and social phobias separately because social phobias require more than just anxiety management. They require training in the specific skills on which the person will be evaluated. In this section, we provide only a brief overview of the treatment approaches but cover them in more detail in later chapters.

Specific Phobias

In many cases, a specific phobia can be thought of as a fear that is unreasonably strong given the actual risk. Yes, occasionally a dog attacks a person, but that is a relatively rare occurrence. Moreover, someone who is reasonably comfortable around dogs can adjust their behavior to make such an attack unlikely to occur. That information is helpful and is worth mentioning to someone who is afraid of dogs. However, it will not reduce their anxiety.

The key to the treatment of phobias is exposure. If we are never exposed to things we fear, the fear will not decrease. We need to see firsthand that the object that we fear is indeed not dangerous. It is virtually impossible to talk oneself out of the phobia, but with appropriate exposure to the phobia, the fear will gradually dissipate. It is important to remember the general theme around anxiety; we are programmed to learn anxiety quickly and unlearn it slowly. Therefore, exposure will require repeated contact with the feared object.

In general, the preferred treatment for any phobia is **systematic desensitization**. This process involves gradual exposure to the feared object coupled with anxiety management techniques. The therapist works with the client to construct an exposure hierarchy, which is a list of items arranged from least fearful to most fearful and with approximately equal differences in fear level between any two adjacent items.

The exposure is the most important part of this treatment, and it works no matter how you do the exposure, provided you move at the proper pace. But you can make the exposure easier by teaching people how to manage their anxiety. One way to manage anxiety is to control the muscle tension that is part of being anxious. This is a skill that people can learn and practice at home and then use during each level of exposure. A second technique is to take a deep breath, which decreases the physiological arousal associated with anxiety. If you do the exposure without these techniques, the anxiety will go down in time and you can overcome the fear. But if you add these techniques, the anxiety will go down more quickly, and you will feel more in control of the process.

Another technique is to use cognitive strategies to manage anxiety. Let me repeat that you cannot talk yourself out of anxiety, so these cognitive techniques by themselves do not reduce anxiety. Rather, they are used to manage the anxiety and prevent it from spiraling out of control. For example, each time you move up one level in the hierarchy, the situation will be more demanding, and anxiety will return. Telling yourself that the return of the anxiety is normal is a reasonably effective way of preventing yourself from overreacting. Telling yourself that you still have the tools to manage the anxiety and that the anxiety will go down at this new level in the hierarchy, just as it did in the previous levels, will

138

make it easier to remain in the situation until the anxiety does go down.

Social Phobias

Treating social phobias also includes gradual exposure to the feared situation. This kind of systematic desensitization is effective in managing anxiety and gradually reducing it, but it may be more challenging to set up the hierarchy with social phobias. If you are afraid of snakes, you can gradually come closer to snakes to create the hierarchy, but if you are afraid of public speaking, you may not have control over the situations in which public speaking is required. However, it is possible to create artificial situations in which one can practice public speaking and the management of anxiety about public speaking. For example, one can give a talk to the therapist or to the therapist and someone else from the office. You can gradually increase the size of the group or the formality of the setting to make it seem more realistic. The advantage of this approach is that it is low-risk and allows you to do the second element in the treatment of a social phobia: improving the person's skills.

Learning to manage anxiety while giving a talk is helpful, but it is far more helpful to be able to manage anxiety and give a quality talk. The hallmark of social phobia is that it occurs in situations in which the person will be judged, and people are judged on their performance. Helping the person to perform better is the single most important thing you can do in treating social phobias. Teaching people how to structure a good talk and how to connect with the audience increases their confidence. Teaching them how to hide their anxiety so that it is a personal experience and not something the audience can see also adds to a person's confidence. Public speaking is a skill, and just like any other skill, it requires practice and instruction.

Because the client will already be anxious about speaking in public, the treatment should also focus on elements that can trigger even more anxiety. For example, it is a hassle when the equipment does not work, but when you are anxious about giving the talk, it

139

can be terrifying not to have the equipment work. It feels like everyone is looking at you and laughing at your inability to even start your talk. Making sure that the person knows what to do to get the equipment to work, has a backup plan in case the equipment does not work, and checks everything out before the talk to avoid a hassle removes these potent triggers. In most cases, the greatest anxiety occurs before the person begins speaking and in the first few minutes of the talk. However, if those first few minutes go well, most people experience a dramatic drop in their anxiety. Working with clients to help them perform well in those first few minutes will get them over that serious anxiety hump.

Giving a talk is anxiety producing for many people but responding to questions after the talk is particularly stressful because that part of the talk cannot be planned. Working with people to help them answer questions will increase their confidence in that part of the talk. Moreover, there are often effective ways of dealing with the most difficult questions. For example, it is always helpful to label a difficult question as a good question. That label alone tends to make the questioner reasonably satisfied even before you give an answer. It is also permissible if you don't know the answer to acknowledge that you don't know the answer. You could say something like, "That is a great question. I had not really considered that issue, so I am not sure what would happen in that situation." The individual could then throw the question back to the person who asked it with something like, "It sounds like you have some ideas about what might happen. Would you be willing to share them?" These approaches to dealing with a speaker's worst fears are like giving the speaker get-out-of-jail-free cards. If they have done a good job of preparing the talk and rehearsing it sufficiently so that they can give it despite being anxious, they have achieved the first step. If they know the topic well enough that they can answer most questions, they have achieved the second step. If they have a way of dealing with questions that they are not prepared to answer, then they feel like they are on top of the situation.

You might think that public speaking anxiety is relatively easy because the principles of what constitutes a good public talk are clear. There are college courses that teach you how to do public speaking, but it is less likely that you will find a college course that deals with dating or job interviews. But those aspects of our lives also have principles, and those principles can be learned and practiced. Therapists who work with individuals who are concerned about dating will often rehearse a variety of strategies for dealing with meeting the person for the first time, striking up a conversation, avoiding topics that could have interpersonal landmines associated with them, and most importantly, focusing on listening to the person you are with. Learning to listen better is often the most valuable skill because almost everyone experiences a good listener as a great conversationalist and almost everyone feels flattered by someone who is interested in what they have to say.

Job interviews also have specific skills and strategies that can be learned. For example, no one would expect to give a good talk if they did not put the time into preparing it. No one should expect to do well in a job interview if they have not done their homework. You should know what the company is about, what your job at the company is likely to involve, and, if possible, who will be interviewing you and their title and background. With that information, you can identify the strengths that you bring to the job and emphasize them in your answers. You can also prepare good questions that will indicate your sophistication and the fact that you have done your homework about the company. You can practice these skills with anyone who has gone through job interviews because they will have an idea of the kinds of questions that might be asked.

First impressions are critically important in a job interview, and those first impressions start before you ever meet the person who will interview you. Your resume should be clear, precise, and flawless. By flawless, I do not mean that you walk on water; what I mean is that there should never be a typo or spelling error in your resume. There should never be a typo, spelling, or grammar error in your cover letter or email. You should be appropriately dressed; what that means will depend on the job that you are interviewing for, the nature of the company, and even the part of the country in which you live. It is best to be a bit overdressed for an interview rather than underdressed. You are likely to shake hands; you want a nice firm handshake that suggests confidence. If you are the kind of person whose hands sweat when you are anxious, your hand is likely to be visibly wet when you shake the person's hands. But that is easy to deal with; simply wear a pair of slacks that are made of absorbent material. When you stand up, rest your hands on the upper part of your thighs, and that sweat will easily be absorbed. With a little practice, this move is entirely natural and effective. Two minutes later, your hands are likely to be sweaty again, but it will not matter because the two of you will have already shaken hands.

Some of these ideas may seem like tricks, but they are anything but tricks. Making a good impression, whether you are talking about giving a speech, going on a date, or interviewing for a job, is a matter of doing what is expected in a way that impresses people. Knowing what people expect and being able to deliver is the key to overcoming any social phobia.

If your skills in public speaking improve dramatically, your anxiety around public speaking is likely to decrease dramatically. With sufficient practice, you can expect to get much better at speaking. In the meantime, you will continue to experience anxiety. Remember, anxiety is a feeling that there might be a risk and that you are not sure that you can handle it. If you are still developing your public speaking skills, you will not be sure that you will be able to give a great talk. It is not the experience of anxiety that is the problem; if it were the problem, almost everyone would have a phobia of public speaking. You do not need to avoid anxiety; initially, all you need to do is hide that anxiety. In time, the anxiety will decrease, and there will be less of a need to hide it. Knowing how to avoid a handshake with sweaty palms is nothing more than hiding normal anxiety. You are likely to be the only one who notices your anxiety if you are prepared and able to perform despite the anxiety.

Chapter Summary

Phobias are divided into two classes: specific phobias and social phobias (now called *social anxiety disorder*). Both represent a fear of an object or situation. Social phobias involve an additional element. In social phobias, there is performance anxiety because people are required to do something on which they will be judged. Since some objects or situations, such as snakes or heights, arouse anxiety in many people, we do not consider it a phobia unless it significantly disrupts a person's life.

Phobias have the potential to affect both the person and his or her loved ones. This is especially true of social phobias. Among other things, an inability to perform tasks that others can handle is often hard on one's self-esteem.

Treatment of phobias always includes exposure, but skills training is also critical in the treatment of social phobias. Reducing anxiety is of little help if the person still lacks the skills needed to perform adequately and thus avoid negative social judgments. Whenever possible, exposure is done gradually using a procedure called *systematic desensitization*. Using anxiety management techniques with gradual exposure keeps the anxiety at a manageable level throughout the treatment process.

Chapter 10

Obsessive-Compulsive Disorder

Obsessive-compulsive disorder (OCD) is one of the most interesting anxiety disorders. It also has an interesting history. Although it has been recognized for centuries as a symptom, it is only recently that we began to understand that it is a more common disorder than we realized. When I was an intern back in the 1970s, we had an individual with obsessive-compulsive disorder admitted to the psychiatric ward. Psychologists and psychiatrists from all over the hospital wanted to meet this patient because the textbooks at the time described OCD as so rare that most professionals would never see a patient with OCD in their career. The estimated base rate for the disorder now is 1.5 percent. Did this disorder suddenly become much more common? It is possible, but not likely. The more likely explanation is that most people with the disorder had the insight that their experiences were unreasonable, and therefore, they hid the symptoms as best they could.

Everyone obsesses periodically; what makes it obsessive is that we feel like we have little or no control. It may be a night when we cannot sleep because we cannot stop thinking about some problem that we are facing. Like many aspects of anxiety, obsessions serve a purpose. They keep us thinking about a problem, and hopefully, that process of thinking about the problem will eventually lead to a solution. However, in OCD, the obsessions seem not to have an off switch. I am emphasizing that everyone occasionally obsesses because when we talk about how extreme the symptoms of OCD can be, they will sound utterly alien. But like many forms of psychopathology, OCD symptomatology is simply an exacerbation of a normal response tendency. People with OCD are simply doing what most people do but doing it much more strongly and with less control.

Defining OCD

The defining characteristics of OCD are obsessions and compulsions. **Obsessions** are thoughts that people find distressing and uncontrollable. **Compulsions** are behaviors; they often feel like they are behavioral reactions to obsessive thoughts, although there is enough evidence to suggest that that link may be more of an illusion than a reality. Some compulsions clearly seem to be a reaction to an obsessive thought. If you obsess about germs, compulsively washing your hands seems to be clearly linked to your obsession with germs. But, as you will see in this section, many of the compulsions seem to have little or no conceptual link to the obsessions that trigger them. Nevertheless, individuals with OCD feel compelled to engage in those compulsive behaviors.

Obsessions

We all obsess about things occasionally. It might be something that we said or did that embarrassed us. It might be something that we feel strongly has to be done and we do not want to forget it. There is an energy behind obsessions, no matter what the focus of the obsession. In OCD, that energy is anxiety, and the level of that anxiety can be overwhelming. The obsessions are impossible to ignore; there is an enormous drive to do something to deal with those obsessions, and most of the actions that one might take to reduce the obsessions are ineffective. The compulsive behaviors in OCD feel like a reaction to the obsessions, but often the compulsive behavior fails to achieve the goal of reducing the anxiety. That is what sets off the obsessions in OCD from the normal obsessions we all experience.

For example, certain appliances could be dangerous if they are left on. This is less true today than it once was because many of those appliances have built-in safety devices that turn themselves off if they are left on accidentally. An example of such a device is a curling iron, which can get hot enough to start a fire. Early curling irons did not have a safety device that turned them off after a period of disuse, and those devices did indeed represent a risk. I

145

know someone who owned a curling iron forty years ago and forgot to turn it off. It started a fire that destroyed her home and killed her dog. The risk of such a tragedy was real, and therefore worrying about whether you turned off such a device was reasonable. If one does not have OCD, you can reduce that risk by finding the device and turning it off or, better yet, unplugging it from the outlet. Once you do that, your obsession with the risk drops to zero or nearly zero. You can leave the house comfortably secure in the fact that it is unlikely to burn down because of that device.

However, in OCD, it is common for that obsession to lead to rational checking behavior, but that behavior fails to reduce the anxiety. Even after checking, people with OCD doubt that they checked it correctly and therefore feel a strong need to check it again, and again, and again. The same might be true of checking to see if you locked the door. Some days, people with OCD can check once or twice and go on their way, but on other days, they might check one hundred times over several minutes with almost no decrease in anxiety. It seems to defy the logic of how our system runs. I have argued throughout this book about how anxiety is a valuable signal that there might be a risk, and that signal drives behavior that reduces the risk. But in OCD, the behavior that is driven by anxiety does not seem to reliably reduce the perception of risk and thus the anxiety. In some cases, it may increase the level of anxiety. You can imagine how frustrating it is because we expect our behavior to have an impact on our feelings.

Some of the obsessions in OCD make sense, such as the examples given above about checking things that might pose a risk if we fail to take proper steps. However, it is not uncommon in OCD to have obsessive thoughts that make no sense. These thoughts have a magical quality, and often the compulsions that are related to those thoughts also have a magical quality. For example, the individual might feel strongly that the first can on the shelf at a grocery store is unsafe and that only the second can is safe. Although it is possible, although extremely rare, that a canned product might be unsafe, there is no reason to believe that the unsafe can will be in a particular position on the shelf.

Another hard-to-understand obsession found in OCD involves a process referred to as **thought-action fusion**. This is a belief that a person's thoughts can cause actions. For example, a person in anger might wish someone was dead. Wishing someone was dead does not cause them to die, but people with OCD often feel like their thoughts can kill. It is important to note that most people with OCD realize that such beliefs are irrational, but nevertheless, they are unable to control them or discount them. In those relatively rare cases in which the beliefs just described feel rational to the individual, treatment is more difficult and generally less effective. It is also worth noting that both psychological and biological treatments are less effective in individuals who believe such irrational ideas to be reasonable.

It is common for people with OCD to experience obsessive thoughts about things that they might have done inadvertently. For example, they are driving down the road and are suddenly worried that they might have hit someone with their car. Certainly, hitting someone with your car would be devastating, but it is highly unlikely that you would not know that you had done it. You likely would feel the impact, even if you happened to be looking away and did not see the individual. There likely would be a body nearby and damage to your car. But even without such evidence, people with OCD will often feel the need to go back and check to make sure that no one was hit. Even when they do not find a body, they obsess about the possibility that the person crawled into the bushes and is dying. There do not even have to be bushes around for them to come up with some semi-plausible reason why they could not find the person they hit. Again, in most cases, the person with OCD recognizes that such obsessions are unreasonable. In other words, they have insight into their symptoms. They recognize that the symptoms are symptoms and not real experiences, but that realization is rarely sufficient to decrease their anxiety and eliminate the obsessive thoughts.

Compulsions

The *compulsions* in OCD are responses to the anxiety that one experiences from the obsessions. As you learned earlier, some of the compulsions make sense, such as washing your hands if you are concerned about germs. Other compulsions make no sense. Although in general, OCD includes both obsessions and compulsions, it is possible to have just one of those. When OCD symptoms are found in children, it is common for there to be compulsions without associated obsessions. In fact, it is rather common for children without OCD to go through periods that involve compulsive behavior. Many children, for example, will have periods in which they either step on every crack in the sidewalk or avoid every crack in the sidewalk. The fact that this behavior is often associated with verbal statements, such as, "Step on the crack and break your mother's back," does not mean that there is an obsession involved. The key here is that there is typically no anxiety associated with that verbal statement. It is almost as if the child is reciting lyrics from a song in a language that the child does not know.

The anxiety associated with obsessions in OCD can be overwhelming, but it is often the compulsive behavior that is most disruptive to a person's life. The constant checking, cleaning, or counting rituals prevent the person from meeting the obligations of a normal life. Although the obsessions are not visible to other people, many of the compulsions clearly are visible and draw unwanted attention to the person with OCD. It is common for people with OCD to try to hide their compulsive behavior, but often the actions of trying to hide the behavior make the behavior even more obvious.

Where Is the Line between Normal and Abnormal?

Everyone obsesses occasionally, and some people obsess quite a lot. Obsessing is a normal behavior until it reaches a level that is outside the normal range. For example, if the economy is bad and you feel like your job is in jeopardy, it certainly would be reasonable for you to try to read into subtle signals from your boss about your job status. It certainly would be reasonable to be anxious about such signals, and one might easily read too much into normal behavior from the boss. For example, the boss might be irritated with you, but the irritation may have more to do with the argument that the boss had with his or her teenage son before coming to work. It may have very little to do with your performance.

The line between normal and abnormal is not always clear, but at the extremes often found in OCD, there is little doubt. Washing your hands because you are concerned about disease is normal. In fact, it is a smart thing to do. Washing your hands with detergent so powerful that it damages your skin and therefore makes you more vulnerable to infection is abnormal. Checking to make sure that you locked your house or car is normal. Occasionally, not being confident that you checked it and thus rechecking it is normal. Checking it one hundred times over thirty minutes and still not being sure that the door is locked is abnormal. People sometimes engage in silly rituals, such as knocking on wood after saying something as a way of undoing what was just said. Such behavior is irrational but common, and we generally do not define behavior that is common as abnormal. Having to engage in a specific and unnecessary ritual or you will be overwhelmed by crippling anxiety is abnormal. Having difficulty deciding what to throw out and what to keep is common. It often seems like as soon as we throw something out, that is when we need it. But not being able to throw out anything for fear that you will need it someday or that there might be something very important being thrown out by accident is unreasonable.

Most of the symptoms of OCD are found in people without the disorder, but at a level that is much lower and more tolerable than in OCD. So the line between OCD and normal obsessions and compulsions is partly one of degree. But there is a second dimension that defines OCD symptoms, and that is the intense level of anxiety that drives OCD symptoms. If we engage in

149

compulsive behavior and, for one reason or another, must prevent that behavior, we experience little or no anxiety. People with OCD are overwhelmed by anxiety if they cannot do their rituals, which is why it is so difficult for them to challenge those rituals.

A silly example from my past illustrates the distinction between obsessive-compulsive behavior under stress and the much more severe obsessive-compulsive symptoms of OCD. I commuted to college during my freshman year, taking a corner of the basement as my bedroom and study area. During the final exams of the fall semester, I was studying hard. Frankly, I didn't study that hard in high school, and college was clearly more demanding than high school had been. So, I was anxious about how well I would do. I would study for about an hour and then take a brief break and walk upstairs. I would walk into the kitchen and open the refrigerator, taking nothing out, and then open the freezer, also taking nothing out. I would go to the sink and remove a glass from the cupboard. I would fill the glass with water, pour it out, fill it again, pour it out, fill it a third time, and take a drink before emptying the glass and putting it in the sink. I would walk into the living room and turn on the TV, but not wait long enough for it to come on before turning it off again and returning to study in the basement. After several such study breaks, my mother finally confronted me. She pointed out what I was doing and noted that opening the freezer repeatedly was frosting it up (this was before frost-free devices were available), that I was adding a lot of dishes (we did not have a dishwasher at that time), and that watching TV was difficult if I did not stand around long enough for the television to come on. I immediately recognized the craziness of my actions and the fact that my mother correctly captured exactly what I was doing. I previously had not been aware of it. I simply thought I was taking a break and was proud of the fact that I kept the break brief. So what did I do? I stopped doing that silly ritual and was embarrassed that I had been doing it. If I had lived in a warmer climate, I might have taken a walk outside instead of through the first floor of my house, but the temperature was below zero that year during my first semester exams. I had fallen into a ritual that somehow eased my stress during this difficult period in my life. However, the ritual was not OCD, because if it was OCD, there would have been no way that I could have simply stopped it without being overwhelmed by anxiety.

Compulsive rituals are often common in stressful life situations. For example, the traditions surrounding death and funerals are ways that people have developed to deal with the unique stress of losing a loved one. The rituals vary by culture, but they seem to provide a measure of peace during a difficult time. Even positive aspects of life, such as graduations or weddings, have traditions and rituals. These may be positive events, but they also represent a transition in life and thus require considerable adaptation. In other words, they may be positive, but they are still stressful transitions, and rituals provide a level of comfort during that transition. Any change is difficult and requires a level of adaptation, even if it is a good change.

OCD versus OCPD

Obsessive-compulsive disorder (OCD) is often confused with **obsessive-compulsive personality disorder (OCPD)**. OCD is driven by intense anxiety. Although it currently has its own category of psychopathology, until recently, OCD was considered an anxiety disorder. In OCPD, we tend to see a compulsive attention to detail but often with little obsessive thinking or the extreme anxiety found in OCD. In fact, someone with OCPD might be a very valuable member of a business or professional team. These are the people who make sure that they dot every "i" and cross every "t." They tend to follow the rules precisely, and some people might think that they follow them too precisely. But there are many professions in which it is important to get every detail correct. It is common for people with OCPD to be willing to work extra time without extra pay to make sure they get everything just right. Moreover, they often are proud of the fact that they can be counted on to get the details correct.

There is a weak relationship between OCD and OCPD. People with OCPD have a slight increase in risk for OCD, but the increased risk is low and of little consequence. Despite the similarity in the labels, these seem to be very different conditions.

Impact on Daily Functioning

It is common for people to experience obsessions and/or compulsions, but they do not qualify for the diagnosis of obsessive-compulsive disorder unless they are severe enough to be having a significant impact on the person's functioning. In severe cases, the individual may be unable to hold a job because the OCD symptoms constantly get in the way of being productive. Some individuals with OCD give up driving because they experience such intense anxiety about whether they hit someone that they are unable to get to their destination. These are extreme cases, and many individuals with OCD can function, but their OCD symptoms interfere with every aspect of their life: personal, professional, and recreational.

Remember that we once believed that OCD was rare, but the data show that it affects roughly 1.5 percent of the population. How could we possibly believe that it was rare? The reason is that many people with OCD hide their symptoms because they are embarrassed by them. Let me clarify that hiding one's symptoms is not the same as dealing with those symptoms. The symptoms are still there, and they have an enormous impact on the person's functioning, but the nature of the symptoms may not be obvious to other people.

One of the saddest cases of OCD I ever treated was a man in his early thirties who had severe OCD symptoms since his late teens. When I met him, he was interested in treatment for both the OCD symptoms, which he knew was a specialty of mine, and the serious depression that he was experiencing after a recent divorce. He had married the love of his life during college. He would have done anything for her. He absolutely adored her, but he was so embarrassed by his OCD symptoms that he could not admit to her that he experienced them. Because she did not know about his OCD, she might suggest that they go out and do something that would have triggered his OCD symptoms. He could not bring himself to tell her the reason why he could not follow her very reasonable suggestions. What he did instead was to snap at her with things like, "That's a stupid idea!" Every time he did that, he experienced enormous guilt for his brutal and inappropriate behavior toward the person he loved more than anything. She stuck with him for years but eventually could not take it anymore and filed for divorce. He did not fight the divorce because he knew that she did not deserve his behavior. As he gained more control over his OCD symptoms, he met with his ex-wife and explained the situation. He was not sure whether she understood, but whether she did or not, it made no difference. She had remarried and was not likely to ever get back together with him.

This is admittedly the most poignant case of OCD I have ever treated. This was an individual who was able to hide his symptoms by behaving in cruel and inappropriate ways. He was not a psychopath! The terrible behavior that he showed toward his wife devastated him emotionally and would likely be a scar that he carried with him forever. But his embarrassment over his symptoms and his embarrassment over his inability to control those symptoms led him to behave in ways that he truly hated.

Many people with OCD hide symptoms, although the symptoms are still interfering with their functioning. For example, they may have checking rituals that they explain in various ways to avoid admitting how extreme their checking is. They may restrict their behavior when OCD symptoms are likely so that they are alone or in a situation in which it is relatively easy to hide what they are doing. Their symptoms may still interfere with their ability to complete their work and therefore will restrict their ability to get promoted. It may even jeopardize their job because they fail to live up to job expectations. Sometimes, individuals with OCD avoid situations that trigger symptoms. This strategy works if the range of situations is small, but for many individuals with OCD, almost any situation can trigger the symptoms.

What Is It Like to Experience Obsessive-Compulsive Disorder?

The impact of obsessive-compulsive disorder is enormous for both the individual and their loved ones. The level of anxiety that is experienced in OCD is extremely high, and when the individual with OCD tries to resist the compulsive behavior, the anxiety can be overwhelming.

For the Individual

There are three elements that have a huge impact on individuals who have OCD. The first is the intense anxiety associated with the disorder. This level of anxiety is well beyond what most people experience, so it is hard to even explain what it is like. The second is that most people with this disorder are aware that their symptoms are unreasonable, and therefore, they are embarrassed by the symptoms. They recognize there is no reason for the symptoms, at least no logical reason, but nevertheless, they cannot control the symptoms. The final element is that the symptoms take so much time and energy that the disorder significantly disrupts every aspect of a person's life. Life is challenging, even when things are running relatively smoothly, and things rarely run smoothly. If we are emotionally worn out by the constant struggle to manage OCD symptoms, adjusting to the challenges of life can be difficult.

The anxiety that one experiences with OCD can be so intense that it has an enormous impact on a person's behavior. Situations that trigger obsessions quickly become aversive, and therefore the person tends to avoid those situations. However, in OCD, almost any situation can trigger a potential obsessive thought and the anxiety associated with it. It becomes impossible to avoid all the situations, and so, in severe cases, the individual's life is almost as restricted as it is with the agoraphobia found in panic disorder. The person feels out of control and helpless, and that is a recipe for depression. Depression is common in OCD. Depression robs us of emotional energy, leaving us with even less coping ability.

One's self-esteem also suffers in part because most people with OCD have insight into their disorder. They understand that the symptoms are unreasonable, and sometimes downright crazy. Knowing how unreasonable the symptoms are and being totally unable to control them because of the intensity of the anxiety destroys one's sense of control. The truth is that many things in life are outside of our control, and the best we can do is roll with the punches. We avoid a blow to our self-esteem by maintaining the illusion that we have more control than we have. Most individuals with OCD find it hard to maintain such an illusion given their dramatic symptoms and the impact those symptoms have on their life.

The severity of the OCD symptoms and the embarrassment that one feels because the symptoms seem so unreasonable encourage many people to avoid social relationships. People with OCD are simply embarrassed by the symptoms, and one way of dealing with that embarrassment is to avoid people who, if they got close enough, would recognize the presence of these unreasonable symptoms. This creates a secondary problem. As we just discussed, life is a challenge, and one of the ways we deal with the challenges is through the support of other people. If we isolate ourselves from those potential sources of support because of our embarrassment, we remove one of the most important tools for our emotional survival.

For the Loved Ones

Earlier in this section, we talked about a case in which an individual managed to hide his OCD from his wife for years by rejecting any activities she may suggest that would trigger his OCD symptoms. This was a tragic case because of the terrible consequences it had, not only for the individual with OCD, but also for his spouse. However, it is an atypical case because it is unusual for someone with OCD to be able to hide the symptoms from someone who is close for any length of time. He was able to hide them by behaving in the most grossly inappropriate way imaginable, but that was one heck of a price to pay to hide the symptoms.

In most cases, the ways in which people with OCD hide their symptoms break down if you observe them across many different situations. If they are a member of your family or someone who works with you in the office, their behavior will seem so unusual that you will be hard-pressed not to investigate. They may give you excuses to avoid admitting the OCD symptoms, but in many cases, the excuses are more bizarre than the symptoms themselves.

The most difficult part of OCD for the loved ones of people suffering from this disorder is that the symptoms are outside of our normal experiences. It is hard to be empathetic with something that we cannot understand. When individuals with OCD describe their obsessive thoughts, we think about the normal obsessions we periodically experience and how we handle them. However, OCD obsessions are much more severe than what most people experience, and they create a level of anxiety way beyond what we experience when we are obsessing about something. For most people, the occasional obsessions might be distracting during the day and might interfere was sleeping at night, but they tend to go away with time or with specific actions that we take. For example, we might obsess about something that someone said to us, and it upsets us for a time. We talk with our friends to deal with our anger and frustration, and we might even confront the individual who upset us. In a worst-case scenario, we might decide to limit our interactions with that individual, and the net result is that the obsessions go away. But it does not work that way with OCD; obsessions keep coming back; compulsive behavior might push them away for a while, but they keep coming back. There seems to be no way to turn them off.

Review of Treatment Options

There are two treatment options that have been demonstrated effective in the treatment of OCD. The first is high doses of medications called *SSRIs*. The second is a behavioral treatment called *exposure with response prevention*. It is generally agreed that other treatments that have been tried are ineffective. But even these effective treatments are not always effective, and they almost never wipe out the symptoms. Even with proper treatment, individuals with OCD continue to struggle with their symptoms, although as they learn to manage their symptoms, they have a chance to get back their lives.

Selective serotonin reuptake inhibitors (SSRIs) are the treatment of choice from a medical perspective. These drugs are used in the treatment of other anxiety disorders, such as panic disorder, and they were originally used as a treatment for depression. In fact, because of their original use in the treatment of depression, they are often referred to as *antidepressants*. The difference between using this drug for treating panic or depression and treating OCD is primarily the dosage. Whereas it is common to have a dosage of 20 mg a day of Prozac (the first SSRI) to treat depression or panic, dosages of 100 mg a day are common in the treatment of OCD. As with all drugs, as the dose increases, the problems associated with side effects and risks increase. Most of the SSRIs that are prescribed for the treatment of depression are prescribed by general practitioners, and that is reasonable because prescribing these drugs for those conditions is well within their areas of expertise. However, I would recommend that individuals with OCD seek treatment from a psychiatrist who is more familiar with managing the high doses of the drug needed to be effective.

Exposure with response prevention is a behavioral treatment that involves exactly what the name implies. Individuals with OCD expose themselves to situations that trigger obsessive thoughts. The obsessive thoughts create enormous anxiety and an incredible drive to engage in compulsive behavior to reduce that anxiety. But the individual resists the compulsions (i.e., response prevention). This treatment is consistent with all psychological treatments for anxiety disorders. One must do exposure to reduce the anxiety; it is not possible to talk yourself out of the anxiety. What makes this treatment different from most other anxiety disorder treatments is that it is impossible in OCD to do gradual exposure. Gradual exposure that allows people to reduce their anxiety and learn to manage it more effectively is called *systematic desensitization.* When you do exposure all at once, it is called **flooding**. With systematic desensitization, the individual is clearly uncomfortable during exposure but never extremely uncomfortable if done properly. With flooding, the individual is extremely uncomfortable. In general, flooding tends to work more quickly than systematic desensitization, but it has a risk. If you stay in the situation long enough, the anxiety will go down with flooding; however, if you are unable to remain in the situation, the anxiety will increase. In other words, if you do not commit to flooding and staying with it, the anxiety may get worse.

I cover both the medication and the behavioral treatment options for OCD in more detail in the section on treatments. For now, I want to make three important points about the treatment of OCD. The first is that the treatment is more uncomfortable and difficult for the client than the treatments for other anxiety disorders. In addition, the prognosis is not as good as it is for many other anxiety disorders. Because it is more difficult, it is important that the individual seek treatment from someone who is knowledgeable about OCD and its treatment. The second point is that the options that are effective appear to be more limited in the case of OCD than with other anxiety disorders. Most anxiety disorders do not respond optimally to traditional insight-oriented talk therapies but do rather well with cognitive behavioral therapy or behavioral therapy. OCD tends not to respond at all to insight-oriented therapy. The third point that I want to make is that one need not completely control the OCD symptoms to have an improvement in one's life. Even a modest level of control may help someone to have a more satisfying life. Because the behavioral treatment is so difficult for the client, and often for the loved ones of the client as well, sometimes it is entirely reasonable for people in treatment to say that they do not have the energy to continue treatment. In effect, they have decided to enjoy the relative freedom from reducing the OCD symptoms. Most behavioral therapists who work with individuals with OCD recognize this. If clients make it clear that they are not ready for the next level, the therapist readily accepts that and praises them for the progress they have made. The therapist encourages them to live the life that they want, and if at some point in the future they want to take it to the next level, the individual is always welcome to come back.

Chapter Summary

Obsessive-compulsive disorder (OCD) is still considered an anxiety disorder, although the more recent additions of the diagnostic manual have created a separate category for OCD and related disorders. OCD is characterized by obsessive thoughts that generate massive anxiety and compensatory behaviors (compulsions) that the individual uses to reduce the anxiety. However, the compulsions are rarely effective in removing anxiety, and the result is that the individual is often overwhelmed by both the anxiety and compulsive symptoms that are extreme and embarrassing.

Though OCD was once thought to be a rare disorder, we now realize it is relatively common (affecting approximately 1.5 percent of the population). Most people with OCD realize that their symptoms are unreasonable and irrational and therefore try to hide those symptoms, which may be one reason why we once thought this disorder was rare. There is more of a recognition of this disorder now and an acceptance that it is a legitimate disorder. Consequently, more people are willing to acknowledge their symptoms and seek treatment.

In general, the symptoms of OCD are dramatic and have a tremendous impact on a person's life. In severe cases, the individual with OCD may not be able to work or live up to other social obligations. Treatments exist, but they are more difficult and less likely to be effective than treatments for other anxiety disorders. Traditional insight-oriented therapy is of little value with OCD. The behavioral treatment called *exposure with response prevention* is the treatment of choice. Very high doses of SSRIs have also been demonstrated to be effective.

Chapter 11

Anxiety as a Secondary Disorder

Anxiety is a symptom; it is not a disorder by itself. We do have anxiety disorders, and all of them include significant anxiety. But as you learned in earlier chapters, these disorders include other symptoms beyond anxiety, and the nature of the anxiety varies depending upon the disorder. Therefore, it should not be surprising that anxiety is a symptom that appears in many disorders. Moreover, anxiety is a normal response to a variety of situations in one's everyday life, and it is a common response to any situation that creates serious uncertainty. Whether we consider those situations as requiring treatment depends on many factors.

In this chapter, we will talk about situations in which anxiety is present but is not a defining characteristic of an anxiety disorder. As I have emphasized throughout this book, anxiety is a normal response, and even though we may not enjoy the discomfort associated with anxiety, it is not our enemy. When we see situations in which there is anxiety, we should not immediately assume that the goal is to eliminate the anxiety. That would be shortsighted because eliminating anxiety may significantly increase our risks of negative consequences. For example, first responders need to be anxious because they routinely face potentially life-threatening situations. They need to be on alert. We do not try to eliminate their anxiety; instead, we teach them to function at a high level despite the anxiety.

Anxiety as a Comorbid Symptom

Anxiety as a symptom is found in many disorders that are not anxiety disorders. For example, it is rare for someone suffering from depression to not also be experiencing anxiety. The reason for the high comorbidity between anxiety and depression has been hotly debated for decades. To us, anxiety and depression feel very different, so we imagine that they must be very different. But anxiety and depression share common biological and psychological elements.

Anxiety can also be found in several disorders in which the primary symptoms of anxiety do not overlap the symptoms of the disorder, as is true with depression. For example, any disorder that interrupts our ability to function almost always increases our anxiety because we are worried about the potential impact on our lives. In this case, anxiety is a reactive symptom that is a signal that there is a problem. Moreover, it is a reactive symptom that motivates the individual to seek appropriate treatment for the problem that generates the risk of failure. In almost every situation in which anxiety is a reaction to the disruptions associated with another disorder, one would not want to treat the anxiety but rather would focus on the factors causing the anxiety.

Anxiety as a Reaction to Uncertainty

In the first section of this book, I argued that anxiety, although uncomfortable, is a critical signal. It tells us when there are potential risks and motivates us to prepare for those risks. Because potential risks are everywhere, the norm is to experience anxiety on a regular basis. Such anxiety is normal and beneficial.

Everyone experiences anxiety because there is always uncertainty and potential risk. We do not consider it a disorder to be anxious in such situations. However, sometimes the situations are so extreme that they are well outside the range of what most people experience. Consequently, the anxiety that one experiences might also be well outside the norm and qualify as a disorder. We refer to such anxiety as *reactive anxiety* in that it is understandable given the extreme situation that the person is in, but at the same time, it is so extreme that it interferes with functioning.

161

Anxiety as a Secondary Effect of a Disease Process

Our bodies are magnificent machines which represent a delicate balance. Everything interacts with everything else in our body. If our body overheats because we spent too much time in the sun on a hot day, we do not just experience feeling hot. Dozens of other body functions will be affected, and some of those body functions are outside of our awareness. Those responses are intense and can be potentially life-threatening. That is true for any kind of disease process. A disease process, such as cancer, may be focused on a particular organ, and the primary symptoms may be a function of the disruption of that organ. However, almost certainly, other organs will be affected because they interact with the organ being attacked by cancer.

The parts of the brain that are responsible for triggering anxiety represent organs that are affected by dozens of other systems in our body. It is not uncommon for the disruption in body functioning due to disease to directly create the feeling of anxiety. Note the careful wording in the previous sentence. It is the feeling of anxiety that is created because the parts of the brain responsible for that feeling are being stimulated indirectly by the disease process. However, it does not matter whether that feeling is an indirect stimulation because of a disease or a direct stimulation because of the situation we find ourselves in. In both cases, we will feel anxious, and in both cases, we will respond to that anxiety.

There is another way in which a disease process can create anxiety as a secondary effect. In fact, many people would argue that this mechanism is not a secondary effect. If you are diagnosed with cancer or some other life-threatening disease, it is hard not to be anxious about that situation. There may not be much you can do other than seek good medical treatment and do your part in the treatment but being in a situation in which you may die is certainly anxiety arousing.

Some people try to cope with this anxiety by maintaining an unrealistic optimistic outlook. Psychologists would call this response *denial*, but there is no rule that says you must always be realistic in your view of the world. I do not recommend denial; instead, I recommend that you understand that the anxiety is indeed something that should be addressed. There are treatments to reduce anxiety, such as the anxiety one might experience when faced with one's own mortality. Moreover, there is evidence that treating such anxiety improves your prognosis for recovery (Yusufov et al., 2020). So if you or a loved one has a life-threatening illness, it would be wise to seek the best medical treatment and to also seek supportive psychological treatment. Not only will the patient be more comfortable during this critical period, but the likelihood of surviving the illness will also be increased.

Anxiety as a Side Effect of Medications

In some cases, the anxiety is not so much comorbid with the disorder but rather comorbid with the treatment for that disorder. This is especially true with medications. Anxiety is the second most common side effect of medications, second only to depression. Let me emphasize that we are not talking only about medications for psychological disorders. Medications used in the treatment of hundreds of other disorders may increase anxiety as a side effect. Powerful medications always have multiple effects.

Years ago, I had the chance to listen to one of the top pharmacologists in the world at a conference. The point of his talk was that every medication has multiple effects, and whether we call the effects *treatment* or *side effects* depends on our perspective. To expect medication not to have side effects is unreasonable. Whenever you get a prescription, it will come with a sheet, which is typically printed in such small type that you may need a magnifying glass to read it. This sheet describes the medication, dosage levels, and potential side effects or interactions with other drugs. The material is typically taken from the *PDR* (short for *Physician's Desk Reference*), which lists every drug on the market and the information just described. If you are experiencing anxiety that seems too intense for the situation, it might be a good idea to investigate the drugs you are taking. You can get that information on the Internet, or you can talk with your pharmacist or doctor about the medications you are taking. If there is reason to believe that your anxiety is a side effect of the medication, it would be a good idea to have your doctor reduce the dosage, eliminate the medication, or try an alternative medication to see if such steps reduce your anxiety.

What Is It Like to Experience Secondary Anxiety?

Sometimes when we modify a word by saying that it is secondary, we give the impression that it is less severe and may even be something that we can ignore. That is not the case with secondary anxiety. It does not matter where the anxiety comes from, because the impact of the anxiety is similar regardless of the cause. In this section, we will talk about the very real problems of secondary anxiety and the impact it has on people's lives.

For the Individual

From the standpoint of the individual suffering from anxiety, it makes little difference whether it is secondary or primary. There might be a small effect of knowing that the anxiety is a side effect of medications that you are taking, but the effect is so small as to not be noticeable. People are still going to be anxious and, consequently, may be unable to function in the way they would like.

Adding strong anxiety to an already debilitating depressive state disrupts a person's life even more. With depression, one finds it difficult to stay focused on anything long enough to complete the task. Adding anxiety simply adds another distraction and an impediment to optimal functioning. The anxiety that one experiences during a life-threatening illness may be a normal response to that situation, but it makes it even harder for the individual to respond effectively. Moreover, there is evidence that the anxiety interferes with the normal body responses to illness, thus making the prognosis worse.

There is a tendency among some people to view the treatment of anxiety in a situation like the ones described in this chapter as unnecessary and even unreasonable. That is a misguided perspective. Throughout this book I have tried to emphasize the value of anxiety, and in most cases, anxiety is something that should be taken seriously, guiding us to adjust our behavior to reduce risks. But when anxiety is secondary to some other process, it often means that the anxiety is no longer a valuable signal encouraging adaptive behavior. Instead, it may encourage behavior that may not be in our best interest. Secondary does not mean that it is weak or easily ignored. If our car is damaged in an accident, one can view the damage to the frame and the panels of the car as primary and the damage to the paint job as secondary. Granted, it is important to repair the frame and the panels, but the paint job must be replaced too. The difference between this analogy and secondary anxiety is that we paint the car after we have fixed everything else. With secondary anxiety, we often must treat the anxiety while we take care of everything else.

For the Loved Ones

The effect of secondary anxiety on loved ones depends on the source of the anxiety and the situation. For example, if the secondary anxiety is due to an individual having a life-threatening illness, it is highly unlikely that the person with the illness is the only one anxious about that illness. If it is your loved one with a life-threatening illness, you will be anxious, too, and your anxiety will not be secondary. Your anxiety is a direct response to the situation in which you find yourself. Our loved ones are important to us; they are what makes life worthwhile. When their lives are threatened, we are anxious for them, and we are anxious for ourselves because of how important they are to us.

165

Sharing our anxiety with someone we love whose life may be at risk because of a disease is both a natural and a positive thing. Sometimes people feel they should hide their anxiety and focus only on the anxiety and the disease process in their loved one. If you do that, it distorts the entire relationship you have with that person. People support and share their feelings with loved ones. Sharing your anxiety with someone who may be dying from a disease gives them an opportunity to continue to be the kind of caring and empathic person who can provide support during difficult times. That can be a very good way to momentarily distract them from their own anxiety and the very real disease process they are fighting.

In situations in which the anxiety is secondary to something like medication, it would be valuable to be empathetic about the anxiety while supporting the individual's efforts to have the medication adjusted to avoid unnecessary anxiety. In some cases, that might involve intervening with the doctor to point out the problem. If that is necessary, I would support it, but I would be more supportive of encouraging the person to deal with those issues directly with the doctor. The reason for that is that the process of taking charge in dealing with one's anxiety, even when the anxiety is not their responsibility because it is due to medication, tends to increase the person's self-esteem and sense of control. In general, anxiety that cannot be controlled weighs heavily on our self-esteem.

Review of Treatment Options

The treatment options for secondary anxiety depend on the nature of the anxiety. Anxiety can usually be attenuated with medications, although you learned in this chapter that some medications increase anxiety. If the medications are the source of the anxiety, a change in dosage or type of medication often improves the situation. If the medication is necessary and alternatives are not available, it is common for people to take medications to attenuate the uncomfortable side effects of medications that are required for the person's health.

If the anxiety is overwhelming because the person is facing situations that seem completely out of control, a combination of social support, medications, and anxiety management techniques can give the person a sense of control over their anxiety. Remember, the goal is not to eliminate anxiety, but rather to manage it. We manage it when the anxiety is appropriate and beneficial, but we do the same thing when anxiety is secondary to some other process. The only difference is that secondary anxiety rarely signals the need to make behavioral changes to reduce some future risk.

When anxiety is associated with a serious illness, the medical establishment is becoming increasingly sensitive to the importance of managing that anxiety. In cancer centers, for example, behavioral specialists are available for the treatment of anxiety experienced during treatment for the disease. For example, chemotherapy or radiation therapy are common treatments for many forms of cancer. They are reasonably effective and have gradually gotten better because of careful research on their effects. However, they are nonetheless barbaric. In chemotherapy, we poison people to within an inch of their life in the hopes that we kill the cancer before we kill the person. That works because cancer cells are growing fast and therefore absorb more of the poison. Your hair also grows fast and therefore absorbs more of the poison, which is the reason why it falls out when you have chemotherapy. I feel confident that in the next couple of decades we will have more effective and less barbaric treatments. But until then, imagine how difficult it is to get into the car and go to the clinic or hospital knowing that they will put a needle in your arm and poison you to within an inch of your life. Not only that, but you also must live through several rounds of chemo to kill off the cancer. Helping people to deal with such treatments is a huge part of successfully treating people with cancer. In fact, there is good evidence that reducing the stress of treatment not only improves the patient's sense of well-being but also significantly improves the likelihood of full remission (Yusufov et al., 2020). You can minimize the distress of chemotherapy with appropriate behavioral treatment.

Chapter Summary

Until this chapter, we have been talking about anxiety as a normal and important signal of potential risk or as a symptom of an anxiety disorder. In this chapter we talked about anxiety that is secondary to other processes. The two most common situations in which this occurs is anxiety that is secondary to other disorders (either physical or psychological disorders) and anxiety that is the result of medications for other conditions.

Secondary anxiety is not necessarily a weaker level of anxiety. In fact, it can be overwhelming. We call it *secondary* because it is the result of some other process than the analysis of potential risks. Because its source is different than most anxiety, it does not serve the same purpose of being a signal for risk. That means that it does not motivate behaviors that could reduce risks. However, the anxiety is still present and still uncomfortable, and it may very well interfere with the person's ability to function. Therefore, we need to manage that anxiety using the control techniques we introduced in previous chapters and discuss in more detail in the last few chapters of this book.

Section III

Treating Anxiety Disorders

Most anxiety is normal, and it is manageable with techniques that we talked about earlier in this book. Some anxiety can become so intense or so disruptive that it qualifies as an anxiety disorder. Even in those situations, the anxiety can be managed, and the disruption caused by an anxiety disorder can be mitigated. Sometimes the treatment involves medications; sometimes the treatment involves psychological processes, such as systematic desensitization, which we briefly talked about earlier in this book.

I have introduced several treatments as I discussed anxiety disorders. In this section, I discuss those treatments in much more detail. I have chosen to organize this section not by disorder but rather by treatment approach. There are certain treatments that have become the standard for specific disorders. However, most anxiety disorders use a combination of treatments to address the various elements of the disorders. Because this book is geared toward managing anxiety, I wanted to organize this section so you could see how the various treatments address the specific issues associated with anxiety and anxiety disorders.

Although I make no claim that this section on treatment approaches is exhaustive, it does represent the most effective and most widely used techniques for treating anxiety. There is constant research focused on developing new techniques that are even more effective or combining techniques to improve the efficiency of a treatment approach. This is an exciting area because there have been dramatic improvements in the diagnosis and treatment of even the most severe anxiety problems. There is every reason to expect that we will continue to make progress as researchers around the world work to improve our technology.

Chapter 12

Behavioral Approaches to Treatment

Behavioral treatment techniques are based on a rich history of research on how behaviors are learned and maintained in the laboratory and in the real world. Although much of the research was done with animals, there is clear evidence that these techniques work well with humans. Since anxiety is both a learned response and a variable that influences other learning, the behavioral approaches have much to offer in both the management of normal anxiety and the treatment of anxiety disorders.

Behavioral Approaches

There are two primary behavioral approaches, and most people have at least a passing familiarity with them. The first is called *classical conditioning*, which is based on research by Pavlov. The second is called *operant conditioning* (sometimes called *instrumental conditioning*), which is based primarily on the work of B. F. Skinner. Most people have heard of Pavlov's dogs, who learned to salivate at the sound of a bell, and the Skinner box, which Skinner used to train rats and pigeons to engage in a variety of behaviors using a combination of rewards and punishments. There is a third approach that has been helpful in the treatment of anxiety, called *observational learning* or *modeling*. I will give a brief introduction to the ideas behind each of these models before introducing the treatment techniques based on these models.

Classical Conditioning

Classical conditioning involves the creation of a response to a specific stimulus by pairing that stimulus with another stimulus that naturally triggers that response. In the case of Pavlov's dogs, Pavlov paired a bell with meat. It is worth noting that Pavlov was not particularly interested in behavioral principles, although he is best known for this work. His research was on the process of digestion, for which he won a Nobel Prize. His work on classical conditioning was a side project triggered by a problem that he encountered in his early research. It is a great example of what an outstanding scientist does with a problem, studying the problem with sufficient clarity so that new principles are discovered.

Pavlov was studying the very first stage of digestion, which occurs in the mouth. That process is called *salivation*. Salivation makes the food slippery so that it will slide into the stomach easily. Pavlov developed a surgical technique to install a small tube in the side of the dog's mouth to measure the amount of salivation. This was a very clever technique, but Pavlov noticed a problem early in the research. His plan had been to present the dog with meat, which automatically triggers salivation. However, the dogs were not cooperating. In short order, they started salivating before the presentation of the meat. In fact, they started salivating when Pavlov or his assistant walked into the laboratory. It was as if they were anticipating that the presence of the researcher meant that they were going to be fed, and they were responding as if feeding would occur soon. This is a response that all of us can appreciate. If we imagine our favorite meal, we often salivate at the thought, and if we walk into the house in which a wonderful meal is being cooked, the smell alone can trigger the salivation response.

A lesser scientist might have viewed this problem as something to solve rather than to study. Pavlov was not such a scientist, so it was not an accident that he won a Nobel Prize for his work on digestion. Pavlov might have figured out a way to sneak into the lab without the dogs noticing, but it occurred to him that the dogs' responses were interesting. Consequently, he developed several brilliant experiments to identify what was happening. Without going into the details of the experiments, Pavlov discovered that whenever a stimulus that triggers a response is paired reliably with another stimulus that does not trigger a response, that second stimulus, in time, will produce the same response as the original stimulus. With his dogs, Pavlov found that meat reliably triggered the salivation response (the first stage of a complex digestion process). The dog apparently did not need to learn this response; it appeared to be already there. Pavlov labeled the stimulus that produced the response without needing to be learned as the **unconditioned stimulus** or **UCS** and the response as the **unconditioned response** or **UCR**. He called them unconditioned because no conditioning was required. Instead of using himself as the stimulus that he wanted to condition, he used something that he could control more precisely, which was a bell. Initially, when he would ring the bell, it caught the dog's attention, but the dog did not salivate to the sound of the bell. Therefore, the bell did not produce the salivation response, but that changed when the bell occurred just before the dog was presented with meat. The meat triggered the salivation response, but after a few trials, the bell was sufficient to trigger the salivation response. The bell was called the **conditioned stimulus** or **CS** because Pavlov could condition the animal to respond to the bell through this process. The salivation to the bell was called the **conditioned response** or **CR**.

This simple approach allowed Pavlov to demonstrate that it is easy to condition almost any response to almost any stimulus by the proper pairing of a UCS and a CS. There was nothing special about the bell except that it did not trigger a response initially. However, after conditioning, it did trigger the same response as the meat. Pavlov believed that this was a simple reflex learning that was the result of pairing these two stimuli. He thought it was a mindless action that was based on how the brain was wired and how it responded to repeated experiences. It turns out it is more complicated than that, but we do not need to worry about this level of detail here. If you are interested in a detailed description of this process and the modern research on it, I recommend Lavond and Steinmetz (2003).

Classical conditioning is critical in psychology because most of our emotions are classically conditioned. We have many basic emotions in our repertoire, and most of them are triggered by specific stimuli. For example, anxiety is a basic emotion, and it is triggered by concerns that we may be facing a situation we are not prepared to handle.

Fear is also a basic emotion, and because it is such a strong emotion, it is easily conditioned. That is one of the principles of classical conditioning. When we have a strong emotional response (a strong UCR), conditioning occurs quickly to other stimuli, thus producing a powerful conditioned response. That is one of the reasons why we see so much avoidance in panic disorder. The intensity of the panic attacks makes almost anything that happens to be present at the time of the panic attack an object that will be feared in the future. Note that you do not need a researcher to pair two stimuli (a UCS and a CS) as Pavlov did. In the real world, when a UCS produces a UCR, any stimulus that happens to be present is a potential CS.

To understand this process, assume that something triggers a panic attack. We do not even need to know what triggered the panic attack. Whatever triggered it, the panic attack is an incredibly strong response (our fight-or-flight response). Therefore, almost any aspect of the situation that happens to be present quickly becomes conditioned to trigger panic attacks (or at least the fear that one might have a panic attack). We say that such intense responses lead to *one-trial learning*—it only takes a single experience to get conditioning—compared to the work of Pavlov, where repeated trials were needed for conditioning to occur. For example, if one has a panic attack in a grocery store, it is likely that every future trip to the grocery store will be frightening for the individual. The grocery store becomes classically conditioned to trigger the fear because it was paired with the panic attack that created a powerful fearful response. Because panic attacks can occur almost anywhere, people with panic disorder are likely to increasingly restrict their activities to a limited set of situations. Panic attacks at the grocery store, on the highway, at a movie, or during a walk in the park make all those situations frightening and therefore lead the person to avoid those situations.

Operant Conditioning

Operant conditioning is based on a simple principle called the **law of effect**. This principle states that behaviors that are followed by positive consequences will tend to be repeated, and behaviors that are followed by negative consequences will tend not to be repeated. To state it another way, if you reward a behavior, you will get more of it, and if you punish a behavior, you will get less of it. This seems so obvious that it is hard to imagine why psychologists make such a big deal out of it.

Although the principles of operant conditioning are straightforward, there is a lot of terminology around it that makes it easier for us to describe precisely what is going on. Although I have generally tried to avoid jargon in this book, the details of operant conditioning are difficult to discuss without some basic terminology.

If a behavior is followed by a positive consequence and that behavior increases as a result, we call the process **positive reinforcement**. We call the stimulus that drives positive reinforcement a **positive reinforcer**. The positive consequences might include such things as food or praise. If a behavior is followed by an aversive consequence and, as a result, the behavior decreases, we call that **punishment**. Punishment is often confused with a concept called *negative reinforcement*. **Negative reinforcement** occurs when a behavior is followed by the removal of an aversive stimulus and, therefore, the behavior increases. Both positive and negative reinforcement increase behaviors, one by applying positive consequences and one by removing aversive situations.

Examples can help to illustrate these concepts. Money is often a positive reinforcer, and so when we get paid for doing something, we are more likely to do it again. If we get paid more money for doing behavior A than behavior B, we are more likely to increase the frequency of behavior A over behavior B. Praise is another positive reinforcer, and it has the advantage of being more controllable. By controllable I mean that you can precisely determine when you will offer positive reinforcement. Payments for services are typically offered sometime after you have completed the services. For example, we might get paid every two weeks, and often that payment is not directly tied to how much work we got done in those two weeks. Even if we are a contractor and getting paid for each job we complete, we are likely to be paid several days or even weeks after the completion of the job because of the normal paperwork associated with such payments. In contrast, if someone does a good job for you, it may take a while to pay them, but you can immediately praise them for their good work. A general rule of operant conditioning is that reinforcement that is delivered reliably and shortly after a behavior is more effective at shaping that behavior than reinforcement that is less reliable or delayed.

Note that a positive reinforcer in operant conditioning is not defined by its characteristics but rather by its effect. If you apply what you believe to be an aversive stimulus after a behavior and that behavior increases in frequency, then that presumed "aversive stimulus" is apparently not aversive; it is, by definition, a positive reinforcer. My father, like many fathers, loved to tell terrible jokes. We would often roll our eyes and moan at those jokes, which appears to be a negative response. But the more we did it, the more often my father told those bad jokes. We may have thought we were punishing him for telling such terrible jokes, but the fact that his joke-telling behavior increased and remained strong was an indication that we were reinforcing it.

The best example of negative reinforcement is taking two aspirin when you have a headache. The likely consequence of taking two aspirin in that situation is that the headache will go away. Your behavior of taking two aspirin is being negatively reinforced by the removal of the headache. If certain foods do not agree with you, eating them may lead to an upset stomach or worse. This is punishment, which involves the application of an aversive stimulus following a behavior. Eat a particular food, and the result is that

175

you will get sick. In general, timing will influence the effectiveness of the consequences in changing behavior. Consequences delivered very soon after a behavior tend to have more impact than consequences that are delayed. If illness occurs immediately after drinking too much alcohol, it will be an effective punishment for drinking too much. However, the most severe aversive consequences of excessive drinking are often experienced years later and, consequently, have little impact on discouraging heavy drinking. There is an interesting exception to this principle that involves food. It is called the **Garcia effect** or **learned taste aversion**. If you eat something that makes you sick even hours later, you will develop a powerful aversion to that food, so powerful that it can last a lifetime. The likely reason for this exception is that getting sick usually involves re-experiencing the taste of the food because of stomach distress and thus linking the food to the illness.

A good example of how the timing of reinforcers has a huge impact is smoking. Smokers are generally aware that smoking is not good for them, but the negative impact of smoking usually takes years to affect the person. In contrast, the pleasant sensations associated with nicotine occur within seconds. That explains why smoking is so addictive. But there is a second reason why smoking is so addictive. As soon as you finish your cigarette, the nicotine in your system dramatically drops, creating an intense biological need for more nicotine. Smokers refer to this by saying they "need a nicotine fix." Smoking is thus being negatively reinforced because the aversive state is removed when one smokes their next cigarette. It is also positively reinforced by an energy kick and a pleasant sensation. It is being punished by long-term negative health consequences, but those consequences are so delayed that they have almost no effect.

What makes operant conditioning so powerful is that it is universal. If someone goes out of their way to help us with something and we thank them for their efforts, they will feel appreciated and will be more likely to want to help us in the future. In this example, the reinforcement of the behavior was deliberate. You were thankful for the help of another, and you wanted to express your thanks. But it makes no difference whether reinforcement is deliberate. The person whose name is associated most strongly with operant conditioning, B. F. Skinner, was famous for building mechanical devices that provided reinforcement based on simple rules. In these devices, called **Skinner boxes**, a rat could get a food pellet by pushing a bar, or a pigeon could get some food by pecking a particular spot on the wall. Mechanical devices do not have intentions in the same way that human beings do; they just follow the rules dictated by their mechanical or electronic construction. Yet they still shape behavior. Think about the last time you put money in a vending machine and did not get the product you wanted. Did the action of the vending machine influence your behavior toward that machine?

You might be telling yourself that teaching a rat to press a bar or a pigeon to peck a disk on the wall is not a very useful activity. But all complex behavior is a collection of simple behaviors that have been organized and learned over time. During World War II, Skinner and his colleagues, on a very limited budget, trained pigeons to fly bombs into ships. Think about that. Kamikaze pigeons! It sounds impossible, but Skinner made it happen. By combining learned behaviors with the right technology, amazing things can be done. Pilots do not actually fly a plane, because pilots cannot fly. However, they can learn to control machinery developed and refined through decades of work that can take off and carry people and cargo thousands of miles to a destination. Their behavior is complicated and was learned through years of experience and thorough training. Most pilots can also deal with significant problems during what might otherwise be a routine flight because of their training.

Pigeons can be taught to fly a bomb into a ship by teaching them to peck different discs to move the image of the ship into the middle of their visual field. These controls do not resemble the controls in a plane because pigeons are not able to manipulate the same controls a pilot can manipulate. But when a technology is married to the capabilities of an organism, the net result can be amazing. For example, you might have difficulty lifting a fifty-pound box, but with the right technology, you can lift several tons. The pigeons learned to peck discs to move the image of the ship into the center of the field. Their pecking moved the fins on the bomb to redirect it toward the ship in the same way that a pilot moves the control surfaces of a plane to direct it toward a destination. When the image of the ship was in the center of their visual field, the bomb was falling directly toward the ship.

All behavior is reinforced, although the reinforcement may not be deliberate and may not be optimal. Even when you are ignored after a particular behavior, that is a reinforcement contingency. You behave, and people ignore you. Being ignored is aversive for most people, so it decreases the likelihood of you behaving in the same way in the future. Even when we are reinforced for behaviors, it is rare that we are reinforced on a predictable schedule. Sometimes people will praise our work, and other times people will not notice it and thus will not reinforce us. People who study behavioral principles can tell you that such a schedule of reinforcement is not optimal for quick learning, although it does have the advantage of slowing the process called *extinction*. **Extinction** is the gradual reduction in the level of a specific behavior over time because the behavior is no longer being reinforced.

We will see shortly that all these principles can be used to optimize the way that we manage anxiety, including the severe anxiety associated with many anxiety disorders.

Observational Learning

It is easy to understand why we would increase the likelihood of behaviors that are reinforced and decrease the likelihood of behaviors that are punished. If you are praised for a behavior, you are likely to increase the frequency of that behavior. If you are given a speeding ticket for driving too fast, you are likely to slow down. Fortunately, we can learn these things without having to experience the consequences. It is called *observational learning*. In **observational learning**, we observe behaviors in others and the consequences of those behaviors. If someone is rewarded for a behavior, not only will the likelihood of that behavior increase for

178

that person, but it will also increase for those who observed the behavior and its consequences. If someone is punished for behavior, both their behavior and an observer's behavior are likely to decrease. Think about what you do each time you see an officer giving someone a speeding ticket. You did not personally suffer the negative consequences of that ticket, but you likely slowed down.

A variation of observational learning is that we can and do learn by just hearing about the consequences of behaviors. We do not have to experience the consequences or even observe others experience those consequences. This is an amazing ability, which allows us to transfer incredible information to guide our behaviors to others in a matter of minutes. The information might be as simple as a student telling other students that a particular professor really loves certain ideas and really hates other ideas. The second student can take that information and use it to craft a paper that likely will appeal to the biases of that instructor.

This book, and any other self-help book, is an example of that principle. The information in such books can change your behavior in positive ways without you having to experience the consequences yourself or vicariously through observation. If the information in this book works for you, the changes in behavior will be maintained because you will enjoy more control over your anxiety and thus your new behaviors will be reinforced.

Relaxation Procedures

It is not an accident that we use the term *relaxed* to refer to a state in which one is not anxious. When you are anxious, you not only feel the anxiety, but also your body responds with increased muscle tension. If you tell yourself to relax, you will quickly discover that it is easier said than done. But you can relax your body by relaxing your muscles. When you relax your muscles, you feel relaxed (i.e., not anxious). It may be extremely difficult to get the anxiety to go away on command, but with practice, you can get your muscles to relax, and, therefore, you will feel relaxed.

179

Muscle Relaxation

In *progressive muscle relaxation therapy*, you simplify the task of controlling your muscles by dividing your body into muscle groups. There are dozens of ways to divide the muscles up. I will introduce you to the technique that I first learned and that I have used throughout my career with clients who experience excessive anxiety. Initially, we start with sixteen muscle groups. With practice, we can easily combine muscle groups to make the relaxation exercises more efficient. With more practice, you can reach the point where you have sufficient control over your muscles and can simply say, "Relax." That is what you try to do right now when you tell yourself to relax, but because you have not trained your body and your body's muscles to respond to that command, you really do not know how to make it happen.

In a moment I will list the muscle groups and the typical order in which you relax those muscles. Memorizing sixteen muscle groups can be a problem, so let me give you a visual image of how to remember them. Imagine your hands above your head; you will relax your muscles from the top to the bottom (from your hands down to your feet). Whenever you have two of something, such as your arms and legs, you will do your dominant side first, followed by your other side. If you are right-handed, you will do your right hand and arm first, followed by your left hand and arm. The same will be true of your legs. This order is not entirely arbitrary. We tend to start with the muscles we have the greatest control over, and we try to avoid relaxing muscles that will be tensed by the process of relaxing the next muscle group.

First, I have a word of warning. This muscle relaxation technique is effective, but it takes time and practice for you to learn it. It is common to take weeks of practice. However, many people who learn these exercises find them almost addictive. They report that they have not felt that relaxed and comfortable in years. Some people routinely use them to improve their sleep. They can fall asleep more easily and awaken more refreshed.

The ideal place to do these exercises is a recliner, but with a little experimentation, you can learn to do them in bed, on the floor, or even sitting up straight in a chair. You are not likely to be able to relax your entire body while you are standing. You can reduce the muscle tension, but if you reduce the muscle tension too much, you will collapse. The only way you can stand up is to maintain muscle tension, and if you want to completely relax all muscle tension, you must have furniture that supports your body.

By the way, there are many sports for which optimal performance is done under relaxed conditions. Golf happens to be one of those sports. Learning to reduce the tension in your muscles when you are on the golf course can help you to have a more fluid swing and, surprisingly, a faster swing. Most people intuitively think that the harder you try, which translates into greater muscle tension to move the club faster, the further you will hit the ball. The ball is moved primarily by clubhead speed, and the highest clubhead speeds are attained when your muscles are relatively relaxed. It is more of a swinging motion than a pushing or hitting motion. The subtle movements for short shots around the green are especially influenced by excess tension muscles. So the techniques we are talking about here could not only help you to manage your anxiety better, but also you may find that they will help improve your golf game.

Here are the sixteen muscle groups in order.
1. Right hand and forearm (assuming you are right-handed)
2. Right upper arm and shoulder
3. Left hand and forearm
4. Left upper arm and shoulder
5. Upper part of the face (forehead)
6. Middle part of the face (nose and eyes)
7. Bottom part of the face (jaw)
8. Neck
9. Chest and upper part of your torso
10. Stomach and lower part of your torso
11. Upper part of the right leg (assuming you are right-handed)
12. Thigh of your right leg
13. Right foot
14. Upper part of the left leg

15. Thigh on the left leg
16. Left foot

If you are seeing a behavior therapist or cognitive behavioral therapist, the therapist will likely walk you through these muscle relaxation techniques in the office. It is helpful to hear the therapist's voice announce the next step. I recorded such instructions and made them available on YouTube. You can access these recorded instructions at https://youtu.be/r8RMivYuZLE. However, with just a little bit of practice, you will not need the instructions. Moreover, as you become better at controlling your muscles, you will find that you pick up the pace with these relaxation exercises. So if you use the recorded instructions, it will not be long before they feel like they are too slow to be optimal.

When you begin to learn muscle relaxation techniques, the strategy is to use some muscle tension to help you visualize the muscles you want to control. For example, if you want to tense the muscles of your hand and forearm, you make a *gentle* fist. Note that I emphasize the word *gentle*. This is a situation in which too much muscle tension is ineffective. The purpose of muscle tension is to help you to see the muscles in your mind, which will allow you to control them better. To illustrate, after you finish reading this discussion, try the demonstration I am outlining. Close your eyes and try to see with your mind your right hand and forearm. You probably have the vaguest sense of where they are but almost no sense of how they feel. Unless we are in pain, we have learned to ignore our bodies to avoid distraction. Now make a gentle fist and notice how it appears like there is a spotlight on those muscles. The tension allows you to see the muscles so that you can learn to control them more effectively. To a degree, the tension also provides a slingshot effect in that a little tension allows you to relax the muscles more completely. Now, close your eyes and try it for yourself.

Could you sense your muscles more clearly with a little tension? We are going to have you do that with each of the sixteen muscle groups. I have listed below the way you will tense the muscles.

Again, you want just enough muscle tension so you can clearly visualize the muscles you are seeking to relax.

1. Right hand and forearm (gentle fist)
2. Right upper arm and shoulder (push elbow down in a recliner or against the body if not in a chair)
3. Left hand and forearm (gentle fist)
4. Left upper arm and shoulder (push elbow down in a recliner or against the body if not in a chair)
5. Upper part of the face (raise your eyebrows)
6. Middle part of the face (squint and wrinkle your nose)
7. Bottom part of the face (gently bite down but without letting your teeth touch)
8. Neck (bring your neck down toward your chest)
9. Chest and upper part of your torso (pull your shoulder blades together in the back)
10. Stomach and lower part of your torso (pull your stomach muscles in until you can feel the tension in your lower back)
11. Upper part of the right leg (move your knee down against the chair or bed)
12. Thigh of your right leg (point your toes toward your head)
13. Right foot (turn your ankle inward and point your toes away from you; be very gentle because it is easy to cramp your foot with this movement)
14. Upper part of the left leg (move your knee down against the chair or bed)
15. Thigh on the left leg (point your toes toward your head)
16. Left foot (turn your ankle inward and point your toes away from you; again, be very gentle)

Before you begin practicing, just a few words of warning. If you have any injuries to your muscles or joints, you may need to adjust the tension procedure to avoid creating pain or potentially doing damage. You can typically find an appropriate muscle tension technique that works for you. Remember, the goal is to make it easy to see the muscle in your mind's eye as you try to control it. Just play with a muscle, and you will discover that there are at least a dozen different ways of creating that visibility.

Initially, you want the exercises to take about twenty minutes, which works out to roughly one minute per muscle or muscle group. Normally, you would use the following procedures.

1. Tense a muscle for three to four seconds and then relax it for roughly twenty seconds. You will typically feel the muscle relax quickly, but if you continue to focus on the muscle, it will relax more over time.

2. Repeat the same cycle.

3. If the muscle is adequately relaxed, move on to the next muscle group and do the same two cycles of tension and relaxation.

4. When you have completed all sixteen muscle groups, take a tour of your body to see if there are pockets of tension still present. It is common to find residual tension in your face and neck. If you find such tension, just do one or two cycles for each of these still-tense muscles.

5. Finally, after you feel completely relaxed, just enjoy it. It is rare for people to take the time to relax so completely. Sometimes it helps to visualize floating on a cloud. Whatever works for you, just feel how good it feels and take pride in the fact that you, without the aid of drugs, have that much control over your own body.

After a week or so of practicing once or twice a day, you will be amazed at how much you can relax your body. You can then combine muscle groups. For example, you can combine the two muscle groups in your arms, the three muscle groups in your face with the neck, and the two muscle groups in your torso. You can easily combine the thigh and calf muscles of your legs. You may still have to do the feet separately, but you may be surprised that if your legs relax, the feet may relax by themselves. Again, you can practice this a couple of times a day for a week and get very good at it. You can shorten the routine even more by putting the right and left arms together and the right and left legs together.

What you are learning with these exercises is to control the muscle tension in your body by focusing entirely on the muscle tension and not the sense of anxiety. What you immediately notice is that the level of relaxation, defined as the absence of muscle tension, is remarkably powerful. As you continue to practice the exercises, you will notice that you can simply command your body to relax without going through the cycles we just described. In fact, in time you can get exceedingly good at it.

My dentist when I was a kid was incompetent, and as a result, I have had many root canals due to substandard work done twenty to forty years earlier. If you have never had a root canal, you are fortunate. Even with sufficient Novocain to dull the pain, the process of hollowing out your tooth and then packing it with something permanent really makes people tense. The tension would gradually build for me through the process until it reached a level that was quite uncomfortable. Because I had trained so many people in how to use these muscle relaxation techniques, I was pretty good at them myself. So when the tension reached uncomfortable levels, I would simply command my body to relax. It drove my dentist nuts. He certainly did not like the fact that I was so obviously uncomfortable because of the extreme muscle tension. But when I exercised my learned skill and relaxed my muscles, from his perspective it looked like I had died in the chair. We were good friends, so we could chat about it, and we decided that he would be much more comfortable if I would just tell him that I was about to release all that tension that had been building up. I tell this story mostly to illustrate how incredibly skilled one can get at controlling tension by learning to control your muscles. It certainly helps to manage anxiety, but it can also manage the tension one develops while someone is crawling around in their mouth and drilling a hole in their tooth. It is also helpful if you are driving on slippery roads during a snowstorm. I lived in Buffalo for twenty years, so I drove in a lot of snowstorms. Staying relaxed and doing everything in slow motion is the best way to maintain control on slippery roads. I would like to tell you that controlling my muscle tension significantly improved my golf game, but that part of my life may be hopeless.

If you have been going through an emotionally difficult period, it is helpful to completely relax even if it is only for a few moments.

185

But the real advantage of these relaxation exercises is that they give you the skills to relax on command. Remember all those times you told yourself to relax, and you simply could not do it? Once you translate that command into controlling your muscles, you will have a way to do it.

Deep Breathing

As you learned earlier, it is also possible to significantly relax your body by adjusting your breathing. Breathing is easier to control than muscle tension and requires less practice. It can also be used in almost any situation because you can take deep breaths without people noticing.

The key to deep breaths is to breathe from your diaphragm, which is a muscle just below your lungs. When you take deep breaths from your diaphragm, your stomach will protrude ever so slightly just below your rib cage. This action expands the lungs vertically to their maximum capacity. By breathing slowly and deeply and holding your breath for a few seconds, you maximize the amount of oxygen that is absorbed into the bloodstream. The increase in the oxygen level of the blood tends to make you feel more relaxed and in control.

Breathing exercises and muscle relaxation exercises work best when you begin to use them as the anxiety is just beginning to build. They will still work if you are extremely anxious, but you will be less effective at managing that anxiety. This means that if you are going into a situation in which you expect to be anxious, such as a job interview, you can control the anxiety and prevent it from building too high by adjusting your breathing or simply relaxing your muscles. There is a secondary advantage to these techniques. Your focus on relaxing your body will shift your focus away from the anxiety. As we have said repeatedly, anxiety tends to feed itself, so the more you focus on the anxiety, the more anxious you get.

Exposure-Based Treatments

You can manage your anxiety with breathing and muscle relaxation techniques, but if you want to be able to overcome anxiety, you must challenge it through exposure. Exposure involves facing the source of the anxiety as you manage your anxiety and perform whatever tasks are necessary. In time, you will gradually get more control over your anxiety and will be able to function at a high level despite the anxiety. Moreover, once you see you can manage the situation, there is less doubt about your ability to handle it and therefore less of a reason to be anxious. I want to clarify this last sentence because I do not want to give you unrealistic expectations. Anxiety is ubiquitous and expecting to have no anxiety is unreasonable. You do not want to make that your goal unless you want to fail. Your goal should be to manage anxiety well enough that it does not interfere with your performance. Anxiety may be uncomfortable, but as you have learned throughout this book, unless it is so intense that it is disrupting your behavior, anxiety is not a problem and may even be beneficial.

Remember the principle that we are programmed to learn anxiety quickly and unlearn it slowly. A way to remember this principle is to imagine that these processes evolved over hundreds of thousands of years, at a time when our ancestors were wandering the grassy plains of Africa. Although we were a formidable species, several other species were perfectly capable of hunting us for food. It was to our advantage to learn to recognize these predators quickly and be appropriately cautious around them. A lion, for example, could easily chase us down and devour us for a meal. However, after a lion has had a large meal, it poses little danger because it has no desire to eat more. Therefore, our ancestors might have occasionally wandered upon lions that were perfectly comfortable lying in the sun and ignoring us. Unlearning the anxiety about the risk that lions pose because of some encounters with well-fed lions would be a foolish move. A well-fed lion might not be dangerous, but the next lion that we run across might well be hungry and dangerous.

187

This principle of unlearning anxiety slowly means that repeated exposure is necessary to be effective. Crossing a long bridge that makes us anxious once may give us a small measure of confidence, but it will never be enough to eliminate the anxiety. Instead, we need to repeat the exposure for the anxiety to be reduced. That is not a deficiency in our anxiety system; the process of unlearning anxiety slowly is a feature. Without it, the value of anxiety would be dramatically reduced.

In this section, I will talk about three exposure approaches. I briefly introduced these approaches earlier in the book but will cover them in much more detail here. The three approaches are *systematic desensitization*, *flooding*, and *interoceptive desensitization*.

Systematic Desensitization

Systematic desensitization has a long history in clinical psychology. It was the first treatment with empirical evidence for effectiveness. Long before there were effective treatments for most psychological disorders, we were able to dramatically reduce anxiety through systematic desensitization.

The effectiveness of systematic desensitization rests on several principles, including the principle of **reciprocal inhibition**. This is just a complicated term for a very simple idea; it is not possible to be tense and relaxed at the same time. Therefore, we teach people how to relax and then expose them gradually to the stimulus or situation that makes them anxious. By doing it gradually, the anxiety-producing effect will not overcome the client's relaxed state. If the client remains in the anxiety-producing situation, whatever anxiety is produced will gradually decrease. At that point, it is time to move on to the next level of stimulation. We create these levels of stimulation by carefully analyzing the situation and producing what we call an *exposure hierarchy*. We will talk about that in just a minute and about the principles that are used in creating this hierarchy.

There is a second process going on that was not immediately recognized when systematic desensitization was first introduced. By facing anxiety situations and learning to control your anxiety in those situations, you are gradually building an expectation that you are in control of your anxiety. Anxiety tends to feed itself, so if we feel in control, this feedback loop that intensifies anxiety can be broken.

The key element in systematic desensitization is the creation of the **exposure hierarchy**, which is a list of items arranged from least fearful to most fearful and with approximately equal differences in fear level between any two items. An example of an exposure hierarchy for treating a snake phobia would be the following.

Imagine seeing the snake through an open window so that there is no way that the snake could ever get close to you.
Imagine deliberately going to see snakes at a zoo in a building in which the snakes have no access to the people.
(1) View a snake in another room in which the snake is in a glass enclosure that does not permit the snake to escape. You are not in the room but rather looking through a window into the next room.
(2) Open the door to that room and remain in the hallway approximately twenty feet from the glass enclosure that holds the snake.
(3) Move a few feet into the room and view the snake from afar but keep the door to the hallway open.
(4) Close the door to the hallway but remain several feet from the enclosure that is holding the snake.
(5) Move closer to the glass enclosure, though the snake is still unable to get out of the glass enclosure.
(6) Stand next to the glass enclosure and look intently at the snake.
(7) Remove the cover to the enclosure but make no effort to reach in and contact the snake.
(8) Allow the therapist to reach in and touch the snake.
(9) Allow the therapist to remove the snake from the enclosure and hold it.
(10) Touch the snake that is being held by the therapist.
(11) Hold the snake.

189

Of course, the exposure hierarchy above assumes that the snake you are using is safe. Reducing one's fear of poisonous snakes is both unethical and stupid. One should have a healthy fear of such snakes, even if one is a snake expert. However, reducing an unrealistic fear of harmless snakes makes sense. Moreover, overcoming such a fear can have a dramatic positive impact. People who overcome their fear of snakes suddenly feel more in control of their lives because something that made them feel out of control has now been conquered.

Exposure is the most important part of systematic desensitization, and it will work no matter how you do the exposure, provided you move at the proper pacing. But you can make the exposure easier by teaching people how to manage their anxiety. We just covered those procedures. Progressive muscle relaxation and deep breathing exercises are very effective at managing the physiological arousal associated with anxiety. If you do the exposure without these techniques, the anxiety will decrease in time. But if you add these techniques, the anxiety will decrease more quickly, and the person will feel more in control of the process.

Cognitive strategies can also be used to manage anxiety during exposure. Let me repeat that you cannot talk yourself out of anxiety, so these cognitive techniques by themselves do not reduce anxiety. Rather, cognitive techniques are used to manage anxiety and prevent it from spiraling out of control. For example, each time you move up one level in the hierarchy, the situation will be more demanding, and the anxiety will return. Telling yourself that the return of the anxiety is normal prevents you from overreacting to that increase. Telling yourself that you still have the tools to manage the anxiety and that the anxiety will go down at this new level in the hierarchy, just as it did in the previous levels, will make it easier to remain in the situation until the anxiety does go down.

It is relatively easy to construct a hierarchy for a specific feared object, such as snakes, and it is relatively easy to find a snake that is harmless and cooperative. When I was in graduate school, treating phobias was one of the few proven treatment techniques. Consequently, we treated a lot of people with snake phobias because this phobia was common and easy to treat. We used a boa constrictor as our snake because, unlike smaller snakes, it was not very good at scurrying away quickly. It is not good to have a snake running around the room with someone who is afraid of snakes. The boa worked well except that he was shy and preferred not to be handled by people, especially people who were anxious about handling him. In time, he got bigger and stronger, and because he was shy, he would often try to get away. Eventually, we had to retire him as our therapy snake because seeing the therapist fight to maintain control of the snake tends to make people who are afraid of snakes more fearful. But it was a simple problem to fix. We just got another younger boa to use in therapy.

For other phobias, it is more difficult to create the kind of hierarchy just described. For example, if someone is afraid of flying, there is a big step in a hierarchy that goes from imagining that one is flying to being on a plane flying to a destination. In an earlier era, one could do exposure treatment at the airport in a situation that was realistic enough that one's imagination could easily invoke relatively high levels of anxiety to be managed. Of course, security requirements now make that impossible. You cannot enter the terminal unless you already have a plane ticket and the intention to fly to a destination. Some airlines offer programs for people who are afraid of flying that include exposure to the actual plane and a brief takeoff and landing as part of the treatment. Such programs are less common today than they once were. I just checked online for such programs and found that all the current programs were from European airlines. It is possible to do treatment of a fear of flying by using small, noncommercial airplanes, but those airplanes are so different from commercial airplanes that it is not clear that such treatment would generalize. Some therapists are using virtual reality technology to avoid the security problems found at airports and to address other phobias for which exposure would be difficult or potentially dangerous (Weiderhold, Bouchard & Loranger, 2014).

A fear of flying is a particularly interesting phobia because in many cases information can attenuate potential triggers for that fear. For example, if one is not familiar with flying, many of the routine aspects of flying might be triggers for anxiety. One might naïvely expect that once a plane leaves the terminal that it will go to the end of the runway and take off. For those of you who frequently fly at busy airports, you realize how naïve that expectation is. You are likely to be in a long line, and the progress of that line can be slow. Two or three planes may take off in a row, and then, suddenly, no planes take off. The reason is likely that other planes are about to land on that same runway, but you cannot see that given the limited visibility that you have from the plane's cabin. So you might imagine that something is going wrong at the airport or with your plane and that is why you are not taking off.

Most fearful flyers find the voice of the pilot to be reassuring, and most pilots will give their passengers information when they have the time to do so. They might, for example, let passengers know that they are seventh in line to take off and that they expect to be in the air in about twelve minutes. They can do that when they are on the ground because they are not nearly as busy as they will be during the takeoff. However, once the takeoff starts, the pilots are busy making sure that everything is smooth until they get to roughly ten thousand feet. A seasoned traveler knows this and does not expect the pilot to say anything during this time, although the cabin attendant usually will make announcements. But a worried flyer might interpret the fact that the pilot is no longer providing information to suggest that something is wrong, when in fact it is normal.

As the plane taxis to the end of the runway for takeoff, the pilots are running through checklists, and some of the items on the checklists may result in experiences that puzzle and perhaps scare a worried flyer. For example, pilots usually check to make sure that backup power will kick in automatically in the event of a normal loss of electrical power. That means that the lights may go off and then come right back on. The pilots will typically check to make sure that the control surfaces on the wings operate, and passengers looking out the window may see parts of the wing moving up and down for no apparent reason. Pilots prepare the plane for takeoff by adjusting the shape of the wing to give it more lift. Again, if you are a seasoned flyer, you may not know why these things are happening, but you do know that all these things are normal and happen on almost every flight. Teaching fearful flyers what to expect can dramatically reduce the likelihood that the situations will trigger a rapid increase in anxiety. Note again that knowing this information does not eliminate anxiety, but it can reduce the impact of events that may trigger anxiety or dramatically increase it.

Finally, a fear of flying may not be so much a fear of flying itself but rather a fear of meeting expectations as a passenger. In other words, the person knows that planes are safe and unlikely to crash, but the person is not sure what to do at the airport. Unless people have flown, they may not know that, even though every airport looks different, they are remarkably similar in their operation. Telling people how to check in, what to expect when they go through security, how they will board the plane, and what they should do when they arrive at their destination will go a long way to making them feel in control of the flying experience. Knowing that they can follow signs to the baggage claim at any airport and that there will be guidance at that baggage claim area about where to get one's bag can reduce a lot of anxiety. Knowing that ground transportation is usually out the door right next to the baggage claim can reduce anxiety about how to get to their hotel.

The point of these last couple of paragraphs is that a careful analysis of the situations that trigger anxiety can often uncover issues other than what is implied by the diagnosis of a phobia. A fear of flying may not be a fear of flying, or at least some of the fear around flying is not what you might expect from that label. Therapists that specialize in the psychological treatment of anxiety and its disorders routinely probe for these subtle features that can lead to a more effective outcome.

Flooding

Unlike systematic desensitization, flooding involves experiencing anxiety at its highest-level right from the beginning. With a snake phobia, for example, flooding would involve immediate contact with the snake. As you might guess, the anxiety during flooding is intense and sometimes overwhelming. Flooding has one major advantage and one major disadvantage. The major advantage is that it tends to work quickly; the major disadvantage is that it can backfire. If you use flooding to treat anxiety, the anxious person must remain in the situation until the anxiety goes down, or the anxiety will be even more intense in that situation in the future.

What if the anxiety does not go down? There is no need to worry; it will. Anxiety will decrease for a very simple reason. Anxiety takes an enormous amount of energy because it involves such high arousal in the body. The body is only capable of putting out that much energy for so long. Then, we are simply too fatigued to be anxious. Think of anxiety in flooding as something akin to running a marathon. Even if you are in superb shape, you will have virtually no energy left when you cross the finish line. If you are not in superb shape, you will hit the wall and not be able to continue long before you reach the finish line.

Flooding is not the treatment of choice if you indeed have a choice. Systematic desensitization has fewer risks and is less stressful for those undergoing the treatment. But there are situations in which flooding is a necessity. In obsessive-compulsive disorder, for example, any exposure-based treatment is almost certainly going to be flooding. The reason is that when the OCD symptoms are challenged, the anxiety experienced is incredibly intense. It is not possible to develop an anxiety hierarchy with this disorder. So behavioral treatment for OCD (exposure with response prevention) only works with individuals who are highly motivated.

Interoceptive Desensitization

Systematic desensitization focuses on the anxiety produced by the object or situation that is feared. However, for many people with intense anxiety, the anxiety itself becomes a source of fear. We introduced this concept when we discussed panic disorder. Many people who develop panic disorder appear to be prone to develop this disorder because of what we call *anxiety sensitivity*. This appears to be an inborn fear of the symptoms of anxiety (McNally, 2002). People with anxiety sensitivity are literally anxious about being anxious. Because they are worried that they will lose control when they are anxious, people with anxiety problems become acutely sensitive to any feeling suggesting that the anxiety is building.

The problem with anxiety sensitivity is that the physiological symptoms of anxiety, which become cues for more anxiety in those who are anxiety sensitive, are not unique to anxiety. When we are anxious, for example, we often feel winded, as if we can barely breathe. We get that same effect by exercising. If you run up three flights of stairs, you will find yourself breathing hard and feeling like you are not getting enough oxygen. Your labored breathing is a reaction to the biological need of your body for oxygen because of exercise. If you are in good shape, you will generally be able to meet that biological need and will experience less stress on your breathing. However, if you are not in good shape, even minor physical exercise will make you feel like you cannot get enough air.

If you are sensitive to the symptoms of anxiety, you will do your best to avoid them. You might, for example, choose to take the elevator rather than the stairs for even a couple of flights. If you avoid exercise because it makes you breathe hard, it will not be long before you are out of shape. Consequently, when you take a single flight of stairs, you will be winded, and if you have anxiety sensitivity, you will be anxious about being winded. In other words, the avoidance of the feelings associated with anxiety may make those feelings more likely to occur in everyday life.

Interoceptive desensitization is a process of deliberately producing the physiological symptoms associated with anxiety so that one can desensitize to those feelings, thus decreasing their ability to trigger anxiety. You can create the feeling of being winded by running in place for a few seconds. You can create lightheadedness by putting your head between your legs for several seconds and then quickly sitting up straight. If you do that, it will take a moment for your blood pressure to adjust sufficiently to push blood into the brain, and thus the feeling of lightheadedness. Each of the symptoms of anxiety can be easily produced in the office or at home with an action like the ones just described.

Interoceptive desensitization involves repeatedly producing the sensations and then managing the anxiety that is a response to those sensations. The therapist starts by assessing which of the sensations tend to trigger anxiety. It is rare that every potential interoceptive trigger is potent for everyone with anxiety sensitivity, so testing for individual sensitivity identifies which sensations produce the greatest level of anxiety. Listed below are the most common sensations and the procedures used to stimulate those sensations.

Although there is no standard set of techniques to produce the various interoceptive feelings associated with panic, there are several techniques that work well. For example, you can increase your heart rate by walking up a flight of stairs quickly or running in place. You can make yourself dizzy by spinning around; to avoid the risk of falling, the therapist will typically have you use a desk chair that swivels. You can make yourself lightheaded by putting your head between your legs for twenty seconds and then quickly sitting up straight. You can give yourself the sensation of not being able to breathe by breathing through a small hose or puckering your lips as if you were breathing through a small hose. Very quickly, you will start to hyperventilate from such breathing. You can create dizziness by shaking your head hard. These are only a few of the many interoceptive triggers that can be produced in the lab or office to desensitize individuals who have become overly sensitive to these feelings.

Virtually every sensation in the list above can be scaled. For example, if the feeling of dizziness creates anxiety, one can create mild dizziness with a gentle shaking of the head and more intense dizziness with more intense shaking. Desensitization of a particular interoceptive sensation starts with a mild level, which the person tolerates and manages with deep breaths and muscle relaxation.

Once that level is easily managed, the intensity is increased, and the process is repeated. In that sense, it is a form of systematic desensitization in which the focus is not on an object or situation but rather on internal feelings.

Other Forms of Desensitization

Interoceptive desensitization is rarely used by itself in treating anxiety. It is typically combined with other exposure treatments. For example, it is common in treating panic disorder to challenge agoraphobic avoidance by leaving the office or home with the therapist and going to those places that have been avoided by the individual. This type of exposure is called **in vivo exposure**. It involves facing the feared situation in the real world rather than through imagination **(imaginal exposure)** or through virtual reality **(VR exposure)**. With panic-disordered individuals, anxiety sensitivity is common, so interoceptive exposure is often included. Because anxiety sensitivity often supercharges anxiety responses, it is common to do interoceptive exposure before or during the early stages of in vivo exposure.

Often the therapist directs the client during each type of exposure. The therapist can usually help the client to manage anxiety, to coach the client about the most effective ways to manage anxiety, and to provide a sense of safety that facilitates taking emotional risks during the exposure. However, the goal of therapy is to eliminate the need for therapy. Therefore, clients are encouraged to continue the exposure exercises as homework assignments, usually at a slightly lower level of intensity. Remember that we are programmed to unlearn anxiety slowly, so repeated exposure will be necessary, and not all exposure requires the presence of a therapist. The homework assignments early in therapy tend to be modest and easily accomplished if the client is motivated to do them. As the client progresses, confidence builds, and the client can take on more challenging homework assignments. Eventually, the therapist is unnecessary. The client understands the process, knows how to design exposure exercises to address any new anxiety issues that might arise, and has the anxiety-management skills to do the exposure successfully.

Skill-Based Treatments

When anxiety is triggered by situations in which people are likely to be judged, how well we perform is directly related to how anxious we feel. Moreover, how well we expect to perform based on experience is also directly related to how anxious we feel. Therefore, anything that can be done to improve performance reduces anxiety in the situation and the anxiety we experience as we anticipate the situation.

Some people judge others based on things that are outside of their control, such as skin color. We correctly condemn such judgments. We condemn such judgments because the individual has no way of improving performance. However, we do not generally condemn judgments of people's performance when improving that performance is possible. For example, when we go to see a play, we expect the actors to be entertaining and engrossing. That takes skill and considerable effort. Imagine doing the same play night after night for months at a time. There will be nights when actors do not feel motivated to give their best. But if they do not give their best, their performance will suffer, and their audience will be rightly disappointed. The same is true for ballplayers, musicians, and colleagues in a business environment.

Performers, athletes, and business professionals are typically well trained so they can compete with others. The skills around which most people experience performance anxiety are rarely at that level. Musicians who have been performing for years are likely to be comfortable with their skills, especially if they have been successful. Those same musicians performing as high school sophomores in a band with friends may likely experience considerable performance anxiety. Business professionals that chair two meetings a day and speak to groups several times a week almost certainly have those responsibilities in part because they perform well in those tasks. But those same business professionals may well have been anxious giving talks in high school. The principle here is that the more skilled you are at any task, the more confident you will be that you can perform that task in front of others who will be judging you. Unfortunately, there is no way to instantly build those skills. Even the most natural of public speakers will initially be little better than average in their speaking performance. They might well stand out compared to their peers, but their skills still need development. But most people are not natural public speakers, and therefore, when they begin giving public talks, they will struggle just to perform at an acceptable level.

Learning to build skills through practice requires a certain attitude. Carol Dweck (2006) identified the ideal attitude, which she called a **growth mindset**. The best way to understand a growth mindset is to look at its opposite: a **fixed mindset**. In a fixed mindset, we believe that our skills are inborn and remain stable throughout life. We might, for example, be intelligent, athletic, or socially effective. We know that we have those skills because of our performance. For example, intelligent people do better in school and learn things easily. But in a fixed mindset, taking on a challenge can be distressing. If you try to learn something difficult, you will likely fail initially and may repeatedly fail until you finally master the new material. Those failures are upsetting because they challenge your sense of being intelligent. So you avoid trying things that are too difficult because you do not want your image of yourself as intelligent to be challenged. The result is that you fail to learn new things and build your skills.

In contrast, in a growth mindset, you view characteristics like intelligence as fluid. Your intelligence increases as you learn more. It is still emotionally challenging to take on difficult tasks because you will inevitably fail until you master the new material, but you understand that such failures are not a sign that you are not intelligent, but rather the cost of becoming more intelligent. In a growth mindset, you understand that public speaking is a skill and that no one is great at this skill without practice. The more public talks you give, the better you become at preparing and delivering the talk. Moreover, the practice also gives you an opportunity to learn to manage whatever anxiety you might be experiencing. Constructive feedback on your talks, instead of being threatening, is a shortcut to getting better. You start to view people who give such feedback as coaches rather than people who doubt your ability. A growth mindset really does promote growth.

Public speaking anxiety is an excellent example because it is so ubiquitous. It is rare for people to be comfortable in public speaking the first time they do it, even if their public speaking skills are unusually good. One reason oral presentations are often required in high school and college courses is that they give students practice in this important skill. Most universities require students to take at least one course in public speaking, and those universities may offer courses that include presentations. But many universities have such large classes that the opportunity for such training is limited. That is one reason why organizations like Toastmasters International exist. This is a group that allows individuals to practice public speaking skills in front of other members of the group. There may be individuals there who can critique talks and suggest ways of improving one's performance, but the most valuable part is simply the practice and the support of the other people in the group as you practice. Listening to other speakers often gives ideas on how to enhance your own public speaking skills. Those examples suggest great ways of capturing the audience. Admittedly, some examples are counterexamples that show approaches that are ineffective, but those examples can also be valuable. They tell you what to avoid doing.

Social phobias often illustrate the principle that the rich get richer. If one overcomes the natural fear of public speaking early, one is likely to engage in public speaking frequently. Each time people give a talk, they get feedback on how they are doing and thus can improve their speaking skills. Moreover, repeated exposure to giving talks gradually decreases anxiety and at the same time builds confidence. If, on the other hand, one avoids public speaking because of anxiety around public speaking, one does not have the chance to either build the skills to be a better speaker or develop the anxiety management techniques to be comfortable in front of people.

One way to understand this process is to think back to your first day of high school. Imagine what it felt like. If you are like most incoming freshmen, you had little idea about what was expected and were overwhelmed by the confidence of the upper-class students. But in a couple of years, you figured out what was expected and developed the same confidence that you so admired in the juniors and seniors when you first started. Imagine what it would have been like had you entered high school and gone into a state of suspended animation for three years. You would now be a junior or senior with the social skills and confidence of a typical incoming freshman. If you thought you were anxious on your first day of high school, imagine how anxious you would be three years later if your skills and confidence had not advanced at all in those three years.

This example illustrates two critical points in understanding the value of treating a social phobia. The first is that you do not need to take someone from 0 to 100 to achieve your goal. For example, if you are focused on a fear of public speaking, you want to get clients to the point at which they can give an adequate talk and manage the inevitable anxiety. That will give them sufficient confidence to give other public talks, which will allow them to build their skills and their ability to manage anxiety. The second point is that if people fail to overcome anxiety early, they will not just fail to progress. They will move backward compared to their peers. In theory, they can always catch up at some point, but it becomes increasingly difficult to work on something when you are so obviously behind other people. Consequently, people with social phobias may very well give up on the idea of catching up.

There are so many situations that involve performance and judgment and thus generate anxiety. Consequently, it is impossible to cover how you would incorporate skills training into each of those situations. Therefore, I have selected two situations that often involve social anxiety as examples of how to incorporate skills training. Since the fear of public speaking is the most common social phobia, I will start with that situation. I have chosen dating as the second situation because it is common to experience anxiety around dating, and the skills used in dating situations are very different from the skills in public speaking, and the way that those skills are typically developed are also different. There are courses to help you improve your public speaking, but there are rarely courses on how to be more effective at dating.

Public Speaking Skills

The skills associated with public speaking have been extensively studied by academics in university communications departments. These skills can easily fill an entire book, and that is not the purpose of this book. It is common for the treatment of public speaking anxiety to utilize existing public speaking training programs in conjunction with the efforts to teach people how to manage their anxiety when giving public talks. However, it is also common for the therapist to provide some basic public speaking training, complete with homework exercises to polish those skills. Remember, social anxieties are, by their nature, performance anxieties. People are afraid of public speaking because they are afraid that they will do it badly and that others will think less of them. Reducing anxiety but failing to improve public speaking skills will never be effective.

There are dozens of trade books on how to improve your public speaking skills. Selectively reading one or two of those books and doing the exercises they suggest will improve your ability to give a good presentation. The books are particularly helpful in creating the content for good presentations. For example, the first paragraph of a talk is very important in capturing the audience. If you do not tell the audience in the first one hundred words why they should listen to what you have to say, they may not listen. If, on the other hand, you think about what is important in your talk and promise to cover that important material in the first few words, you will capture the audience. Consequently, the rest of the presentation is likely to go much better. The same is true of the last one hundred words. Too many people end their talks abruptly with no closure. With just one hundred words, you can provide closure that will tie up the most important points of your talk. This is the take-home message you want your listeners to remember. Your audience will be left thinking about the important ideas you shared with them. These are skills, and like all skills, they can be learned. These are not easy skills, so they will not be learned quickly, but if you improve those skills, you will improve the effectiveness of your speaking.

Other skills that can be taught are how to use slides effectively. How often have you heard a talk that included PowerPoint slides that were, at best, distracting? They added nothing and often were useless. Many of the books on public speaking now cover how to do effective slides. Effective eye contact with your audience can make a huge difference, but if the speaker is reading a presentation, it is hard to look up and maintain eye contact. However, if you practice giving a presentation from an outline or from the implicit outline on your slides, you will be better at maintaining eye contact, which is critical to connecting with your audience.

Humor is often effective in presentations, but not always. If the humor is forced and out of context, it is more likely to turn off the audience than to help you to connect with the audience. Humor is one of those delicate skills that can be difficult to master unless it is part of your personality. Humor is never just a function of words; it requires timing and facial expressions to make it work. If you plan to use humor, practice it out loud in front of a mirror. Do not rush it, and do not overdo it. Humor can break the ice with the audience; however, it rarely transmits the most important aspects of your message.

It is important for speakers to explain things clearly and in a language that can easily be followed. If you are reading something and you do not understand some aspect, you can always reread that section. However, audiences do not have that option, so it is your responsibility as a speaker to be as clear as possible. Details can be important in buttressing an argument, but in a traditional talk, there is not a lot of room for details unless you want to put your audience to sleep. These are the kinds of principles a speaker needs to develop over time. Even the very best speakers have violated these principles, but because they violated them and saw the consequences, they learned to do their talks differently. That is how they became good speakers.

Finally, most people think of giving a public talk as getting up and speaking. That perspective fails to appreciate that some of the most difficult time is waiting your turn to speak. This is when anxiety builds and sometimes overwhelms a person. The natural tendency in such situations is to focus on your talk, but unfortunately, such a focus will usually increase your anxiety. Preparing people with public speaking anxiety to handle their anxiety before the talk is critical. It is also important to cover details that seem unnecessary, such as how the equipment works. If one is presenting a talk with PowerPoint slides, it is important to be confident that you can start the slide show quickly and correctly. The best way to trigger panic before a presentation is to discover that you cannot get the slides to work while everyone is watching you try. Things like how to load the PowerPoint presentation, how to advance the slides, and how to use the microphone effectively may seem like they are unimportant, but trust me, if any of those are not working, they can absolutely overwhelm.

Dating Skills

Dating can be one of the most difficult social tasks that we are ever asked to do. Technically, we are not asked to do it, but most of us feel a great need to find a suitable partner, and the way we do that is through dating. What makes dating so difficult is that it is one of the most important situations in which we are evaluated, and we are evaluated on dimensions that are usually very important to our self-esteem. Moreover, both parties on a date are evaluating each other. Imagine what it would be like if you tried to buy a car but the car had a say in whether it wanted to be bought by you. Many people find buying a car difficult enough because they want to make sure they get the best car, but what if you found the best car and it said, "No thanks"? That is what dating is. You are looking for the best person for you, but there is no guarantee that that person will feel the same about you.

It is possible to learn some things about dating from reading books. There are a few trade books that cover ideas on how to be successful at dating, but I find it interesting that there are more books published on how to be a pickup artist. Being a pickup artist is essentially using dating not to get to know someone but rather to take advantage of them. Dating is a common topic in most novels, but I am always amazed at how most people in novels are immensely skilled at dating. They are knowledgeable, personable, well-read, and great conversationalists, who have little difficulty connecting emotionally with other people. Most people are not that skilled, and even the ones who do become that skilled do not start out that way.

So how do you learn how to be better at dating? How can a therapist help you to be better at dating? The single best thing that you can do is become better at conversing with people outside of dates. You can practice these skills by carrying on conversations with people at work, people you meet in other settings, and your own friends and family. Although it may be possible to include sexual innuendo that is not obnoxious in conversations with a date, it is a risky ploy. The best first dates usually involve just a lot of discussion. One misconception that many people have about discussions on a date is that they think that the goal is to show your brilliance in the conversation. It is far more important to show your interest in your partner by listening to what they say and asking them questions. This skill can be learned easily with a little practice and a desire to focus on your date.

Of course, when you are having casual conversations with friends or people you meet, you may not be expecting a sexual relationship or the kind of long-term relationship found in marriage. That is a big transition in a dating relationship, and it is not always clear when and how that transition will happen. Many people are anxious about dating because they do not know how to make that transition. They worry that they might be going too slow or too fast. This is not something that is taught easily, and there are no simple rules that guide this transition. Dating is like a dance in that one partner makes a move and the other either reciprocates or not. If the partner reciprocates, the first individual makes the next move. A move might be something as simple as touching the other person's arm, and the reciprocation might be no more than not pulling away or looking into the other person's eyes. Although one can ask, "Do you mind if I touch your arm?" it is rarely that explicit. Of course, touching one's arm is an intimate gesture but not so grossly inappropriate as touching their bottom or some other sensitive part of their anatomy. Such behavior is inappropriate and may represent sexual harassment.

Although it is possible to go too slowly in a relationship, most experts encourage people to be patient rather than to push it too quickly. Do not be fooled by what you see in the movies. There are rare occasions in which people fall into each other's arms and end up in bed together. It is far more likely that that natural process will happen over weeks than over minutes. But movies usually last two hours and not weeks, so they tend to give a false impression of how quickly a relationship develops.

As much as possible, you want to make dating fun. Find out what your potential partner likes, and if possible, find something that both of you like. Have fun together; do not put too much pressure to make this the love of your life. It is highly unlikely that the first person you date will be the love of your life. But you can still have a good date and a good time and accept that you might not be right for one another. There is research that suggests that trying too hard to have every date lead to marriage and children can create overwhelming anxiety that makes successful dating almost impossible (Prisbell, 1987).

Finally, if the goal of dating is to find a potential partner, never forget what most potential partners desire. They want someone they can trust, someone who is warm, caring, and dependable. They want someone who will think about the ones they love first and not about themselves. It would be nice if they were wealthy, extremely successful, physically attractive, and respected by everyone. The best way to find the kind of person you want to partner with is to be the kind of person they will want to partner with. Dating can be frightening because it can be very hard on one's self-esteem. However, it is good to remember that the other person is likely equally frightened that their partner will not find them attractive. Be yourself but do your best to be the best human being possible.

Chapter Summary

The behavioral perspective introduced the first effective treatment for anxiety (systematic desensitization), and it continues to provide new insights and effective approaches for the management of anxiety and anxiety disorders. The key element required in all successful treatment of anxiety (exposure) is a behavioral concept. Without exposure, it is highly unlikely that anxiety will decrease. You can either use gradual exposure, such as systematic desensitization, or a more aggressive exposure technique, such as flooding. Although most exposure is to the objects or situations that make us anxious, recent research suggests that for some individuals, the feelings of anxiety themselves make the person anxious. In that case, the exposure is focused on those feelings in addition to the objects or situations that create anxiety.

Behavioral techniques have also given us ways of managing anxiety during exposure. Progressive muscle relaxation and deep breathing effectively reduce anxiety without resorting to drugs. They give people a way of managing their anxiety during exposure.

In many situations, the primary reason for anxiety is that there is doubt about whether the person can perform adequately in each situation. In that sense, the anxiety is doing exactly what it is supposed to do: be a signal that there might be risk and a motivator to prepare to handle that risk. When performance is an issue, anxiety treatment must go beyond the management of anxiety. The treatment must also seek to improve the performance so that there is less of a reason to be anxious. In situations in which our performance is judged, there are usually clear criteria by which we are judged and instructing people on how best to meet those criteria can make a huge difference in their treatment.

Chapter 13

Cognitive Approaches to

Treatment

The cognitive approach to therapy has a long and powerful history. Cognitive treatment approaches are among the most effective and the most flexible treatments that we have. Cognitive therapy rests on the idea that we respond not just to reality but also to our interpretation of reality. We interpret situations, trying to make sense of them, and that interpretation will affect how we respond both behaviorally and emotionally. For example, if we fail to effectively handle social interactions, we might assume that everyone makes mistakes and that we need to apologize and move on. However, people who are depressed tend to make very different interpretations, viewing their mistakes as proof that they are failures. That interpretation tends to feed the depression, making it worse and, unfortunately, also making it more likely that they will continue to berate themselves for every single mistake they make.

The cognitive approach to treating anxiety has an intriguing contradiction. Although we are perfectly capable of talking ourselves into anxiety, we are generally incapable of talking ourselves out of anxiety. That is one of the reasons why the cognitive approach is almost always coupled with the behavioral approach; without behavioral exposure to the things that make us anxious, the anxiety is unlikely to decrease. So, you might ask, if it is almost impossible to talk ourselves out of anxiety, what good is the cognitive approach to the treatment of anxiety?

The cognitive approach may not help us to unlearn anxiety, but it can help us to take the behavioral steps that are necessary to unlearn anxiety. If we feel that a situation is dangerous and therefore do not want to put ourselves into that situation, we will continue to avoid the situation and thus never conquer the anxiety. The cognitive approach can convince us that there is little reason to be anxious even while it fails to reduce our anxiety. If we can convince ourselves that the risk is low, we can get ourselves to take that risk and begin an exposure-based treatment.

The second value of the cognitive approach is that cognitions often amplify anxiety. We need to learn how we increase our anxiety through our thoughts so that we can reverse that process and prevent it. We might, for example, notice our feeling of anxiety in a situation and start to get anxious about being anxious. Cognitively, we are telling ourselves something like, "If I get anxious, I will lose control," or, "I am the only one who gets anxious in such situations." Recognizing such negative statements and challenging them can be valuable in preventing the vicious circle often found in anxiety disorders.

Before we jump into the process of cognitive therapy for anxiety, I want to make one last comment. People who experience anxiety often get upset with themselves when they learn that their own cognitions may be enhancing that anxiety. They take that information as evidence that they are responsible for their anxiety. Not only is such a feeling unwarranted, but it also fails to recognize that having our cognitions contributing to our anxiety is an asset. Although it is possible that other species besides humans can communicate about danger, it is unlikely that they do it as well as we do. Someone can tell us how a disease is transmitted and encourage us to do something as simple as washing our hands to prevent disease. Pilots can be trained to avoid situations that might lead to the loss of control of their plane without having to experience those situations. Factory workers can be told about specific dangers, which might not be obvious, that may harm them if they fail to take appropriate precautions while working around heavy machinery. The ability of human beings to understand risk after no more than just an explanation of its existence is one of the most valuable skills we have. It means that people can dramatically reduce their risks by simply learning where the risks are and how to avoid them.

Our cognitions do have the potential of increasing our anxiety, but what gives our cognitions that ability is the same thing that gives us the ability to dramatically reduce risk through communication. In other words, such cognitions are a two-edged sword, sometimes getting in the way but more often being enormously valuable. With practice, we can overcome the negative aspects without affecting the positive features of those cognitions.

Cognitive Errors and Distortions

The most pervasive cognitive distortion around anxiety is the idea that anxiety is a weakness, and one that to be avoided or eliminated. Some of you may be reading this and saying to yourself that that statement is true. If you have had to deal with anxiety, and you have berated yourself for not being able to handle the anxiety, it is hard to imagine anxiety as anything other than a weakness and a problem. The easiest way to understand why this statement is false is to imagine what it would be like if you had no anxiety. If you had no anxiety and you had an important deadline coming up, you likely would have little incentive to work hard to get everything done by the deadline. If you had no anxiety, you probably would not be bothered by individuals thinking you were irresponsible, hateful, or hurtful because of things that you did, did not do, or said. Our anxiety about how people view us is one of the driving forces that socializes us. As I pointed out earlier, there is a group of individuals that experiences much less anxiety than the typical person. We have a name for that group: psychopaths or sociopaths. I am guessing that if you are reading this book, joining that group is not your goal.

Another common cognitive error surrounding anxiety is that your anxiety level is much higher than that of your peers. The likely reason for that belief is that you fail to appreciate that you judge the anxiety of others by what you see. In contrast, you judge your own anxiety by what can be seen and what you feel, which cannot be observed by others. Consequently, comparing our anxiety to the anxiety of others is really a comparison of apples and oranges. More accurately, it is a comparison of apples with apples plus oranges, with apples being the external signs of anxiety and oranges the internal feelings of anxiety.

This leads to another cognitive error: the belief that the anxiety that we feel is the anxiety that others see in us. In learning to deal with anxiety, the first task is to learn to hide it from outside observers. If you tend to be anxious, the idea of hiding that anxiety seems impossible, but it is much easier than you imagine. At very high levels of anxiety, your body may physically shake, your face may flush significantly, and your voice may crack. However, it takes incredibly high levels of anxiety for these things to occur in most people. The truth is that the anxiety we feel is largely invisible to other people unless we give them a clue. The most likely clue is that we tell them we are feeling anxious. Once we tell them that, they might well be able to observe subtle clues to our anxiety, but those clues are often so subtle they likely would not have been noticed had we not told people we were anxious.

Yet another cognitive error is the idea that you will be unable to control your anxiety. Often this idea involves feeling that others can control their anxiety, and therefore your inability to control your anxiety is yet another sign of weakness. Everyone can control their anxiety with sufficient practice and experience. That includes you, even if you think your anxiety is stronger than that experienced by anyone else. The belief that you cannot control your anxiety can easily be a self-fulfilling prophecy. You feel anxiety, and you doubt that you will be able to handle it. That doubt increases your anxiety, which gives you additional evidence that you may not be able to handle it. In short order, the anxiety starts to spiral out of control.

Note that all these cognitive distortions will feed the anxiety you are experiencing. Anxiety is normal, and everyone experiences anxiety. We are more aware of our own anxiety because we can feel the emotion; when we judge the anxiety of others, all we can see are the external manifestations of anxiety. The internal feeling of anxiety is often much stronger than the external manifestations, so we judge ourselves as lacking in our ability to manage anxiety. That judgment leads to more anxiety.

Finally, we are often unaware of these distorted cognitions, although we can typically infer their presence based on the thoughts we are experiencing. For example, if we are criticizing ourselves for being unable to manage our own anxiety and note that others seem to be able to manage their anxiety easily, we must be telling ourselves that we have more anxiety than other people are experiencing. Although that might be true, often that assumption is inaccurate. We simply cannot see the anxiety that others are experiencing, and at the same time, we are assuming that they can see our anxiety. In the next section, we will be talking about how to challenge these cognitive distortions. In most cases, we can simply assume that the distortions exist and actively challenge them even if we are unaware of which distortions are occurring.

Challenging Cognitions

Cognitive distortions are self-statements that influence the way we feel. We challenge those cognitive distortions with other self-statements that reinterpret our experiences. For example, a common self-statement in individuals who are troubled by anxiety is that anxiety is a sign of weakness and is something that should be eliminated. By now, you know better. Anxiety is a valuable response that facilitates our planning for difficult and potentially dangerous situations. It not only is not a sign of weakness, but it is also an indication that our planning and preparation system is functioning properly.

We can counter ineffective cognitive distortions by emphasizing alternative perspectives. For example, we can tell ourselves that anxiety is normal and healthy. We can tell ourselves that we do not like anxiety, but that does not mean anxiety is bad. We can tell ourselves that our anxiety is a powerful motivator that will help us be successful. We need to actively tell ourselves these things because the alternative cognitions have typically become so ingrained that they play automatically in our heads. However, we cannot tell ourselves any of these things unless we first learn to recognize that we have cognitive distortions that need to be challenged.

We can take almost any behavior, including thoughts, and make them automatic through repetition. If you are young enough to remember when you first learned to drive, you likely can vividly recall that it took all your concentration to remind yourself what you needed to do. You needed to constantly remind yourself to check the mirrors, check your speed, scan the sides of the road for potential hazards, and leave sufficient space in front of you in case the car in front of you stopped suddenly. We even had to remind ourselves to use the signals to tell people our intentions to change lanes or make a turn. It took so much concentration to be an adequate driver during those early months of driving that we found it difficult or impossible to carry on a conversation. Even after driving became second nature, we were often overwhelmed if we were suddenly driving in heavy traffic in a city that we had never driven in before. If you have been driving for years, most of what I just described is no longer true. In fact, you probably have had the experience of driving home and not remembering the drive. Driving has become so automatic that you can easily carry on conversations or get lost in your own thoughts and still manage to drive with reasonable safety.

This ability to take tasks and turn them into automatic behavior is incredibly valuable. We are only capable of doing one thing at a time if that thing requires concentration. However, if we overlearn the task to the point that it is now automatic, we can do more than one thing at a time. We can, for example, drive while carrying on a conversation with our passengers.

Automatic tasks require much less energy and therefore much less concentration, but the disadvantage of automatic tasks is that we typically sacrifice control. When we feel we need more control, we often check out of the automatic nature of a task and take over control. For example, you might be a skilled driver and rarely need to do much thinking when you are driving. But if you suddenly find yourself in heavy and fast-moving traffic, you likely will stop

213

conversing with your passengers and focus more on what is going on around you. You do the same thing if you find yourself in a bad snowstorm with slippery roads. Under those circumstances, you need more concentration and more control, so you exercise that control. You do not trust your automatic driving behavior because you do not have control over it in the same way you do when you pay attention to what you are doing.

There are situations in which tasks become so automatic that exercising voluntary control will interfere. If you are a good typist, you likely are at the point where you just think about what you want to type, and it magically appears on the screen. You are not paying attention to where your fingers are going or even to how the words are being spelled. These things have become so automatic that they seem to happen magically. We need them to be that automatic if we are going to be able to write while sitting at a computer. It takes concentration to write. We must think about what we want to say and how we want to say it, and we must think about where our writing is headed. We simply could not do that if we had to focus our attention on moving our fingers to hit individual letters or selecting letters to type individual words. This is an excellent example of the value of turning routine behavior into automatic behavior.

Being able to type automatically while you are thinking about the ideas is a wonderful thing. I cannot imagine trying to write this book if I had to think about spelling individual words and moving my fingers to type individual letters. But if you want an example of a situation that is easily disrupted by trying to take over conscious control, try thinking about typing when you are doing it. If you are a good typist, the words seem to appear magically with very few errors. However, if you pay attention to your typing, you will find that the typing deteriorates. There is hesitancy and missed letters, and you find it increasingly difficult to keep track of where you are headed.

Fortunately for us, the self-statements that influence our emotional responses are rarely so ingrained that they are disrupted by our efforts to think about them and challenge them. In that sense, they are different from the ability to write at the computer and have the words seem to appear magically. Moreover, what we will be doing is replacing some self-statements with other self-statements. We might be replacing a statement like "If I am anxious, it means that I am weak," with a statement like, "Anxiety is normal, and I need to pay attention to the anxiety to be better prepared." You might note that these two statements are mutually exclusive. If anxiety is normal, it should not be a sign of weakness. If you are doing things to be better prepared for the future, it makes no sense to criticize yourself for this positive activity. These ideas are obvious when we think about them, but the key aspect of automatic behavior and automatic thoughts is that we are not thinking about them. They are simply happening. Until we start to think about them and actively challenge them, automatic thoughts and behaviors will continue, even if they are detrimental. A cognitive therapist working with someone experiencing anxiety problems helps that person recognize their automatic thoughts and coaches them on effective ways to challenge them.

Let's look at some automatic thoughts that are common in individuals who are troubled by anxiety and see how we might challenge them by practicing alternative thoughts. A common automatic thought is that we believe that others can see our anxiety. That thought is not entirely untrue because, if our anxiety is strong enough, there will be observable elements. However, most of the time the anxiety that we are experiencing internally is not visible to other people. We can challenge the feeling that others will know when we are anxious by simply stating that our internal feelings are personal and only available to ourselves. People cannot see what we are thinking or feeling; they can only see what we are doing. If we are feeling anxious and yet are still able to function, people will notice that we are functioning and assume that that means that any anxiety that we might be experiencing is under control.

A variation of the issue just described is a self-statement that our anxiety is worse than what other people experience. We can challenge that by deliberately telling ourselves that it only appears that our anxiety is worse because we can see something that no one else can see. That something is the feeling of anxiety. They can only see our behavior, and we can only see their behavior. If we want to judge our anxiety against other people's anxiety, we need to leave out our internal feelings and focus only on behavior. Only then can we make a legitimate comparison of our anxiety with the anxiety of others.

Breaking the Vicious Cycle

Our thoughts or cognitions can often increase our anxiety. We have already talked about how those thoughts can increase anxiety and how we can challenge those thoughts to prevent that increase in anxiety. Let me remind you that virtually all our anxiety is a result of our thoughts, and that fact is a good thing. Our ability to think about risks that we might face, which can lead to an increase in anxiety, also motivates us to prepare for the future.

The cognitions we have looked at so far increase anxiety because they create unrealistic demands on us. This is a very real effect and is often the source of a good deal of our excess anxiety. Note that I say *excess anxiety* because I want to separate it from *productive anxiety*. We want to manage excess anxiety; we never want to suppress productive anxiety. Instead, we want to use productive anxiety as a motivator to be better prepared.

There is a second class of cognitions that generates excessive anxiety, and this class is particularly troublesome because it generates anxiety rapidly and with little opportunity for us to challenge our thoughts. This class of cognitions involves the anxiety feeding itself. We talked about this phenomenon several times; here we will look at it from the standpoint of how to manage this source of this excessive anxiety.

Chances are you were drawn to the title of this book because you have viewed your anxiety as the enemy. You perhaps have viewed yourself as weak because of that anxiety, and I hope by now you have convinced yourself based on the arguments presented that you are neither abnormal nor dysfunctional. Experiencing anxiety is a healthy thing. Using that anxiety to motivate behavior is not only not dysfunctional but also is perhaps the greatest advantage that human beings have over other species.

Part of the reason that you may view anxiety as the enemy is that it feels to you like it is outside of your control. If you feel that way, you very likely respond to the anxiety by getting more anxious. If you view anxiety as a weakness, you will want to eliminate anxiety, but that is not possible unless you are brain-dead. If you are thinking, there will always be legitimate reasons to be anxious. But your contention that anxiety is a weakness will feed a panic response whenever you see yourself getting anxious. You literally become anxious about being anxious, and unlike productive anxiety, which leads to useful preparation, being anxious about being anxious does not lead to anything other than more anxiety.

In this section, we will talk about the things that you can do to prevent anxiety from feeding itself. The two management strategies involve focusing your attention away from the anxiety and reinterpreting the anxiety with a different label. They are both effective, although they work in different ways. In the initial phases in which anxiety is feeding itself, the refocusing option is the best because it prevents runaway anxiety. However, over the long run, learning to reinterpret the anxiety will, in time, give you automatic responses that will give you even better control of your anxiety.

Refocusing Attention

You cannot become anxious about being anxious unless you realize that you are anxious and focus your attention on that fact. But you learned earlier in this book that it is virtually impossible for us not to think about something by trying not to think about it. The more we try not to think about something, the more we think about it. In fact, the more we try not to think about something, the more likely we are to obsess about it. Everyone has experienced that. You go to bed hoping for a good night's sleep, and you start to think about things that worry you. The more you try not to think about those things, the more you think about them, until sleep becomes impossible.

217

There is a much more effective way to not think about something, and it takes advantage of the fact that our attention is a limited resource. For us to process anything, we need to focus our attention on it, at least if we want to process it effectively. Trying to read a book while you are watching your kids is likely to result in either a failure to absorb what you are reading or a failure to keep track of your kids. Doing two things at once is difficult. That means that the best way to not think about something is the think about something else instead. Psychologists refer to that as *refocusing your attention*. We need to focus our attention to process information effectively, but if we focus our attention on one thing, we will automatically be focusing our attention away from other things. Remember that crazy research study in which people were asked to watch and count the number of passes of a basketball? Focusing on counting those passes was enough to prevent most of the subjects from even noticing a guy walking through the scene in a gorilla suit.

The key to using this refocusing strategy is to identify things that are likely to capture our attention and do so successfully enough that they will work to distract us from whatever anxiety we might be feeling. There are certain things that tend to capture our attention easily. One item in that category is sudden, unexpected, and potentially dangerous events. You might be absolutely absorbed in reading the book in front of you, but if someone on the street loses control of their car and piles into your house, your attention will immediately be drawn to that event and away from the book in your lap.

Another category of events that tends to draw our attention is things that are personally interesting to us. A fascinating phenomenon that has been studied extensively is called the *cocktail party phenomenon*. You are at a party with a lot of people and loud background music. The noise is so loud that you can barely hear the people next to you. Yet somehow you hear someone across the room mention your name. This is not paranoia; this is a natural phenomenon of your attention being drawn to things that are relevant to you. Someone is talking about you; of course, you want to know what they have to say, and you hope that what they have to say is nice. The cocktail party phenomenon not only indicates how personally interesting material can draw our attention but also that part of our attention is always scanning background activity for things that might be of particular interest.

Human beings are social creatures. People vary on how outgoing they might be, but even introverted individuals are interested in social relationships and in people in general. People watching is perhaps the most interesting activity people do. Whether we are at the mall, taking a walk through the neighborhood, or sitting in a crowded theater waiting for a movie to start, it is hard not to watch what people are doing and speculate on the meaning of their activity. If there is something about the people that we find interesting or attractive, we will be even more inclined to watch them. For example, it is hard not to pay attention to a celebrity who happens to be where you are. If someone is engaged in an activity that is unusual or perhaps even bizarre, we are likely to be mesmerized by watching. This is the equivalent of rubbernecking as you drive by a serious traffic accident. You feel compelled to watch. If you see someone that you find sexually attractive, well-dressed, or unusually commanding in their manner, your interest will be aroused, and your attention is likely to be focused on them.

You can use these principles to shift your attention away from your anxiety or the source of your anxiety to something else. Again, you are taking advantage of a weakness in our attentional system. We are terrible at paying attention to two things at once. Focusing our attention on something else is often all it takes to reduce the spiral of anxiety that we experience when we focus on our anxiety. The question is, what can we pay attention to that will distract us from our own anxiety?

You will want to focus your attention on things that are so important that they will naturally grab your attention. For most people, your loved ones are the best example of items that can easily command your attention. You might remember the pride you felt when your daughter performed so well at a concert or the warm feeling you had as you cuddled with your spouse in front of a fire. You might focus on the vacation you are planning or the vacation you enjoyed so much last summer. You might focus on things that are simply important to you, such as how you want to handle a particular problem at work. The things you focus on do not even have to be real. The world around us might be real, but it is not always that fascinating. However, you may have fantasies that are perhaps unrealistic but certainly strong enough to capture your full attention. Sometimes tasks in front of us are more than demanding enough to capture full attention. We may be able to drive on a deserted road on intellectual cruise control, free to think about anything we want. However, if there is heavy traffic, our attention will be drawn to the demands of navigating that traffic.

Often the best thing to focus your attention on is right in front of you. For example, if you are in a job interview, you want to focus on the person doing the interview or on the nature of the workplace in which the interview is taking place. If you are focusing on those things, you will not be focusing on your own anxiety. If you must give a talk, focus on the audience and how they are responding to what you said. By focusing on them, you will not be focusing on yourself. If several other people are speaking before you, do not focus on the talk that you will be giving. Presumably, you worked hard on that talk, and you will be ready to give it when it is your time. Instead, focus on the other people who are speaking and see if you can formulate some good questions based on what they have said. That will completely capture your attention and thus focus your attention away from any anxiety that might be building.

Reinterpreting the Situation

There is a principle in cognitive therapy that we never respond to the situation but instead respond to our interpretation of the situation. A corollary of this principle is that we interpret situations subjectively. If people's interpretations were truly objective, we would all interpret those situations the same. It may be too strong to say that the interpretation of the situation is arbitrary, but it is certainly reasonable to argue that many situations could be interpreted in more than one way. If that is the case, it makes sense to use an interpretation that is both reasonable and serves us well.

A typical example is often used in the treatment of depression. People who are depressed often interpret a single mistake as evidence that the person is incapable of being successful. Clearly, that interpretation is neither objective nor does it serve people well. Everyone makes mistakes, and making mistakes is certainly not evidence that we can never be successful again. So, in treating depression, we seek to identify those interpretations that increase the person's sense of failure and thus contribute to an even deeper depression.

The kind of destructive and inaccurate cognitions found in anxiety situations usually involves an exaggeration of potential risk. For example, if one is concerned about public speaking, they may believe that their entire life will be ruined if they are unsuccessful with a given talk. Even the best public speakers have delivered some flat and ineffective speeches. Their lives were not ruined. A more reasonable interpretation is that it is important to do the best you can, but it does not need to be a perfect talk for it to be successful. Moreover, the way to become a good speaker is to keep speaking to give yourself a chance to improve those skills.

Here are some other examples of cognitions that can be modified to help manage anxiety. You can learn to interpret anxiety as a mechanism to motivate adaptive behavior rather than as a sign of weakness. You can consider anxiety as an appropriate response to a thorough assessment of the situation rather than as an unreasonable response to a situation in which bad outcomes are possible. You can challenge the idea that your anxiety is unreasonable because other people would not be anxious in the situation. It may very well be that the real problem is that these non-anxious people do not appreciate the potential risks. If you think about each of these situations, you will realize that the way you feel about yourself really does depend on how you interpret the situation and your emotional response to that situation. I am not suggesting that you should be Pollyannaish and ignore potential risks just so that you do not feel anxious. The entire theme of this book is the opposite argument. Rather, I am suggesting that sometimes it is easier to be comfortable with your own anxiety when you interpret that anxiety not as a weakness but as a potential strength.

Chapter Summary

Cognitive therapy can add a significant element to the treatment of anxiety and anxiety disorders. Most often, it is combined with behavioral therapy because little progress is possible for anxiety disorders without exposure. What cognitive therapy can add is a justification for doing the exposure and a mechanism to avoid the anxiety spiral that is so common in anxiety disorders. You cannot talk yourself out of anxiety, but you can talk yourself into challenging the anxiety because your rational analysis suggests that the anxiety is exaggerated. For example, you may be afraid of flying. Thinking about the statistics regarding the extremely low risk of flying will not stop your anxiety, but it may be enough to seek treatment and eventually fly. You will still be anxious when you do fly, even with treatment, because we are programmed to unlearn anxiety slowly. However, if you continue to fly, the anxiety will gradually decrease.

Although you may not be able to talk yourself out of anxiety, we all know that it is easy to talk yourself into anxiety. In fact, all of us are guilty of this at one time or another. When we see that we are anxious and we believe that we should not be anxious or that people will think less of us because we are anxious, we often over-respond. We start to get anxious about being anxious, which creates a vicious spiral. Learning to recognize and challenge early cognitions that contribute to the spiral essentially eliminates that process. We may still be anxious, but our anxiety is no longer spiraling out of control.

Chapter 14

Medical Treatments

I wish I could tell you that we have magic pills that can alleviate any anxiety. There are drugs, some legal and available from pharmacies and others illegal and available on the street, that can reduce the impact of anxiety. However, many have significant side effects, which we will cover in this chapter. But there are also medications that have proved themselves to be effective in controlling anxiety in those individuals who are at least momentarily overcome by it, though they have risks and side effects like everything else in life. In this chapter, I will cover the primary pharmacological treatments that are available to reduce anxiety, especially those that have been used effectively with anxiety disorders.

In addition to traditional medications, there are some other biological treatments that have been suggested for the treatment of anxiety. The research on these is less extensive and, in general, less persuasive, but in the interest of completeness, I will cover them in as fair a manner as I can.

I want to make one final point before we jump into the topic of this chapter. Medications are big business, and common problems like anxiety are the focus of extensive research to develop new drugs that are more effective. Therefore, this chapter will probably be outdated before many of the other chapters in this book. So, if you are reading the book 10 years after it was published, I would encourage you to do a little research to find out what things may have changed in the field.

Anti-Anxiety Drugs

We tend to label most of our drugs by their effect. Generally, those names include a problem with a prefix that indicates that it is the solution to the problem. So we have anti-diarrhea pills for those people who are experiencing diarrhea, and we have anti-constipation pills for those people who are experiencing constipation.

We have dozens of such pills. Some of the pills were developed to do something else. Antihistamines are an example. They were originally developed to reduce histamine-induced swelling and vasodilation, but we discovered that they were also effective in reducing the allergic response that many people experience to pollens and other airborne irritants to our respiratory system. Some antihistamines tend to make people drowsy, and so we warn about those effects on the label, suggesting that we should be careful driving or operating heavy equipment while taking the medications until we know how they will affect us. At the same time, we market those medications as potential sleep aids. Other antihistamines not only do not make people drowsy but are central nervous system stimulants. Antihistamines have even been found to be helpful in the treatment of certain cancers when combined with other medications. There are more than a dozen conditions that are treated by one or more antihistamines, but we still use the name that suggests that they only have one effect.

The class of drugs that we call **anti-anxiety drugs**, also known as **anxiolytic drugs,** tend to reduce the physiological sensations associated with anxiety. As a result, we feel less anxious. But like every drug, their effects are not nearly that specific. The largest class of currently used anti-anxiety drugs are benzodiazepines. These drugs have a long history and tend to be used extensively because of their effectiveness and relative safety. One of the first of these drugs was called Valium (the generic name is diazepam). It was once the most widely prescribed medication on the market, with almost all the prescriptions written by general practitioners for their patients who complained of anxiety. It was made famous by the Rolling Stones' song *"Mother's Little Helper."* At the height of its popularity, Valium was often referred to as the "little blue pill" (which was the color of the 10 mg tablet of diazepam). Today, if we referred to it as the "little blue pill," people might be confused because we have another popular little blue pill (Viagra, for erectile dysfunction).

All benzodiazepines tend to reduce anxiety but also tend to make one drowsy. Different benzodiazepines tend to emphasize one of these effects over the other. The ones that have a stronger anxiolytic effect are marketed for that purpose. Valium was in that category. The more commonly used benzodiazepine prescribed today is Xanax (the generic name is alprazolam). Benzodiazepines that tend to produce sleepiness (sedation) are marketed as sleep aids. One such drug is Ambien (the generic name is zolpidem tartrate). The evidence suggests that these drugs have their effect by influencing the neurotransmitter GABA. GABA is an inhibitory neurotransmitter, which means that it tends to reduce brain activity. This process of reducing brain activity seems to calm the entire system, which may explain both the anxiolytic and sedative effects of this class of drugs.

Anti-anxiety drugs tend to be used in two ways. Because many of them are fast acting, they can be taken only when one is anxious. Doctors will use phrases such as "as needed" or simply PRN (short for the Latin term *pro re nata*, meaning "when needed"). When prescribed in this way, the drugs are intended to reduce anxiety in specific situations and have a minimal effect on the body in other situations. If, for example, someone has a serious fear of flying but is required to fly to a funeral of a loved one, an anti-anxiety drug might be the most effective short-term treatment to allow the person to get on a plane and make it to the funeral. When used in this manner, these drugs tend to be safe and have minimal side effects other than inducing drowsiness.

The other way in which anti-anxiety drugs are used is to take them on a regular basis to manage the everyday anxiety that one experiences. Often doctors prefer to use benzodiazepines that have a longer half-life for this purpose because drugs with a longer half-life stay in your system longer and therefore maintain a constant blood level in between doses. The reason for this strategy is that

225

once your body becomes accustomed to these anti-anxiety drugs, it is common to experience a rebound phenomenon when the dosage of the drug is reduced. A rebound phenomenon is an increase in anxiety because the normal calming effect of this drug is no longer available and the body has become used to its calming effect. When a drug leaves the body quickly, it feels like a cut in dosage, and a rebound is experienced. An example that many people can relate to is nicotine, which is fast acting and has a very short half-life. Consequently, smokers quickly start craving a cigarette if they have gone any length of time without one.

When we discussed panic disorder earlier in the book, I noted that anti-anxiety drugs are not considered the treatment of choice. The reason is that the level of anxiety found in panic disorder is so high that the dosage of anti-anxiety drugs must be high to be effective. The dosage of anti-anxiety drugs to control the anxiety in panic disorder would put most non-panic individuals to sleep. Once the body has become accustomed to that dosage level, reducing the dosage is problematic. The rebound phenomenon from high-dose benzodiazepine regimens can be intense, and with panic disorder, that usually means anxiety levels high enough that panic attacks are common. [Remember, panic attacks are not the same as anxiety attacks. But when we believe that we are in potential danger (i.e., we are anxious), the alert system that is part of our fear response is on a hair trigger.]

Most prescriptions for benzodiazepines are still written by general practitioners. However, one should be careful about using this class of drugs with anxiety disorders. The general practitioner can easily handle occasional anxiety problems with such medications, but I would recommend seeing a psychiatrist for more serious anxiety problems because a psychiatrist is more likely to be familiar with the complications associated with the management of intense anxiety. Moreover, the behavioral and cognitive-behavioral approaches described in this book are often superior to drugs in their ability to manage anxiety without side effects and risks. However, there is a market for anti-anxiety drugs because not everyone is willing to put in the time and work that it takes to learn to manage anxiety without drugs.

Antidepressant Drugs

Antidepressants are called that because they were originally used to decrease depression. In general, they are reasonably effective at that goal. However, as you have learned, drugs have multiple effects. You might be surprised to hear that antidepressant drugs are currently more likely to be used in the treatment of anxiety disorders than depression.

There are three classes of antidepressant medications on the market: MAO inhibitors, tricyclic medications, and selective serotonin reuptake inhibitors (SSRIs). The MAO inhibitors were the first antidepressants, and they are still in use, but their use is limited because they have potentially lethal interactions with certain foods. Tricyclic medications are effective antidepressants, but they tend to have side effects that are uncomfortable, and therefore, many individuals find these drugs difficult to tolerate. SSRIs are about as effective as tricyclic medications, but they tend to have fewer side effects and are therefore tolerated more readily. For the treatment of anxiety disorders, SSRIs appear to be the most effective and are the most frequently used.

SSRIs are called that because they momentarily block the reuptake of serotonin from the synapse after their release. Without going into all the details of how nerve cells (i.e., **neurons**) function, we can break down the passage of signals along neurons into two phases. The first is within a neuron, in which the movement is fast and the result of a neurochemical process called *firing*. An electric signal is generated by changing the permeability of cell walls to specific ions, thus generating this electrical signal. You need not understand the process, but it is important to realize that this is an all-or-none process. The cell either fires or does not fire; there are no degrees of firing. Intensity is coded by how frequently the cell fires. Between neurons, a very different process occurs. At the end of the neuron, chemicals are released into a small gap between neurons called the **synapse**. These chemicals are called **neurotransmitters** because they transmit information from one neuron to another.

There are more than forty known neurotransmitters operating in the human brain, but less than a dozen have significant effects on psychological functioning. Different regions of the brain tend to use different neurotransmitters, and most neurons use several different neurotransmitters. Neurotransmitters are complex chemicals that take considerable energy to produce in the cell. Our bodies wisely recycle these chemicals by releasing them into the synapse to signal that a cell has fired, but then will reabsorb those chemicals into the releasing cell to be used again and again. This reabsorption process is called **reuptake**. SSRIs (selective serotonin reuptake inhibitors) tend to slow the reuptake of the specific neurotransmitter serotonin while having little or no effect on other neurotransmitters. Inhibiting reuptake increases the amount of the neurotransmitter in the synapse, making the synapse behave as if the cell releasing the serotonin is firing more frequently, thus releasing more serotonin.

Other antidepressant medications have their effect on different neurotransmitters, such as norepinephrine, or on a combination of neurotransmitters. For example, tricyclic antidepressants affect both serotonin and norepinephrine, and it is believed that the most serious side effects are due to the impact of those drugs on norepinephrine. That is presumably the reason that SSRIs have fewer side effects while still being effective for depression. There are drugs that are selective norepinephrine reuptake inhibitors that show modest effects on both depression and anxiety disorders, but the research evidence and clinical experience with these drugs are more limited than with SSRIs. The take-home message is that SSRIs are the drug of choice for treating both panic disorder and obsessive-compulsive disorder.

Alcohol, Tobacco, and Street Drugs

Perhaps the most widely used self-medication for anxiety is alcohol. The problem is that alcohol can have significant costs to the individual. If one has a couple of stiff drinks when anxious and only does it once, the cost is minimal. But the problem is that a couple of stiff drinks works, which means that you are more likely to take a couple of stiff drinks the next time you are anxious. As you have learned in this book, if you are breathing, there will be things in your life that make you anxious. Therefore, you are likely to use alcohol to self-medicate regularly.

Alcohol has served the very useful function of storing calories for times when normal foods are in limited supply. Alcohol also has the advantage of preventing bacterial growth, which is how those calories can be stored safely. Alcohol can even be used to sterilize a surface area, such as the skin before one gets an injection. But the obvious psychological effects of alcohol have been recognized for millennia, and people have deliberately consumed alcohol to obtain those psychological effects.

Alcohol is a central nervous system depressant. If you drink enough alcohol, your nervous system will be depressed to the point that you will no longer be breathing, or your heart will no longer be beating. At a blood-alcohol level of approximately .50 (roughly six times the level for being legally intoxicated), you will die. At levels closer to legal intoxication, your central nervous system will be depressed to the point that anxiety will be attenuated. Because anxiety is aversive and the act of drinking can remove this aversive state, the act of drinking is negatively reinforced. Remember that negative reinforcement is not the same as punishment. In negative reinforcement, a behavior is increased in frequency because it removes an aversive state. Taking Advil when you have a headache is negatively reinforced because the headache is likely to go away.

One problem with alcohol as a treatment for anxiety, or any drug that depresses the anxiety response, is that you have lost the signal value of anxiety. You do not feel the anxiety and therefore have less incentive to analyze what is causing it and what you can do to reduce the potential risk.

Another problem with alcohol is that one quickly develops tolerance. **Tolerance** means that it takes more of the substance to have the same effect. So initially, two strong drinks might be enough to calm you, but it is not likely to be enough to calm you a year later if you drink regularly to self-medicate. You are likely to need three or four or even five drinks to have the same effect. Moreover, anxiety is so common that you will need to drink heavily and frequently if that is your primary way of managing anxiety. Such heavy drinking has enormous biological consequences. People who drink heavily for years rarely make it to retirement age, because they die of one or more disease processes that are the result of chronic drinking. For those who happen to make retirement age, their brain is significantly compromised by their heavy drinking. In the normal course of things, tens of thousands of brain cells die every day, but because of the way our brain is wired, we are normally able to function well despite the loss of so many neurons. We do notice some deterioration. For example, older people often find that their memory is not as good or that they cannot recall a word or person's name. This is annoying, but it is normal. But because the rate of neuronal death is much higher when you are intoxicated, the collective loss of so many neurons will eventually lead to serious cognitive decline, known as *dementia*.

I will not moralize about whether one should drink. Most people who drink do so responsibly. Do they occasionally use alcohol to relieve unpleasant sensations such as anxiety? I suspect they do. They may not even do it deliberately. They might be having social drinks with friends on a bad day and discover that they feel better after a couple of drinks. However, when you start to find that you are drinking more often and in higher quantities, you now have another problem. Alcohol is an addictive substance. It may require several years for a full addiction to develop, but once it does, it is very difficult to kick. Alcohol addiction can interfere with your personal and professional responsibilities, leading to a breakup of important relationships and even the loss of a job.

Some people find that smoking also reduces unpleasant states. Nicotine, the addictive substance in cigarettes, is a complex chemical that has several effects on the brain. It can give people an energy boost, reduce such uncomfortable states as anxiety, and even inhibit appetite. Some people find that when they quit smoking, it is very hard to control their weight. Smoking is even more addictive than alcohol, and it is far more dangerous to one's health. Smoking causes far more deaths than all other drugs combined, both legal and illegal.

Alcohol and tobacco are legal, but there are other drugs available on the street that are not legal and have the potential to reduce anxiety. To be blunt, using such drugs is a foolish thing to do. People who sell drugs on a street corner are not at all concerned about the health of their clients. They rarely know or care about how the drugs are produced and whether they are safe. Most are trafficked in a concentrated form and then diluted for street sale, and there are no standard procedures for this dilution process. Consequently, the concentration of any purchase of street drugs can vary dramatically from one dealer to the next or one batch to the next. All drugs have a lethal dosage level, so not knowing the dosage may very well be a life-or-death mistake.

Central nervous system stimulants, such as cocaine, can dramatically increase energy levels and give one a very pleasurable sensation because of their impact on the pleasure center of the brain. Central nervous system depressants, such as heroin, can dramatically reduce unpleasant states and even induce sleepiness. However, heroin also affects the pleasure center of the brain. Both classes of drugs are highly addictive and a very dangerous way to manage your anxiety. The drug fentanyl is a synthetic opiod, which was originally developed for pain management. It is 50 to 100 times more potent than morphine. Currently, fentanyl is most likely to be used as a street drug, and because it is so inexpensive to manufacture and so powerful, it is often mixed with other illegal drugs to increase their potency. Unfortunately, even in modest doses it is lethal, accounting for more than 50,000 overdose deaths a year in the United States.

Cannabis currently is somewhere between legal and illegal drugs. It is legal in some states, although in many of them, it is legal only for medical purposes. Other states have legalized it for recreation, but as of this writing, it is still illegal at the federal level. Because it is legal in some jurisdictions, it is grown commercially and sold in licensed stores. It may not yet have the quality control standards of the pharmaceutical industry or even the alcohol industries, but

231

its standards are likely to be comparable to those found in the tobacco industry.

Does marijuana relieve anxiety? The informal evidence suggests that it does. Is it dangerous? The jury is still out on that question, although available evidence shows that both alcohol and tobacco represent significant risks that may well exceed that of marijuana. Almost forty years ago, I coauthored with one of my graduate students a pair of review articles on the neurological impact of cannabis (Wert & Raulin, 1986a, 1986b). We found little evidence of neurological dysfunction from cannabis use based on measures that clearly documented the neurological damage due to heavy and prolonged drinking. Admittedly, none of the studies we reviewed were experiments with strong controls; cannabis was illegal, so doing such studies would have been illegal. Is our decades-old review still relevant? Not really. The marijuana sold today is between five and ten times more potent as measured by the THC content compared to the marijuana of that era. THC is the active ingredient in marijuana. Without further study, it is unclear what the long-term impact of this drug might be.

I suspect that the various forms of cannabis will be legal soon. That is the direction that things are going. I do not have a basis for discouraging the use of marijuana as an informal treatment for occasional anxiety. I am concerned that heavy use of this drug may have negative impacts that have yet to be determined, and I know that productivity suffers when one is under the influence, whether from alcohol or marijuana. I will leave the discussion of legalization to others to address. However, I discourage people from using any of the drugs described in this section as their way of managing anxiety. There is no need to use such drugs for that purpose because, as you have learned in this book, there are other effective options for managing your anxiety.

Other Biological Treatments

Although drugs are by far the most used medical treatments for anxiety and anxiety disorders, there are other treatments that have been used. I will briefly describe some of them.

Psychosurgery and Other Neurological Treatments

Psychosurgery for psychological disorders has a checkered history and therefore tends to rarely be used today and only used in situations in which other less invasive treatments have not worked. Historically, the frontal lobotomy was introduced in 1935 by Dr. Egas Moniz for the treatment of schizophrenia, and he was awarded the Nobel Prize for this work. Lobotomies were also used for treating severe depression and anxiety. The lobotomy was a crude procedure, which often resulted in significant loss of neurological function in patients. All psychosurgery is irreversible, which is one reason to be cautious about using it; that is the primary reason why it is usually a treatment of last resort.

There is some evidence that psychosurgery may be effective for some individuals with severe OCD that has not responded to other treatments. For example, bilateral cingulotomies have been used to treat severe OCD with success. This procedure, unlike lobotomies, focuses the surgery on a specific brain area (the anterior cingulate cortex), which is thought to play a major role in regulating emotion. Several other surgical procedures have been tried with modest success in severe OCD cases, although the research shows that irreversible neurological dysfunction is a risk in at least some of the cases.

A nonsurgical procedure called *deep brain stimulation* also shows promise and with less risk than surgical procedures. It is not yet a routine treatment for OCD, but it may be a treatment available in the future for those cases that are unresponsive to traditional approaches.

There is little work in psychosurgery for anxiety disorders other than obsessive-compulsive disorder. Those other disorders

233

typically respond well to either medications or focused psychological treatments, so there is no need to explore such risky treatment options.

Nutrition

Few would argue the fact that good nutrition is important. Foods provide us with both the energy on which our body runs and the nutrients to promote health. If you search the Internet, you will find dozens of articles on the value of specific diets to manage anxiety. My reading of this literature is that it has little scientific background. Often, even the theoretical bases for the proposed diets are weak and with little evidence for their validity. I would encourage everyone, whether anxious or not, to be concerned about their nutrition, but I am skeptical that a change in diet can begin to compare with the proven treatments already available for anxiety and anxiety disorders.

One diet restriction that may influence anxiety, especially in the case of panic disorder, is caffeine consumption. Most people tolerate caffeine easily, and many people feel that they cannot function without caffeine. But some individuals are sensitive to caffeine, with even moderate doses of caffeine increasing their level of anxiety. Before scientists discovered the effectiveness of CO_2 for triggering panic attacks, caffeine was one of several substances used in laboratories because it tended to trigger panic attacks so they could be studied. Many individuals with panic disorder voluntarily restrict their caffeine consumption because of the anxiety they feel after consuming caffeine.

Chapter Summary

Every psychological experience is mediated by our biology. Note that I did not say that it is caused by our biology. We tend to think of biology and psychology as if they are somehow different, but we are simply one person, and our biological and psychological responses to the world around us are interconnected. Because of that fact, we can use biological interventions to change our psychological state.

Through trial and error, people have learned about chemicals that can change their state. Besides alcohol, people have noticed the psychological effects of smoking a variety of substances, such as tobacco and cannabis. Many illegal street drugs also have an impact on anxiety levels, but in modern times we have developed a sophistication that has allowed us to develop substances with more specific and powerful effects on anxiety. Many of these substances are now available as prescription drugs for the treatment of anxiety and anxiety disorders.

The two most common drugs to treat anxiety are anti-anxiety drugs (also called anxiolytic drugs) and so-called antidepressant drugs (specifically, SSRIs). These drugs are generally safer than alternative biological treatments. They are easier to manage and tend to have fewer side effects. However, like all drugs, they have side effects, and there are potential dangers. But they are useful tools in the management of chronic anxiety, anxiety disorders, and occasional unpleasant anxiety states.

There are other biological treatments that have been offered for anxiety, but in general, they do not have the kind of scientific evidence to support them that traditional drugs have. For a drug to be on the market, it must demonstrate some level of efficacy and must be found to have risks that are minimal and acceptable given the benefits the drug offers. Other treatments have no such requirements before they can be made available to the public.

Chapter 15

Taking Back Your Life

They say that the only certainties in life are death and taxes, but if you have a good enough accountant and tax lawyer, you may be able to avoid most taxes. However, you will never avoid death. The best you can hope for is to postpone it. It may make more sense to say the only things that are certain in life are death and anxiety, because anxiety is almost as certain as death. Perhaps for that reason, most people fear anxiety and would be happy if it could simply go away.

I hope by now that you have come to understand that anxiety, although uncomfortable, is valuable to not only your survival but also your prosperity. Anxiety motivates behavior that prepares us to deal with potential problems. Our ability to think hypothetically into the future and envision such problems, coupled with the motivating effects of anxiety, drives us to act now to prepare us to be successful when faced with difficult situations in the future.

In this chapter, I will be summarizing the ways in which you can not only accept anxiety as a normal part of your life but also embrace it as the price you pay for success. Successful people experience anxiety like everyone else, but they use their anxiety to enhance their future success through preparation. If life were easy, we would not need anxiety. Life is not easy, and it is not likely to become easy. Our anxiety simply reflects this reality.

Accepting Anxiety as Valuable

We accept uncomfortable states all the time, and we do so because they represent value to us. The phrase, "No pain, no gain," is widely used to express the idea that improving your physical conditioning is going to be hard work and uncomfortable, but the price is worth the reward.

Perhaps we are willing to accept the pain associated with significant exercise because it is a choice on our part. We can avoid the sore muscles and other effects of intense exercise by simply not doing it. If we make that decision, we have decided that we will not be in the best physical condition because we do not want to endure the pain that is the price of such conditioning.

Anxiety is rarely a choice. In that respect, it is like the pain associated with injuries or disease. We can accept the pain that we know is the consequence of intense exercise, but more often the pain that we experience is an incredibly valuable signal. It tells us that there is something wrong and that it requires immediate attention. If you break your leg, the pain you experience if you try to walk on it will be unbearable. Consequently, you are likely to realize immediately that you are not capable of walking. By making that decision, you dramatically reduce the likelihood that you will do further damage to an already damaged leg.

Pain is an excellent metaphor for anxiety. Although it is triggered by different situations, it plays the same signal role. The example of a broken leg is a good indicator of how pain can tell us what actions to avoid. What if we were able to eliminate pain? Most people would consider that a wonderful thing, but in fact, the outcome would be devastating. People with spinal cord injuries not only have lost the use of their limbs because of the injury, but they have also lost the feeling from those limbs. A simple example that plays a huge role in spinal cord injuries illustrates the importance of pain. As you learned earlier, if you sit for any length of time, especially if you sit on a firm surface, your bottom will start to hurt. Your bottom is hurting because you are cutting off the blood supply by putting weight on a small surface area. When your bottom starts to hurt, you shuffle around in your chair, and that movement relieves the pressure that has been blocking blood flow. But if you have a spinal cord injury, you may have no feeling in your bottom and therefore have no idea that you have been cutting off the blood supply. If you did have feeling, you would be experiencing pain and would find it impossible to not shift your weight to return the blood flow to your bottom. The result, which is far more common than you might imagine in people with spinal cord injuries, is that the tissue dies from lack of blood flow. The patient will develop severe ulcers, sometimes the size of a person's fist and almost as deep as their bones because of the tissue loss. You might imagine the danger associated with sores that severe. Infection is common and potentially life-threatening, and extensive surgery is often required to repair the damaged tissue.

It is hard for us to imagine that pain is a good thing, but an example like the one above illustrates just how critical it is to our survival. Spinal cord injuries are not the only medical problems that can disrupt pain, and every medical problem that disrupts pain enough has severe secondary consequences. Pain is critically important to our health and survival. In much the same way, anxiety plays a critical role.

Just like pain, anxiety is a signal that some action is necessary. Also, like pain, the signal starts out gentle, providing a nudge to focus our attention on a potential problem. However, if we choose to ignore this gentle nudge, the intensity of the anxiety is likely to increase until it is impossible to ignore. If we let anxiety build to that level, we have created two problems. The first is that the anxiety is so intense that it is difficult for us to concentrate on the actions required to deal with the situation. You likely have experienced that. When it gets that bad, you feel that the anxiety owns you and that you cannot think clearly about what to do. The second problem can be even more severe. A problem that can easily be handled when addressed early may become overwhelming if we wait too long.

An example might help you to understand how these two problems can develop if we ignore anxiety. Imagine that you are having problems at work and the problems are preventing you from being able to do the job that is expected of you. Of course, you are aware of the potential consequences if those problems are not resolved, and that knowledge makes you anxious. If you use a process that psychologists call *denial* to deal with the situation, you are essentially saying to yourself, "Don't pay attention to the anxiety; there is no reason to be concerned." Consequently, you will ignore the problem and it will continue to affect your performance. At some point, your poor performance will be recognized by those in control, and they are likely to let you know that your poor performance is unacceptable. In fact, they might up the ante by saying that if you do not turn things around immediately, you will be fired. At that point, your anxiety might be so high that it is difficult for you to even think about the problem. Moreover, at that point, it may be impossible to turn the situation around even if you could correct whatever problems are getting in the way of your performance.

If one listens to the signal value of anxiety early, it may be possible to engineer a completely different outcome. For example, perhaps your poor performance is a result of the distraction at work that you are experiencing because of serious problems in your marital relationship. Perhaps, with the aid of marital therapy, the relationship can be improved and its negative effect on your work performance reversed. Perhaps, part of the problem in your marital relationship is that your boss believes that working seven days a week should be the norm for someone in your position. Let's assume, for the sake of argument, that the boss works seven days a week and assumes that is what everyone should do. Let's also assume that you do good work and that is why your boss depends on you so much. Your boss will probably not want to lose you, so if you approach your boss and honestly talk about the negative impact of the workload on your family, the boss may well realize that he or she is about to lose a superstar unless some accommodation can be made. Perhaps you can negotiate a position that is somewhat less demanding and thus allows more time for your family, recognizing that that position may slow the pace of your promotions. There is no question that approaching your boss about such issues or talking with your spouse about such issues would be difficult, and frankly, many people might be so anxious about doing that that they avoid the situation. But it would be easy for you to imagine that avoiding that situation long enough could almost certainly lead to irreconcilable differences with your spouse and perhaps the loss of a job.

The examples that I have just given are rather dramatic, but anxiety gives us hundreds of indications of potential problems every day. The roads are slippery, or perhaps the traffic is heavier, and we find ourselves uncomfortable driving. We respond to that discomfort by driving more carefully and therefore reducing the likelihood of an accident. We are tempted by sweets that would ruin our diet and perhaps put us at risk for diabetes, and our response is to either avoid those sweets or reduce the volume of those sweets. We encounter someone in a bad mood and find ourselves anxious about what to expect from them because, in the past, they have been unpredictable when in a bad mood. Therefore, we tend to avoid them and tend to avoid potential interpersonal problems that might occur if we spend too much time with them when they are in such a mood. We barely notice the anxiety in these situations because we act on it so quickly. The truth is that some anxiety leads to appropriate action with little effort on our part and other anxiety may lead to exactly the opposite. That is the issue we address in the next section.

Turning Anxiety to Your Advantage

Anxiety is a valuable signal, and when it works well, it focuses our attention on potential problems before they become serious problems. We have an opportunity to adjust the situation or adjust our reaction to the situation to avoid more serious problems. However, anxiety can also lead to avoidance of situations, and sometimes that avoidance is the worst possible action. In this section, I talk about when such avoidance is likely, how to recognize that it is occurring, and what to do to avoid the problems that such avoidance creates.

The value of anxiety is that it both signals potential danger and motivates action to reduce that potential. When this occurs naturally, it is an amazingly effective strategy. However, there will always be situations in which this system does not work. In such cases, the anxiety may be recognized, but the action to prepare for the situation that could be a problem is postponed. Often, the postponement is explained by suggesting that one is just adjusting priorities. For example, a person is anxious about the idea of asking the boss for a raise. This scenario raises anxiety because asking for a raise could lead to a negative response. The boss could deny the raise, which would be bad enough, or the boss could deny the raise and make it clear that your work is not considered to be worthy of a raise. This latter response would be devastating to one's self-esteem.

The example of asking for a raise is a typical one in which the anxiety signal might not work effectively. Part of the reason why it may not work is that it is possible to avoid the situation. If one does not ask for a raise, there is no chance of being turned down. Of course, if you do not ask for a raise, it is less likely that you will get a raise. Some of you may be thinking that it makes good sense not to ask for a raise. Perhaps, you work in a system in which raises are rarely given other than through a negotiated contract. Perhaps, you believe that asking for raise will make your boss like you less because the boss will think that you are less committed to the job. The truth is that it is perfectly reasonable to decide that things like asking for raise, asking your roommate to be more considerate, or asking friends to help you when you are moving are not things you want to do. I am not here to tell you what your values should be or what behavior you should engage in. However, I am going to assume that the thought of asking for a raise occurred to you because (1) you know that you are doing a good job and putting in a lot of extra time, and (2) you feel that you deserve the extra money for all the good work you are doing. If those two premises are true, asking for raise is perfectly reasonable. If you also happen to know that someone who is doing much less work or lower-quality work is getting paid more than you, not getting a raise is unreasonable.

If anxiety is a signal that some future situation might be dangerous and some action now is appropriate to reduce that potential danger, failure to act on such anxiety is a signal that something is wrong with your adaptive system. It is unlikely that the anxiety system itself is the problem because this is a virtually foolproof system. It

241

is more likely that you are sabotaging your potential success because of some belief about whether you deserve such success.

Psychologists would argue that you are likely experiencing unreasonable beliefs that are affecting your behavior. If such beliefs exist, they may be out of your awareness and therefore difficult to challenge. The strategy in such a situation is to ask yourself why you find it so difficult to address this issue when you routinely address other issues without difficulty. Let's focus on the example of asking for raise. What could explain your reluctance to ask for raise that you feel you deserve? There are several possibilities. The first is that you may not be confident that you deserve a raise; in fact, you may be confident that you do not deserve a raise. Asking for raise in that situation is asking to be told what you already fear is true (that you are not a valuable employee). Another possibility is that you are ambivalent about staying with the company. That might be true if the company's values and your values are at odds. For example, the company may be more concerned with profit and less concerned with customer satisfaction than you are, and it distresses you that you must represent their values. If you ask for a raise and the boss decides to give you that raise, you have essentially committed yourself to that company and its values. There are probably at least a dozen other potential ideas that could underlie your reluctance to ask for that raise, and it will be up to you to figure out which of them are relevant to your situation.

The key to turning your anxiety to your advantage is to not allow other forces to block your natural response to the anxiety. Anxiety is different from fear. Fear involves an immediate danger, and in the face of such danger, escape is a very reasonable response. Anxiety is a response to potential danger, but the potential will only be realized if one fails to take appropriate action. The anxiety is your motivation for such action. If you follow the natural course, the anxiety will likely direct appropriate action. Whether the action is effective is another matter because its effectiveness depends on the quality of your analysis of the risk and the ways to minimize the risk. But cutting off that analysis because some other aspect of your personality is preventing you from facing a difficult situation and seeking a solution will guarantee that you will not be prepared for some of the risks that you will face.

How do you take these principles and address the issue of asking for a raise? Start by identifying reasons that you deserve a raise. Perhaps you were instrumental in achieving a company goal. Perhaps you put in lots of extra time to complete a major project on schedule. Perhaps you have been incredibly reliable, not calling in sick and working your vacation around company schedules. Perhaps you have learned knew skills that make you more valuable as an employee. If you cannot find good reasons to justify asking for a raise, you might conclude that you need to change your behavior to make you more valuable to the company. But if there are good reasons, you might develop a strategy to make those aspects of your work more visible before you ask for a raise. You have taken the anxiety about asking for a raise and used it to identify strong reasons to support a raise (or committed yourself to building such reasons before you ask). Asking for a raise without giving good reasons and the evidence to support those reasons is less likely to be successful than asking with persuasive arguments for why you deserve it.

Taking Pride in Your Anxiety Management

Let me repeat a principle that I introduced early in this book and have repeated several times. We are programmed to learn anxiety quickly because it is in our best interest to learn it quickly; we are also programmed to unlearn it slowly because it is not in our best interest to unlearn it too quickly. That is the way the system works, but we can function at a high level within these constraints.

For most of us, anxiety is more of a benefit than a problem, although we would love to be able to take away the discomfort associated with anxiety. If you are in that category, your goal is not to eliminate anxiety but to manage it effectively. Managing it effectively means using it to your advantage and keeping it to a level that benefits you instead of hinders you. If you address the potential danger that is the source of the anxiety by taking steps to prepare, you will be more effective. If you take every opportunity to imagine potential danger, analyze its likelihood, and put together the resources you need to deal with the danger if it were to occur, you will be more successful than those people who fail to take such action. Most successful people experience anxiety, but they do not experience their anxiety as a threat to their success. Instead, they accept the idea that their neurotic focus on the risks in life is what helps them to be successful in situations in which others fail.

I started out this book by focusing on the simple concept that anxiety is not your enemy. I hope by now that I have convinced you that anxiety is not only not your enemy, but also it can be one of the greatest resources you have. It may never be your friend, but it does not need to be. If you deal with anxiety effectively, you will be more successful. Use the techniques of this book to manage your anxiety and profit from the value your anxiety provides. Most importantly, take pride in your ability to manage your anxiety and face the difficulties of life with an open mind and a creative spirit.

Although anxiety often is not the enemy, I would be the first to admit that sometimes it is the enemy. We call those *anxiety disorders*. They represent anxiety that is so intense or so disruptive that it interferes with life. If you are experiencing one of those anxiety disorders, I hope I have been able to give you insights into the nature of the disorder and ideas about how even that level of anxiety can be managed with appropriate treatment. Managing such intense and/or inappropriate anxiety is difficult, which gives you even more reason to be proud of your efforts to take it on and to focus once again on what you want out of life.

Focusing on Your Goals Instead of Your Challenges

Life is always a challenge, and it comes with unpredictable twists and turns. Novelists do their best to create such twists in their plots, and if they fail to produce sufficient twists, the novel is simply not believable. Life throws challenges every day, and it is our task to carry on despite the challenges. It is hard in the face of challenges to not focus on these constant threats to our goals, but if we want to be successful, we need to never lose sight of the goals. The goals are what give us direction; the challenges are what knock us off our path to our goals. I would be lying if I told you that all challenges could be overcome. You know better than that. But many challenges can be overcome, and often they can be overcome sufficiently so that we need not compromise our goals.

Throughout this book, the theme has been that anxiety is not your enemy. You also learned that anxiety is often a valuable resource. Think of anxiety as an early warning system, something like the radar that was developed during World War II to observe attacking airplanes early enough to allow us to get our fighter planes into the air to stop them from reaching their targets. Your anxiety system works by actively contemplating what might go wrong. Some people might call that *pessimism*; I call it *optimistic realism*. One deliberately focuses on what can go wrong only if one believes that it is possible to overcome each of these challenges.

If I were to leave you with a single theme, it would be that anxiety gets a bad rap. The discomfort associated with anxiety is not a problem; it is not a bug in the system. It is how the system works. I do not know where the idea that life should be easy and pleasant came from. To the best of my knowledge, no one made such a promise. Life is a challenge, but you are up to the challenge. I have lost count of the number of times that I have heard people say, "Life is a bitch and then you die." Usually, they are just being funny, although sometimes they are being funny because it is their way of dealing with the feeling that this statement may be true. It is certainly true that we will all die at some point, so let me concede that part of the statement. I also must concede that sometimes life can be a bitch. But I believe that this statement leaves out a very important element. I believe that life also offers many sources of satisfaction, and I am betting it will not take you long to list those sources for yourself. The goal in life is to create situations that are satisfying for you, your family, and your friends. Effectively managing your anxiety is a critically important tool in achieving this goal.

Chapter Summary

There is no question that anxiety can be uncomfortable and sometimes disruptive. But the thesis of this book is that these facts do not support the argument that anxiety is the enemy. It is precisely the discomfort associated with anxiety that makes it so valuable. It motivates action that will reduce that discomfort, and if we choose the right action, it will increase the likelihood of our success.

We often see successful people as not experiencing the anxiety that we struggle with, but that is an illusion. Their success is built on anxiety, but their anxiety is a positive force in their lives. Over decades, they used their anxiety to drive behavior that led to success. Their success increased their confidence that they could handle challenges others could not begin to handle. Consequently, we see them as confident, successful, and willing to take chances. They were not born with these traits; these traits developed as a function of actions that led to success. In time, those actions became a part of their style, which reduced their level of anxiety while also increasing their effectiveness. They learned early to listen to their anxiety and use it to their advantage. I doubt they ever learned to enjoy anxiety; if they had, its value would have been lost. I doubt they would ever consider anxiety their friend, but I feel confident that they have long since understood that anxiety is not their enemy.

Glossary

agoraphobia: The fear typically found in panic disorder in which the individual avoids situations in which either panic attacks are likely, or it would be difficult to escape if one were to experience a panic attack. The avoidance can become so severe that the person is virtually housebound.

anti-anxiety drugs: (also called anxiolytic drugs) Drugs that reduce anxiety levels. The most-used anti-anxiety drugs are benzodiazepines. This class of drugs tends to both reduce anxiety and promote sleep.

antisocial personality disorder: A disorder that is characterized by a stable and consistent disregard for the rights of others. Such individuals typically are superficially charming, lie easily and convincingly, and often get into legal trouble because of their behavior. This group of individuals often shows remarkably little anxiety. The terms sociopath and psychopath are often used to describe this group of individuals.

anxiety: A feeling of apprehension about potential risk in the future. The intensity of the anxiety often varies depending on the probability of the risk, the severity of the risk, and the closeness in time to the risk.

anxiety sensitivity: The tendency to view symptoms of anxiety as dangerous. Anxiety sensitivity increases the risk of panic disorder because the occasional panic attack is much more threatening to someone with anxiety sensitivity. Hence, they respond more strongly and begin to fear the possibility of other panic attacks.

anxiolytic drugs: Another name for anti-anxiety drugs.

autonomic nervous system: A system with two branches that tend to be mutually inhibitory: the sympathetic and parasympathetic. The sympathetic branch operates when we are stressed, and it allows us to devote more energy to dealing with stress. The parasympathetic branch is active when we are not stressed, and it focuses the body on taking care of itself (digesting food, removing wastes, healing). It is called *autonomic* because it tends to respond automatically to our situation.

autonomic restrictors: Individuals who show an attenuated sympathetic nervous system response when anxious. People with a generalized anxiety disorder (GAD) often show this pattern of physiological response to worrying.

behavioral activation system: The part of our brain that influences behavior that leads to positive consequences. It encourages behavior that is likely to be rewarded.

behavioral inhibition system: The part of our brain that influences behavior that avoids negative consequences. It discourages behavior that is likely to lead to aversive consequences. The behavioral inhibition system appears to be deficient in people who qualify for the diagnosis of antisocial personality disorder.

classical conditioning: The type of learning studied by Pavlov in which the pairing of a stimulus that previously did not trigger a specific behavior with another stimulus that did trigger a specific behavior will in time lead the first stimulus to trigger the same behavior as the second stimulus.

compulsions: Behaviors that often feel like they are a reaction to the anxiety generated by obsessions in obsessive-compulsive disorder (OCD).

conditioned response (CR): The response that is produced by a conditioned stimulus after it has been repeatedly paired with an unconditioned stimulus. Salivation to a bell following the conditioning experiments of Pavlov is an example.

conditioned stimulus (CS): A stimulus that initially does not trigger a response but will, in time, trigger a response if it is paired with a stimulus that already triggers that response (i.e., a UCS). Pairing a bell with food eventually produced a salivation response to the bell alone.

consciousness: The awareness of oneself and one's feelings, which gives the sense of control over one's decisions and actions.

evolution: The process of gradual change in organisms because of occasional mutations and the pressures to compete with other organisms. Genetic traits that increase survivability and the likelihood of having offspring are more likely to be present in future generations.

exposure hierarchy: This is a carefully constructed list of exposure items that gradually increase the anxiety challenge in the treatment of a phobia. Early items in the list might include imagining the feared object or situation, but later items will involve close contact with the feared object or situation. With each consecutive item, the anxiety will likely increase, but if done properly, the anxiety will be manageable at each level and will decrease with repeated exposure.

exposure with response prevention: A behavioral treatment for obsessive-compulsive disorder (OCD) in which the client is asked to approach situations that will trigger powerful obsessions and to avoid responding to those obsessions and the anxiety that they produce by engaging in compulsive behavior. This is the only psychological treatment with demonstrated effectiveness for treating OCD, but it is a very difficult treatment for the client because the anxiety level is extremely high.

extinction: A process by which learned behaviors decrease in strength over time because they are no longer being reinforced.

fear: An intense emotional response to an immediate danger. Fear is often called the *fight-or-flight response* because it involves a generalized activation of the body to encourage either escape (if possible) or a fight to the death when escape is impossible.

fight-or-flight syndrome: The body's response in the face of danger, which involves activation of the body to either run like crazy to escape or fight to the death if escape is impossible. This response is triggered in the brainstem in a location called the *locus coeruleus*. It is found in every species that has even a primitive brain.

fixed mindset: The idea that your skills are inborn and fixed rather than subject to improvement with practice and study or deterioration with disuse or neglect. For example, if you are good at academic tasks, you might consider yourself "intelligent" and thus expect that all academic tasks will be easy because of your innate intelligence.

flooding: An exposure-based treatment for anxiety in which the exposure is intense rather than gradual as done in systematic desensitization.

Garcia effect: See *learned taste aversion*.

generalized anxiety disorder (GAD): A disorder that is characterized by constant worrying. Unlike normal worrying, worrying in GAD does not seem to trigger behaviors that would reduce the need to worry.

growth mindset: The idea that your skills can be improved with study and practice and will also deteriorate if you do not continue to use them. In contrast to a fixed mindset, in which taking on difficult tasks is threatening to one's self-esteem because initial failure is likely, in a growth mindset, one expects initial failure but recognizes that the effort will eventually lead to even better skills.

imaginal exposure: Exposure-based treatment in which the individual imagines each of the elements of the exposure hierarchy and manages the anxiety that such imagination produces. It is rare that the entire hierarchy is imaginable, but it is common to have some of the items of the hierarchy be imaginable.

in vivo exposure: Exposure-based treatment in which the individual confronts the situations and/or objects that are

250

anxiety producing. For example, if the person is afraid of snakes, the person will gradually come closer to a real snake and eventually handle the snake as part of the exposure.

individual differences: The idea that most characteristics show considerable variability among people. For example, people range from very tall to very short, with most people in a middle range of height. There are individual differences in physical characteristics, behavioral tendencies, skills, and emotional responses.

interoceptive desensitization: The process of deliberately producing physiological sensations that mimic anxiety symptoms and trigger intense anxiety in people with anxiety sensitivity. This process decreases the sensitivity of such experiences in much the same way that systematic desensitization decreases the anxiety produced by feared objects or situations. This process is often included in the treatment of a panic disorder.

law of effect: The principle that states that the strength or likelihood of a behavior is affected by the consequences of that behavior. Behaviors that are rewarded become more likely; behaviors that are punished become less likely.

learned taste aversion: A special example of classical conditioning in which one develops an aversion to the taste of a specific food because it is paired later with illness. What makes this classical conditioning special is that normally the UCS (the illness) would need to be paired closely in time with the CS (the food), but with learned taste aversion, the two might be separated by several hours.

locus coeruleus: Part of the brainstem that triggers the fight-or-flight response, which we experience as intense fear. The brainstem is the oldest part of the brain in terms of evolution, and this fight-or-flight response is found in all animals with a brain, including those animals that have little more than a brainstem.

mutations: Random changes in genes that result from copying errors. Such changes are almost always devastating to the organism and result in the organism dying, often before birth. However, occasionally such mutations can give an organism a selective advantage that increases its likelihood of survival and passing on its genes to the next generation. This is the process that permits evolutionary change.

negative affect: The unpleasant feeling that accompanies several negative emotions, such as anxiety, fear, anger, and extreme hunger. This unpleasant feeling intensifies the desire to activate behavior to deal with the situation that created the emotion.

negative reinforcement: The increase in the strength of behaviors because of the removal of an aversive stimulus following the behavior.

neurons: Nerve cells that specialize in carrying signals to other neurons or to the muscles and organs of the body.

neurotransmitters: Specialized chemicals that are released into the synapse between two neurons when the first neuron fires. These chemicals communicate to the second neuron that the first neuron has fired.

observational learning: Learning to change our behavior by observing the behavior of others and the consequences of that behavior.

obsessions: Unwanted thoughts that generate enormous anxiety and often trigger compulsive behavior in obsessive-compulsive disorder (OCD).

obsessive-compulsive disorder (OCD): An anxiety disorder in which the individual experiences obsessive thoughts that are difficult or impossible to control and that generate enormous anxiety. In response, the individual engages in one or more compulsive behaviors, which may reduce the anxiety but often fail to reduce it sufficiently to allow the person to function normally.

obsessive-compulsive personality disorder (OCPD): A personality disorder that is characterized by obsessive attention to detail. These individuals tend to follow rules precisely and are willing to work overtime with no additional pay to get projects done precisely the way they believe those projects should be done.

operant conditioning: The principle that you can influence the strength of behaviors by manipulating the consequences of those behaviors. Behaviors that are rewarded will increase in strength, whereas behaviors that are punished will decrease in strength.

panic attack: A fear response (fight-or-flight) that is a false alarm (i.e., there is no actual danger present). People usually describe this false alarm as coming out of the blue. Because it is so intense and there appears to be no reason for it, people often interpret the feelings to mean that they are experiencing a heart attack or going crazy.

panic disorder: An anxiety disorder that is characterized by frequent panic attacks and the fear that one will have more panic attacks. The secondary fear of more attacks is critical to the diagnosis; most people who have panic attacks never develop this secondary fear and therefore do not qualify for this diagnosis.

parasympathetic branch (of the autonomic nervous system): The portion of the autonomic nervous system that is activated when one is not stressed. During parasympathetic arousal, most of one's energy is devoted to the housekeeping chores of the body, such as digesting food, removing wastes, and healing injuries.

positive reinforcer: Any stimulus that when presented immediately after a behavior tends to increase the strength or likelihood of that behavior.

positive reinforcement: The increase in the strength of behavior because of having a positive consequence following that behavior.

progressive muscle relaxation: A procedure to reduce one's anxiety by relaxing the muscles of the body. To make this effective, we divide the body into several muscle groups and relax each muscle group in turn. The procedure uses a mild tensing of the muscle group to heighten our awareness of the muscles followed by an effort to let the tension drain away.

punishment: The reduction in the level of behavior because that behavior is followed by an aversive consequence.

punctuated evolution: A model of evolution that suggests that most evolutionary change is slow and gradual but that dramatic changes in the environment can trigger equally dramatic changes in the pace of evolution as organisms struggle to adapt to the new environment.

reciprocal inhibition: The idea that it is not possible to be both tense and relaxed at the same time. This process is used in systematic desensitization during which the person is taught to control anxiety during exposure to feared objects or situations by controlling the tension of their muscles.

reuptake: The process by which neurotransmitters are recycled through a process of reabsorbing them into the axon terminal that originally released them.

selective serotonin reuptake inhibitors (SSRIs): A class of drugs originally developed to treat depression but now known to be effective in the treatment of some anxiety disorders. They work by inhibiting the reuptake of the neurotransmitter serotonin after it is released into the synapse. By slowing the reuptake, the volume of this neurotransmitter in the synapse is increased.

self-handicapping: The process of acting (or not acting) in a way that has the result of making you less likely to succeed at a task. Such behavior is often found in situations in which success is possible but failure is also possible. Using self-handicapping to make the chance of success extremely low allows the individual to reduce the level of anxiety because the result is almost preordained.

Skinner box: A mechanical device that automatically rewarded or punished specific behaviors in animals and recorded the rates of those behaviors. Named after B. F. Skinner, who conceived and built these devices to study the laws of learning.

social anxiety disorder: The current DSM diagnosis for what used to be called *social phobias*.

social phobias: Social phobias involve a fear of a situation in which one is likely to be judged, such as a fear of public speaking. Because performance is the basis on which one is judged, treatment must go beyond managing the anxiety to also improve the performance skills of the client.

specific phobias: Fear of specific objects and/or situations. Common specific phobias are the fear of snakes, spiders, heights, or flying.

sympathetic branch (of the autonomic nervous system): The portion of the autonomic nervous system that is activated during periods of stress, fear, or anxiety. During sympathetic arousal, one can devote more energy to dealing with the immediate problems in front of them.

synapse: The small space between the axon terminal of one neuron and the dendrite of the next neuron. The signal from one neuron to another is passed with chemicals called *neurotransmitters* that are released into the synapse at the axon terminal of the first cell when that cell fires.

systematic desensitization: A gradual exposure technique for the treatment of a phobia that pairs the exposure with anxiety management strategies, such as relaxation exercises or deep breathing, until the anxiety level drops significantly. The gradual exposure is achieved by creating an exposure hierarchy that ranges from items that create minimal anxiety to items that create intense anxiety. Once a level of exposure hierarchy results in minimal anxiety, the individual is asked to increase the exposure to the next level.

thought-action fusion: A belief that a person's thoughts can cause things to happen. This is found in obsessive-compulsive disorder (OCD), although in most cases, the person with thought-action fusion realizes that such ideas are unreasonable (i.e., they have insight into this symptom).

tolerance: A process that involves an adjustment of the body when exposed repeatedly to a substance. In time, it takes more substance to achieve the same effect. This is especially true with addictive drugs.

unconditioned response (UCR): A response to a specific stimulus (a UCS) without any need for conditioning. An example is salivation for food.

unconditioned stimulus (UCS): A stimulus that produces a specific response (a UCR) without the need for any conditioning. An example is food, which produces a salivation response.

VR (virtual reality) exposure: Exposure-based treatment in which the individual confronts frightening situations and/or objects using virtual reality (seeing and interacting with computer simulations). Virtual reality allows exposure to things that are difficult to address in today's world, such as boarding a plane and experiencing the sensations of taxying, takeoff, and landing. You can also experience driving over long bridges without the need to drive for half an hour or more to get to such a bridge for exposure.

References

American Psychiatric Association. (2022). *Diagnostic and Statistical Manual* (5th ed, Text Revision). Washington, DC: American Psychiatric Association.

Bandelow, B., Michaelis, S. & Wedekind, D. (2017) "Treatment of Anxiety Disorders." Dialogues in Clinical Neuroscience, 19, 93-107.
doi: 10.31887/DCNS.2017.19.2/bbandelow.

Barlow, D. H. (2002). *Anxiety and Its Disorders: The Nature and Treatment of Anxiety and Panic* (2nd Ed.). New York, NY: Guilford Press.

Becraft, M. B. (2014). *Bill Gates: A Biography*. Santa Barbara, CA: Greenwood Biographies.

Black, R. (2022). *The Last Days of the Dinosaurs*. New York, NY: St. Martins.

Craske, M. G., Wolitzsky-Taylor, K., & Barlow, D. H. (2021). "Panic Disorder and Agoraphobia." In D. H. Barlow (Ed.), *Clinical Handbook of Psychological Disorders: A Step-By-Step Treatment Manual* (6th ed) (pp. 1-63). New York, NY: Guilford Press.

Demarais, A., & White, V. (2005). *First Impressions: What You Don't Know About How Others See You*. New York, NY: Bantam Books.

Denefrio, S., Myruski, S., Mennin, D., & Dennis-Tiwary, T. A. (2019). "When Neutral Is Not Neutral: Neurophysiological Evidence for Reduced Discrimination Between Aversive and Non-Aversive Information in Generalized Anxiety Disorder." *Motivation and Emotion, 43,* 325-338. http://dx.doi.org.eps.cc.ysu.edu/10.1007/s11031-018-9732-0.

Dror, O. E. (2017). "Deconstructing the 'Two Factors:' The Historical Origins of the Schachter-Singer Theory of Emotions." *Emotion Review, 9,* 7-16. http://dx.doi.org.eps.cc.ysu.edu/10.1177/1754073916639663.

Dweck, C. S. (2006). *Mindset: The New Psychology of Success.* New York, NY: Ballantine Books.

Epstein, S., & Fenz, W. D. (1965). "Steepness of Approach and Avoidance Gradient in Humans as a Function of Experience: Theory and Experiment." *Journal of Experimental Psychology, 70,* 1-12. doi: http://dx.doi.org.eps.cc.ysu.edu/10.1037/h0021990.

Friedman, B. H. (2010). "Feelings and the Body: The Jamesian Perspective on Autonomic Specificity of Emotion." *Biological Psychology, 84,* 383-393. doi: http://dx.doi.org.eps.cc.ysu.edu/10.1016/j.biopsycho.2009.10. 006.

Gazzaniga, M. (2018). *The Consciousness Instinct: Unraveling the Mysteries of How the Brain Makes the Mind.* New York: Farrar, Straus and Giroux.

Gould, S. J. (2007). *Punctuated Equilibrium.* Cambridge, MA: Belknap Press.

Kheriaty, E., Kleinknecht, R. A., & Hyman, I. E., Jr. (1999). "Recall and Validation of Phobias Origins as a Function of Structured Interview versus the Phobia Origins Questionnaire." *Behavior Modification, 23,* 1-78. doi: http://dx.doi.org.eps.cc.ysu.edu/10.1177/0145445599231003.

Lang, P. J. (1985). The Cognitive Psychophysiology of Emotion: Fear and Anxiety." In A. H. Tuma and D. Maser (Eds), *Anxiety and the Anxiety Disorders* (pp. 131-170). Hillsdale, NJ: Erlbaum.

Lavond, D. G., & Steinmetz, J. E. (2003). *Handbook of Classical Conditioning.* New York, NY: Springer Science+Business Media.

McNally, R. J. (1994). *Panic Disorder: A Critical Analysis.* New York, NY: Guilford Press.

McNally, R. J. (2002). "Anxiety Sensitivity and Panic Disorder." *Biological Psychiatry, 52,* 938-946. http://dx.doi.org.eps.cc.ysu.edu/10.1016/S0006-3223(02)01475-0.

Prisbell, M. (1987). "Factors Affecting College Students' Perceptions of Satisfaction in and Frequency of Dating." *Psychological Reports, 60,* 659-664. doi: http://dx.doi.org.eps.cc.ysu.edu/10.2466/pr0.1987.60.2.659.

Schachter, S., & Singer, J. (1962). "Cognitive, Social, and Physiological Determinants of Emotional State." *Psychological Review, 69,* 379-399. doi: http://dx.doi.org.eps.cc.ysu.edu/10.1037/h0046234.

Weiderhold, B. K., Bouchard, S., & Loranger, C. (2014). "Fear of Flying (Aviophobia): Efficacy and Methodological Lessons Learned from Outcome Trials. In B. K. Wiedenhold and S. Bouchard (Eds.), *Advances in Virtual Reality and Anxiety Disorders* (pp. 65-89). New York, NY: Springer Science + Business Media.

Wert, R. C., & Raulin, M. L. (1986a). "The Chronic Cerebral Effects of Cannabis Use: I. Methodological Issues and Neurological Findings." *International Journal of the Addictions, 21,* 605-628.

Wert, R. C., & Raulin, M. L. (1986b). "The Chronic Cerebral Effects of Cannabis Use: II. Psychological Findings and Conclusions." *International Journal of the Addictions, 21,* 629-642.

Yusufov, M., Grebstein, L., Rossi, J. S., Redding, C. A., Ferszt, G. G., & Prochaska, J. O. (2020). "Development and Implementation of a Psychological Service for Patients with Cancer." *Cognitive and Behavioral Practice, 27,* 290-305. doi: http://dx.doi290305..org.eps.cc.ysu.edu/10.1016/j.cbpra.2020.05.001.

www.ingramcontent.com/pod-product-compliance
Lightning Source LLC
LaVergne TN
LVHW051226080426
835513LV00016B/1439